Strategic Luxury Management

Strategic Luxury Management is a case-rich and practical overview of how luxury creates value and why some firms are more successful than others. The focus of luxury study has traditionally centered on the clients' drivers of consumption, their perception of the brand and the way to effectively engage with them. Luxury is rarely, however, discussed from a strategic perspective: how luxury managers make complex decisions relative to their competitive environment.

The book provides insight into the luxury industry and how companies face market complexity across three key areas. First, the company itself, determining what defines a luxury firm. Second, the book offers a specific framework to assess creativity across management and not simply as an individual talent. Third, the book considers the competitive landscape and the principles that allow companies to compete consistently and meaningfully. Each chapter includes pedagogical features to ensure comprehension, including chapter objectives and self-study questions.

With examples and case studies from international firms illustrating each chapter, *Strategic Luxury Management* is essential reading for postgraduate, MBA and executive education students studying luxury management, luxury brand management, luxury creativity and innovation, and strategic management, as well as reflective practitioners within the luxury industry.

Online resources include chapter-by-chapter PowerPoint slides.

David Millán Planelles is Adjunct Professor of Strategy at IE Business School, Spain, and Adjunct Professor at the International University of Monaco. He creates teaching materials for the strategy of luxury and creativity-driven firms and was awarded the European Foundation of Management Development (EFMD) best case of the year in 2017.

Mastering Luxury Management

The luxury sector is a rapidly evolving and competitive global industry, requiring premium brands to be dynamic and innovative in their business and management decisions to remain relevant. This series meets the need for thorough yet practical and accessible textbooks that address the complexity of the luxury industry and challenges facing its management.

Mastering Luxury Management is a valuable resource for Luxury Management courses, helping readers to acquire an in-depth understanding of contemporary theories and how they apply in practice, alongside recognising trends and developments that may shape the future marketplace. Individually, each text provides essential reading for a core topic. A range of consistent pedagogical features are used across the series, including international case studies that demonstrate practical applications in the luxury context.

Each text will be invaluable reading for advanced undergraduate and postgraduate students, in particular those studying for a Master's or MBA in Luxury Management or Luxury Brand Management, as they provide tools and strategies for a successful future career in luxury.

Strategic Luxury Management
Value Creation and Creativity for Competitive Advantage
David Millán Planelles

For more information about this series, please visit: www.routledge.com/ Mastering-Luxury-Management/book-series/LM

Strategic Luxury Management

Value Creation and Creativity for Competitive Advantage

David Millán Planelles

Routledge
Taylor & Francis Group
LONDON AND NEW YORK

First published 2022
by Routledge
2 Park Square, Milton Park, Abingdon, Oxon OX14 4RN

and by Routledge
605 Third Avenue, New York, NY 10158

Routledge is an imprint of the Taylor & Francis Group, an informa business

© 2022 David Millán Planelles

The right of David Millán Planelles to be identified as author of this work has been asserted in accordance with sections 77 and 78 of the Copyright, Designs and Patents Act 1988.

All rights reserved. No part of this book may be reprinted or reproduced or utilised in any form or by any electronic, mechanical, or other means, now known or hereafter invented, including photocopying and recording, or in any information storage or retrieval system, without permission in writing from the publishers.

Trademark notice: Product or corporate names may be trademarks or registered trademarks, and are used only for identification and explanation without intent to infringe.

British Library Cataloguing-in-Publication Data
A catalogue record for this book is available from the British Library

Library of Congress Cataloging-in-Publication Data
Names: Planelles, David Millán, 1976– author.
Title: Strategic luxury management: value creation and creativity for competitive advantage / David Millán Planelles.
Description: Abingdon, Oxon; New York, NY: Routledge, 2022. | Series: Mastering luxury management | Includes bibliographical references and index.
Identifiers: LCCN 2021023179 (print) | LCCN 2021023180 (ebook)
Subjects: LCSH: Luxury goods industry—Management. | Luxuries. | Strategic planning.
Classification: LCC HD9999.L852 P53 2022 (print) | LCC HD9999.L852 (ebook) | DDC 338.4/7—dc23
LC record available at https://lccn.loc.gov/2021023179
LC ebook record available at https://lccn.loc.gov/2021023180

ISBN: 978-0-367-85834-6 (hbk)
ISBN: 978-0-367-85837-7 (pbk)
ISBN: 978-1-003-01532-1 (ebk)

DOI: 10.4324/9781003015321

Typeset in Optima
by codeMantra

Access the Support Material: www.routledge.com/9780367858377

To Gabriel, Mª Carmen, Ángel, Emilia, Pachelo, Miquel, Marina, Marisa, Carlos, and Josela
In loving memory of Miguel A. Carbonell and Carlos Delso Mión.

Contents

Introduction	1
Part 1 The concept of luxury	**5**
1 The concept of luxury. Past, present and future	7
Part 2 Principles of luxury value creation. The *essence* of luxury	**33**
2 The need of a managerial approach. Luxury and strategy	35
3 The *essence* of luxury. Unveiling the luxury value creation process	60
Part 3 Principles of creativity-driven industries. The *nature* of luxury	**97**
4 The luxury firm and the role of creativity	99
5 Luxury as a creative industry. The creative value system	132
Part 4 Principles of luxury competition. The *means* of luxury	**163**
6 Principles of business level rivalry. The *means* of the luxury firm	165
7 Principles of corporate level rivalry. Diversification and the conglomerate power	205
8 The future of luxury	226
Index	241

Contents

Introduction 1

Part 1 The concept of luxury 5

1 The concept of luxury. Past, present and future 7
   Introduction and objectives 7
   Luxury and mankind. An anthropological perspective 8
   A brief history of luxury 9
       Early civilizations. There has always been luxury 9
       Greece and Rome. Luxury as the enemy of man 10
       Middle Ages and the Renaissance. From the darkness to the light of arts 11
       Eighteenth and nineteenth century. A new luxury paradigm: luxury as an economic factor 14
           The luxury debate 14
           Luxury and art. Appreciation and refinement 17
       Contemporary luxury. The luxury "market" 19
   Lessons from the concept of luxury. What the luxury manager needs to know 21
       Luxury as constant change. The challenge of defining luxury 21
       Luxury as relativity. A mirror of society 22
       Need versus desires, or basic versus sophisticated needs 24
       Luxury as a threat. The negative perceptions 24
       The notion of quantity versus quality 25
       Refinement and appreciation. The link with art 25
       Luxury as a development force before being an industry 26
   Breaking the stereotypes, the road to analysis 26

Contents

Luxury as superficiality   27
Luxury as unfairness or inequality   28
Luxury as classic or everlasting   28
Luxury as craftsmanship means it is opposed to technology   30
Summary   30
Self-study questions   31

**Part 2   Principles of luxury value creation.
The *essence* of luxury**   **33**

2   The need of a managerial approach. Luxury and strategy   35
Introduction and objectives   35
Luxury and its managerial challenges   36
    The creativity challenge. The tension between management and
        creator   38
    The growth challenge. The tension between mass and exclusivity   39
    The change challenge. The time dilemma   40
    The control challenge. The issues to sustain value on creativity-driven
        firms   42
*Luxury from the lenses of the consumer: traditional marketing and its
limitations   43*
    The classic paradigm   46
    Limitations of the "value driven by consumers" view   47
    Luxury is not a zero-sum game   47
    The luxury paradigm   48
Traditional competitive strategy and its limitations for luxury   50
    The competitive mindset   50
    The economic logic   52
    The assessment of value   54
    The traditional external analysis   55
The need of a luxury strategy   55
*Case study. Maggie Henríquez arrives to Krug
Champagne   56*
Summary   57
Self-study questions   58

3   The *essence* of luxury. Unveiling the luxury value
    creation process   60
Introduction and objectives   60
Luxury and value creation. Is luxury valuable?   61

Type of benefits 62
The functionality trap 64
Normal competition 65
Going beyond normality: excess competition 73
The essence *of luxury.* Excess *as extraordinariness to ensure luxury*
competitiveness 78
Conceiving extraordinariness: luxury as a choice 79
Achieving extraordinariness: the role of resources and capabilities 83
The limits of luxury 88
The role of consistency. The fine line between normality and excess 88
Managing the "entry-level" category 92
Case study. Porsche Macan, beyond the limits of luxury? 93
Summary 95
Self-study questions 96

Part 3 Principles of creativity-driven industries.
The *nature* of luxury   **97**

4   The luxury firm and the role of creativity   99
Introduction and objectives 99
Why is creativity key for the firm analysis? 100
A conceptualization of creativity for luxury firms 102
The concept of creativity 102
Shapes of creativity: art and fashion 105
Role of innovation and technology 107
Role of creators; founders and designers 108
The assessment of creativity for the luxury firm. Lessons
for managers 110
Embracing creativity requires will and adaptation 110
Firm creativity has multiple forms beyond design 112
Firm creativity is not only about individual talent (Firm
        versus Creator) 115
Management and creativity are complementary skills 117
Classic versus modern style is not a problem; it's a choice 119
Static versus dynamics companies. That's the problem 120
Technology is not a conflict with creativity 124
Case study. Creativity at MB&F (Part 1) 124
Summary 128
Self-study questions 129

xi

Contents

5   Luxury as a creative industry. The creative value system   132
Introduction and objectives   132
Why creativity is key (too) for the external analysis?   134
The creative value system   135
  The firm   136
  The partners   136
  The location   137
  Appreciation and its 3T's   139
*Creative versus non-creative markets. The three types of business
environments   153*
  Creative market   154
  Traditional markets   155
  Networked market   155
Case study. Maximilian Büsser and Friends (Part 2)   157
Summary   160
Self-study questions   162

Part 4   Principles of luxury competition. The *means* of luxury   163

6   Principles of business level rivalry. The *means* of the luxury firm   165
Introduction and objectives   165
Business strategy into practice. From formulation to implementation   166
Differences across luxury categories   168
  Powerful categories in personal luxury   171
  Differences across business models   174
*Fundamental problems of luxury rivalry. What can go wrong in the
market?   177*
  Poor strategy formulation   177
  Poor strategy implementation   184
  Poor assessment of threats. Dealing with change   186
*The means of luxury. Principles of luxury rivalry and the 3C's of luxury
competition framework   191*
  The need for control   192
  The need for consistency   194
  The need for confidence   197
Lessons from luxury turnarounds and transformations   198
Summary   201
Self-study questions   203

Contents

7 Principles of corporate level rivalry. Diversification and the conglomerate power   205

Introduction and objectives   205

The business level and the corporate level of strategy   206

A short review of corporate strategy fundamentals   208

    The notion of synergies to approach corporate strategy diversification   208

    Why the analysis of synergies is so complex   209

    The analysis of the diversified firm   210

    Operational-driven approach. Cost side synergies   211

    Value-driven approach. Value side synergies   212

    The analysis of the diversified conglomerate   216

    Operational driven approach. Cost side synergies   216

    Value-driven approach. Value side synergies   217

From complexity to potential. Creating synergies to achieve corporate success   218

    The limits of potential. Possible does not mean it makes sense   218

    Creating business success from synergies   219

Case study. LVMH and watchmaking   220

Summary   223

Self-study questions   224

8 The future of luxury   226

Introduction and objectives   226

An observation of change. The luxury that is coming   227

    A note on the post-pandemic luxury   229

    The role of digitalization   230

The role of corporate social responsibility   233

Social change. The analysis beyond generational change   236

Summary   239

Index   241

Introduction

Motivations. Why write this book?

This book is the result of more than 15 years of study, teaching, practice and research in the area of luxury strategy. The motivation for the book was born in 2011 with my initial course of luxury strategy at IE Business School, and then also at the International University of Monaco.

The book is therefore a notebook of my journey to provide the best possible understanding of the luxury management challenges. And it reflects the passion I have always had when teaching luxury strategy. After all these years, the book is the outcome of the different materials like notes, case studies and examples prepared for the classroom. The preparation of all those materials helped me in the first place to observe and better understand the luxury phenomena so that I could then share them in the classroom.

Of course, this journey would not have been possible without the contribution of the luxury executives and faculty I have encountered in this path. Their kindness in sharing their experiences have enriched me and provided me a unique learning opportunity. And, of course, the second pillar of this book are the amazing students I was privileged to encounter. Their support and enthusiasm always pushed me to provide the most vivid, profound, and yet practical tools for their future careers in the luxury universe. To all of them I am truly grateful.

DOI: 10.4324/9781003015321-1

Introduction

Objectives. What unique value does the book offer?

The book aims to provide a comprehensive review of the competitive issues that luxury firms face. Once you, the dear reader, have completed the book, you might have gained an advanced knowledge of the complexity that managing and leading a luxury firm entails. The book hence provides specific analytical tools to deal with complex managerial issues.

The book's uniqueness relies on the approach to custom-made strategy and creativity frameworks to respond to the luxury-specific challenges. Traditionally, luxury has been studied from the consumer's eyes, where the focus is placed on perception and consumption of luxury. This book, however, approaches the managerial complexity from the perspective of the firm.

Ultimately, this is a book on strategy. As such, the book aims to answer a very intriguing question: why some luxury firms perform better than others? To do so, the book offers tailor-made frameworks based on the study of luxury. This is needed given the particular reality of the luxury market, where creativity plays a fundamental role. Creative markets offer unconventional forms of value creation that require specific analytical tools. The book covers the relationship between creativity and management in-depth to help students and practitioners understand the challenges of luxury as a creative entity. This is intended to complement and fine-tune the classical lessons on strategy and marketing. As a result, the book offers a unique approach to the managerial needs of luxury students and practitioners.

Organization. How the content is organized

The book is organized into four parts. The first part clarifies the concept of luxury, while the remaining parts cover the principles of the three main components of a luxury strategy.

- Part 1. The concept of luxury
- Part 2. Principles of luxury value creation. The *essence* of luxury
- Part 3. Principles of creativity-driven industries. The *nature* of luxury
- Part 4. Principles of luxury competition. The *means* of luxury.

Part 1 is dedicated to the concept of luxury. Chapter 1 delves into the study of the origins of luxury. The aim of the approach is not to provide a mere description of historical facts, but to provide a source of crucial knowledge for every manager. A profound understanding of luxury as a sociological factor can unveil essential managerial insights.

Part 2 argues the principles of luxury value creation, which is referred to as the "essence" of luxury strategy. This part depicts the luxury value process as a genuine and distinctive process. Chapter 2 explores how current knowledge in strategy and marketing to deal with the most common luxury management problems is limited. In this way, the chapter justifies the need for luxury-specific management tools.

Chapter 3 focuses attention on the way luxury creates value. The chapter sets the ground for the competitive discussion of luxury as it unveils the fundamental principles that explain a luxury firm's ability to compete meaningfully in the marketplace. To do so, two alternative forms to conceive value creation are discussed. Each of them represents a distinctive way to understand market rivalry: normal competition and excess competition. The former considers luxury as extraordinariness, an essential tool to reason how luxury can create meaningful value.

Part 3 focuses on the principles of creativity-driven industries, referred to as the "nature" of luxury strategy. To start, Chapter 4 provides a conceptualization of the concept of creativity for luxury firms and discusses the role of creativity within the firm's boundaries. The chapter highlights how creativity shapes the firm's ability to compete meaningfully and their value creation process.

Following that, Chapter 5 enhances the view of creativity to argue why creative firms cannot be understood in isolation. The chapter discusses how it is the collaborative ability of different entities that enhances value creation. As a result, the creative value system framework is presented as a sound approach to analyzing creative markets. This also provides an opportunity to explore the differences between creative markets and noncreative markets. To that end, the creative, the traditional, and the networked markets are described. This comparison is a meaningful way to explore and better appreciate each type of market's proper characteristics.

Finally, Part 4 covers the principles of luxury competition; this is referred to as the "means" of luxury strategy. Chapter 6 discusses luxury rivalry at the business level. The chapter explores the competitive challenges that firms face when implementing their strategy and how they can effectively deal with market rivalry. The chapter identifies the core principles that rule luxury rivalry into the 3C of luxury competition framework. Chapter 7 complements luxury rivalry by exploring the corporate level, which is commonly known as diversification. The chapter explains the potential and limitations of diversification moves and sets the foundation to understand the strategy of luxury conglomerates.

This final chapter (Chapter 8) concludes the journey with an observation of change and an approximation to luxury evolution. This chapter focuses attention on some of the drivers of that change, summarizing the main themes that luxury managers should consider when evaluating how updated their strategy is.

PART 1

The concept of luxury

The concept of luxury. Past, present and future

Introduction and objectives

Luxury is today a widely used concept. This is mainly due to the growth that the market has experienced over the past decades. The luxury market has increased at an unprecedented rate over the last decades. The luxury we know today is undoubtedly a much bigger industry than just three decades ago. Consequently, the reach of firms, the audience interested, and the published content on luxury have flourished.

But the extensive use of luxury is also a consequence of its general adoption. Today, all kinds of businesses want to be related to the idea of luxury. The rationale is quite simple; luxury can help to manage consumer perceptions and convey a higher price. This has also created a certain reticence for luxury firms to use the word "luxury".

As a result, today, there is an extensive use of the "word" luxury. All sets of perceptions and meanings have started to be associated with that word, and its real meaning has become blurred. It is quite frequent to observe luxury as a synonym of premium or expensiveness.

This chapter aims to address this situation and explain the concept of luxury. To that end, the chapter's main objective is to provide a solid knowledge of the concept of luxury and stimulate a proper use of it.

The chapter delves into the study of the origins of luxury, not as a mere description of historical facts, but as a source of crucial knowledge for every luxury manager. A profound understanding of luxury as a sociological factor can unveil essential managerial insights.

The concept of luxury

Learning what luxury has always been and how it has changed can help students and managers to face the complex challenges luxury firms face on a recurrent basis.

By the time you have completed this chapter, you will be able to:

- Understand the origins of the concept of luxury.
- Contextualize what luxury has meant and how it has impacted different societies.
- Identify the main anthropological aspects that luxury managers need to consider when evaluating their current strategies.
- Assess the complex balance between static identity and constant change that the concept of luxury represents.

Luxury and mankind. An anthropological perspective

Some concepts are linked in their nature to society and culture, so it will not be possible to understand one without the other. This is precisely what happened with luxury. Its meaning and representation are heavily linked to the society where it belongs. So luxury and society cannot be separated if one aims for understanding it. In fact, some of the most significant contributions to the knowledge of luxury have emerged from sociologists and economists, like Thorstein B. Veblen, Christopher J. Berry, or Gilles Lipovetsky.

This is why the study of luxury should start with an anthropological quest to understand what luxury has meant for different societies. Of course, this study does not aim for an in-depth anthropological discussion, but provides the primary evidence to show how luxury has historically evolved.

Luxury has always accompanied the evolution of humankind. In any historical period, there has always been a conception of luxury. However, this notion of luxury has not always been the same. Over the years, the facets through which luxury has been expressed or acquired have significantly changed. In other words, what has changed over the years is the representation of luxury.

As a consequence, we aim to unveil two components of luxury. The first one is the core component, which has remained stable for all societies and

Concept of luxury. Past, present & future

helps explain its meaning. And the second component is its evolving shape and how different societies have understood and represented it.

Therefore, this chapter aims to briefly describe the evolution of luxury so that we can dig into the immutable meaning of luxury. Only then will we be better positioned to start understanding its changes in form, content and shape.

A brief history of luxury

The idea behind this section is to provide a short historical overview of luxury. This section unites the principal authors who have studied the evolution, sociology and anthropology of luxury.

This section will be divided into five main different historical eras to highlight the most relevant difference in the relationship between man and luxury. Likewise, this will also serve as a basis to search for its mutable and immutable aspects over its evolution.

Early civilizations. There has always been luxury

Luxury has always had a strong link with power. Gilles Lipovetsky describes in his essay, *Le luxe éternel*[1] how the individual possession of goods did not drive early civilizations; on the contrary, it was the circulation and share of wealth—for instance, gifts to the other components of the tribe or the goods—that was relevant. It is with civilizations with a notion of State, Lipovetsky argues, and when societies became stratified, that wealth accumulation started to be significant and valuable.

Here, we can observe the relativity of luxury, regardless of whether we consider a technology early adopted by the elites or scarce know-how only available to those elites. As that technology advances, it passes into other (lower) layers of society. The improvement of that technology or the refinement of that know-how becomes a luxury for the elites. For instance, a giant pyramid was only available to the Pharaoh. The constructive technology would improve, and the next Pharaoh would build even more giant pyramids. This also impacts society, as the techniques spread to other layers of societies, and the elites can benefit from improving their constructions.

It is then a misunderstanding to try to learn luxury from an absolute perspective in terms of their representation. The representation of luxury keeps evolving. Hence, we cannot define luxury by its form, but by unveiling what is underneath that representation. That is what would be called the "relativity" of luxury.

We can see this also today. In their origins, back in the beginning of the previous century, owning a car was a luxury. It was a revolutionary product that improved the lives of the very few who could afford it. As with any change, some people were reluctant to adopt its use. It was perceived as a complicated machine. But the technology was not the only change. The first cars that could achieve 20 km/h made drivers and passengers sick and dizzy given the "high speed".

Today, owning a car is not a sign of luxury. Our society has adapted to this transportation means, and we have the infrastructure and the technology to use a vehicle daily. However, owning a specific type of car, like a Porsche or a Pagani, is what we know as luxury today.

In summary, as we observe, even in early civilizations, luxury is, in principle, a quantitative aspect (ownership), which becomes more refined later on. This balance between quantity and quality is something that characterizes the evolution of luxury.

Greece and Rome. Luxury as the enemy of man

Plato, one of the most renowned philosophers of ancient Greece, can serve as the basis to explore luxury in this age. Christopher Berry's extraordinary book *The Idea of Luxury*[2] performs the best study on the concept of luxury and its historical evolution. This is, without any doubt, a must-read book for any manager willing to enter into the luxury universe.

Berry suggests that one essential aspect is the interplay between "need" and "desire" and how this has influenced the natural order of different societies. This is one more piece of evidence supporting the fact that luxury is a sociological concept that evolves in line with society.

For Plato, the idea of "desire" was divided into the natural or necessary and the unnatural or unnecessary. The natural desire was the desire for food, while food beyond the simple food or plain food was unnatural. Therefore, unnecessary desires were defined as those eradicable and of no good positive use.

This relevancy of this conception of desire relies upon categorizing what is perceived to be of good (rational) use and what goes beyond that. This is one example of the conflict between luxury and rationality. Luxury is a generator of desires and makes man fall into unnecessary desires. This is also seen in Socrates's association between luxury and going beyond the body's natural needs.

Berry further elaborates why luxury was perceived as an enemy to society and hence the basis of some of the negative perceptions of the luxury as we know today. According to Plato, this notion of desire was a potential threat to society and government. As a driver of human desires, luxury can enter into a conflict with the government's expectations of its citizens. In simple terms, a warrior has to defend his home and his city. Falling into luxury (unnecessary/unnatural desires) will blunt his capabilities.

It is then not surprising that as a threat, luxury was defined with harmful and offensive definitions. One clear example is how luxury was perceived to emasculate a man. Plato's disciple Aristotle placed luxuriousness as an opposite to hardiness and endurance. There was no greater offense to a man than making him lose his core value in protecting society. Therefore, luxury is not just a matter of wealth or ostentation. Luxury was understood as a significant threat to the natural life of man.

This notion of luxury as a threat to society, and hence the need to regulate it, was also very present in the Roman Empire. Luxury was for Rome a political issue since it represented the potential disruptive power of human desires. A key concept for Romans was the simplicity and frugality of natural life. Berry provides multiple pieces of evidence for this point. For instance, the Stoicism school of thought considered the man of virtue as the man who understands the natural life and acts accordingly. Since luxury could soften that natural life, luxury was regarded as a severe threat to society. Controlling human desires was behind many political decisions, such as the sumptuary laws and censors' role.

As luxury evolved, quantitative aspects became less relevant. Luxury is then related to a qualitative refinement. The critical element here is that this refinement is not present in nature, and thus it is beyond or against the basic natural needs of man. For instance, wealth to serve personal satisfaction was perceived to generate dangerous consequences, such as self-indulgence, greed and ambition. And luxury was the leading cause of that. As a threat, luxury received very negative associations. The thought of going against natural life was perceived to be the reason behind corruption and a soft society.

Middle Ages and the Renaissance. From the darkness to the light of arts

Middle Ages did not provide any significant change to the concept of luxury. On the contrary, the strong negative perceptions of luxury remained and intensified.

The concept of luxury

As a menace to man and society, the mechanisms to control luxury effectively, like the sumptuary laws, persisted. Luxury was identified as an enemy. Perhaps one of the most evident examples is to see how luxury was placed as a sin by the Christians. The strong connection between lechery and luxury comes from that age. Etymologically still today, the link persists. For instance, in French, we have *luxure* (lechery) and *luxe* (luxury), and in Spanish, we have *lujuria* (lechery) and *lujo* (luxury).

We shall observe today why the negative perception of luxury we have today is so strong. For centuries, luxury was regarded as an enemy in our collective mindset. So the etymology, the meaning and the values have a mighty harmful component—something which luxury managers need to break down if aiming to manage luxury firms effectively and with real purpose, as Chapter 2 will discuss.

It is during the Renaissance when the concept of luxury started to evolve and to acquire additional meaning. Berry provides more evidence on how philosophers and economists, like Nicholas Barbon, impacted the demoralization of luxury and the change in the perception of desire.

The Renaissance was a shake to the society, and thus to the concept of luxury. Lipovetsky highlights how the most significant contribution of this age to the concept of luxury was the link between luxury and culture. The source of power changed. As said before, luxury and power have always been linked. Luxury was no longer hereditary and started being concentrated in specific social classes, such as the burgesses and aristocrats. Hierarchy and religion were no longer the only sources of wealth. Those new elites found in culture and the refinement of arts a source of distinction.

The first artisans that abandoned their role as mere craftsmen and became artists were the painters. Ancient painter Giorgio Vasari wrote in 1568 *The Lives of the Most Excellent Painters, Sculptors, and Architects*.[3] This is an excellent example of the link between art and luxury. Power was the sponsor of the greatest Renaissance artist, and the appreciation in the arts generated an artistic explosion. While artists still worked for the Church (Raphael and Michelangelo are clear examples), many of their works were based on aristocrat families sponsoring them. For instance, the Duke of Milan sponsored Leonardo, and Raphael or Michelangelo also started with sponsor families.

This notion of appreciation is significant. What we see here are two aspects that reinforce each other. One is the fact that arts improved. Better

Concept of luxury. Past, present & future

techniques and more skilled artisans can generate a more refined outcome. If we know Raphael, Leonardo, or Michelangelo even today, it is for the beauty of their work. They (very significantly) improved the quality work of their predecessors. The second aspect was that clients started to appreciate that work. When the client demanded an artistic creation (let's say a painting), it is also implied that the client knew what to expect or had higher expectations. When the skills were more complex, and so was the outcome, the client could no longer dictate, but appreciate the artist's work.

This appreciation empowered the creator versus the client. Wealthy families hired artists to work for them, but they also needed to refine their taste to appreciate the outcome. The quality of paintings pushed the need to appreciate a more refined work on the client side.

The difference between artisan and artist was another major shift in the evolution of luxury. An artisan learned a job and replicated as it was told. An artist was based on skills to make something on their own, to create. There was a notion of inspiration and personal creativity in artists that couldn't be found in artisans. The work of an artist was irreplaceable and differentiated. And so the artists became the new stars.

The first written document describing the importance of inspiration is attributed to Raphael. This is to say that his work is not only based on the skills he learned (and could be replicated) but on his inner ability to create. Some other art researchers disagree he was the first. In any case, the fact is that this discussion on inspiration is a clear signal of the transition of artisans into artists. This is the entry door to the fundamental conception of creation. The ability to create (beauty in this case) is not only linked to skills that can be learned (artisanship) but also, and sometimes more importantly, to the inner abilities of certain (gifted) individuals.

The difference between artisans and artist is essential.[4] Julian Gallego describes this transition in-depth in his book, *The painter, from artisan to artist*.[5] This new consideration as artists is critical. Artists have a better social position. To start, artists would pay fewer taxes and have the consideration of a liberal work, and "liberal" here meant "performed by a free man". Artists can decide what and when to create while their clients hire artisans and it is for the clients to determine the outcome (including size, technique, time or color). Artists are not measured by their manual effort, but by the inmateriality of their work.

13

The concept of luxury

Eighteenth and nineteenth century. A new luxury paradigm: luxury as an economic factor

The eighteenth century is a turning point for the concept of luxury and the transition toward a more favorable social consideration of luxury. Up to the seventeenth century, luxury was perceived as being pernicious and harmful. But this changed significantly the moment luxury was started to be perceived as an economic issue, which positively influenced society's development. This transition to modernity changes the luxury paradigm, as Berry denotes, by a demoralization of luxury.

The luxury debate

The European Enlightenment is a turning point in the evolution of luxury. Maxine Berg and Elizabeth Eger provide a magnificent compilation in *Luxury in the Eighteenth Century*.[6] In their first chapter, Professors Berg and Eger offer a detailed description of how luxury became central to Enlightenment debates. But this situation was not a simple mutation from bad to good.

This period represents a confrontation between two ways to understand luxury. In Professors Berg and Eger's words, an old (or ancient) view of luxury confronts a new (or modern) idea of luxury. Old (or ancient) luxury was characterized by excessive wealth display, status and power. In contrast, modern luxury was embodied by the expansion of commerce, utility and a discussion of taste and comfort.

It was then when the concept of luxury evolved in its meaning. What once had been "excess" was now "surplus," and what once had been "vanity" was now "refinement". Rather than a complete change in the perception of luxury, this period represented a new emerging way to consider luxury. These two confronting views of luxury started a passionate debate about the idea of luxury, a discussion about how beneficial or harmful luxury can be for society and its economic development. This would be a debate very rich in content touching on the idea of national virtue, economic expansion, canons of taste, and definitions of the self and the social distribution of wealth.[7] Those are aspects that have a significant impact on the role of society.

Once again, we see how luxury is a mirror of society. In this transformational era, luxury became a central topic in the economic and political thought in Europe. A clear example is that *The Cambridge history of the*

14

eighteenth century on political thought[8] has a specific chapter dedicated to the debate on commerce and luxury.

This chapter, written by Professor Istvan Hont, is an excellent and detailed description of the debate evolution toward a more constructive view on luxury. Professor Hont follows the same dichotomy of ancient versus modern luxury to illustrate the debate on luxury and provides an excellent summary of each view's foremost thinkers.

Among the prominent figures that advocated for the old view of luxury were Archbishop Fénelon (tutor of Louis XIV's grandson and promotor of antiabsolutist politics) in France, and Francis Hutcheson and Bishop George Berkeley in Ireland. Archbishop Fénelon had a strong view and considered luxury a poison to society or even worse to society than despotism, in an explicit critique of Louis XIV's legacy.[9]

Despite being more sensitive to the need for economic growth, Berkeley and Hutcheson also considered luxury as a peril to society. As an example, both defended, like Fénelon, the use of sumptuary laws.

On the other hand, the modern view of luxury supported a new perspective linked to modernity, economic growth, nations' power and citizens' well-being. Among the leading advocates of that view, we find Anglo-Dutch philosopher and economist Bernard Mandeville. He is considered one of the first thinkers of this movement. Famous for his *The Fable of The Bees: or, Private Vices, Publick Benefits*[10] (1714), he ridiculed the example of virtuous and frugal bees in it. For Mandeville, there was not a superior morality in basic needs than in superfluous goods.

But, furthermore, in Mandeville, we find that idea of superficiality was never complete, and even a good that was needed only by kings could be regarded as necessary. Mandeville believed that it was in human nature to be self-interested and pleasure-seeking. But this was a positive thing for society as it fueled commerce and employment. Mandeville had a very provocative view of luxury.

Some years later, the French economist Jean François Melon published *A Political Essay Upon Commerce* (1735), considered one of the most vivid defenses of luxury. Melon identified three stages in economic development, from necessary goods to luxuries. It was built again in the same discussion between the type of necessities. However, Melon stated the difference between the necessary and the superfluous, not in terms of moral or perils, but as different forms of commerce. And this is a crucial point, as Melon observed luxury as a natural and necessary stage in the economy's progress.

The concept of luxury

This view is also supported by the two prominent French thinkers of the time, Montesquieu and Voltaire. Both made contributions to the debate of luxury supporting its positive role. Montesquieu dedicated chapters to luxury in his treaties of political economy and, against common wisdom, described that Rome's fall was not due to luxury. Montesquieu believed the main reasons were war and institutional confusion. He also thought that the development of policy required the development of arts and science. In Voltaire's work, there is also a defense of arts and science as a way to achieve social progress. The classic dilemma of luxury versus corruption is also a recurrent theme. However, in the form of refined goods, luxury is considered a natural consequence of development and not a threat to it.

Still, the way to make luxury "politically and morally benign," as Professor Hont describes, was up to discussion. Melon suggested that luxury was an adequate incentive for economic development, only if sufficient democratic. And Mandeville also made considerations on taming luxury. This is what Professor Hont describes as a second debate among the thinkers advocating for a modern luxury consideration.

The consequence of this political debate on luxury and society is the formation of the luxury market. This period provides the two needed components for the creation of the luxury market. First, luxury is perceived as an economic factor, and second, luxury consumption is demoralized. What once were goods for the court and the aristocratic elites expanded greatly to other layers of society.

Professor Maxine Berg describes with great detail this transformational period in Great Britain in *In Pursuit of Luxury: Global History and British Consumer Goods in the Eighteenth Century. Past & Present.*[11] The trade increase in luxury goods represented then a significant force behind the British (and European) economy's transformation. Professor Berg highlights how luxury goods were imported from Asia (cotton, silk, calicos or porcelains), but the production processes were not. Among other reasons, the production techniques in Asia were related to secrecy and small family business. Artisans often lived in semipoverty conditions since most of the value was captured by merchants (note here the difference stated before between artisan and artist). Instead, new techniques were developed to cope with this new and large demand. As Professor Berg states, Asian consumption was transferred, but not Asian production systems.

Asian imports had a tremendous impact on European consumption and production, especially in Britain. New resources and manufacturing techniques were developed to adapt the Asian luxury and meet the European consumption requirements. This was the origin of what Professor Berg calls "British new consumer goods," which would become, by the end of the eighteenth century, "distinctive modern alternatives to former Asian and European luxuries".[12]

While the British example is perhaps the most important one, this transformational period can be observed in other European countries. Professor Matt Erlin describes a similar situation in Germany.[13] Professor Erlin illustrates how culture development is a form of luxury and explains the example of books as a luxury good. This example shows the same controversy of the value of artistic work and the need for refinement in its appreciation as seen in the development of Asian luxury imports in Britain.

The Enlightenment debate on luxury shaped its meaning. There was no complete change from an old (negative) perception into a new (positive) perception). This debate on luxury challenged previous notions on luxury being a pernicious risk to the self and how society was organized. The values of self-indulgence can be positive in the same way that the production, commerce and consumption of luxury can bring positive economic development to society. This is the reason this era is typically considered a turning point for the notion of luxury.

Luxury and art. Appreciation and refinement

There is a second factor. Perhaps even more critical if one observes this situation from the lenses of management. In this period, the first considerations of luxury consumers and the luxury market appear. And, furthermore, the consumption of luxury is related to the appreciation of art. From now on, luxury would be related to the appreciation of art and refinement of the senses.

The vital role of the appreciation of art is evident in David Hume's work. Its initial treaty is evident in his *Of Luxury* (1752), which was later changed to *Of Refinement in the Arts* (1760). As Professors Berg and Eger argue, most likely modifying luxury for refinement was a way to counterbalance the more vivid language of Mandeville. This is an example of how semantics matter in the historical study and evolution of luxury. For Hume, luxury had a positive impact thanks to commerce and development. But luxury was also positive as it brought politeness, civility and refinement.[14]

Art was also a way to limit the negative perception of luxury as a corruptive force for men or as a way to foster unconscious excess. Hume argues that refinement is the way to avoid such excesses. In his *Of Refinement in the Arts*, he states that "the more men refine upon pleasure, the less will they indulge in excesses in any kind, because nothing is more destructive to true pleasure than such excesses". Also, in Voltaire's thinking, we observe a similar idea. To refuse the concept of luxury as a corruptive force to people, he described luxury as flourishing of the arts and sciences.[15]

The fact that luxury is related to the appreciation and the refinement of art is, indeed, not new. In the Renaissance, as seen in the previous section, the difference between artist and artisan was discussed. As said earlier, the artistic output was no longer dictated by the aristocratic client (artisan view), but seen as a creation by the artist (artistic view). This requires an appreciation of the refinement in art by both the client and the artist. What we see in the Enlightenment is the expansion of this situation to other layers of society, layers that, while still an elite of society, we now can call luxury consumers.

But not everyone agreed on the benefits of luxury and art. One of the clearest examples is Jean-Jacques Rousseau. In his *Discourse on the Arts and Sciences* (1750), Rousseau challenges luxury and art's benefits to society. For him, luxury and, in the same way, arts and sciences result from man's vanity, making society more corrupted.

Consequently, the Enlightenment debate between art and luxury pushed further its meaning—the increasing appreciation of aesthetics results in the development of different forms of culture like museums or theaters.[16] The impact of art is the idea of appreciation and refinement, which will also shape luxury consumers' perceptions. The way society sees and consumes luxury from the eighteenth century would be shaped by refinement and appreciation of the arts.

In summary, this period had a fundamental impact on the concept of luxury and its evolving meaning. More positive perceptions are based on two principles. The first one is the understanding of luxury as an economic factor that supports trade and commerce for society's benefit. The second component is the counterargument against luxury being the driver of corruption. The appreciation and refinements in the arts offer a new perspective of luxury, which tries to help men improve social interaction rather than destroy them. Of course, this was open to debate, and the belief of luxury being pernicious to society and men still persisted.

This period witnessed the first consideration of luxury as a market and luxury clients in a broader sense. It is not a coincidence that the eighteenth century was when the first "luxury companies" were born.

Contemporary luxury. The luxury "market"

The luxury debate and the evolution in its perception were the seed of the luxury market we know of today. Social and economic development went hand in hand with luxury development. The increasing social acceptance of luxury and the economic development triggered the expansion of luxury consumption toward more and more society layers. In the same way, artisans became artists and workshops became companies.

The Enlightenment debate on the benefits of luxury evolved into an economic discussion in the nineteenth century, where income distribution played a central role.[17] In this period, we observe the first steps of the appearance of a consumer-driven market. This is described in great detail for different goods in *Consumers and Luxury: Consumer Culture in Europe, 1650–1850*.[18] Among the different types of luxury goods described, the chapter dedicated to fashion transformation in France is of particular interest.[19] Here Professor Fiona Ffoulkes describes the role of fashion merchants (or in French, *marchands de mode*).

Different factors are accountable for expanding fashion from the small aristocratic elite to the more extensive and growing middle class. As Professor Ffoulkes describes, one key element is the new production techniques enabling the increase in output. This, combined with the arrival of new forms of distribution, like department stores, made the goods more accessible. But fashion merchants themselves played a central role in shifting the perception of fashion as a necessity to fashion as a luxury. Fashion merchants were the cornerstone of the idea of obsolescence, an idea that still today drives the fashion industry. Furthermore, fashion journals supported the creative role of fashion merchants.

In the twentieth century, the luxury market continued its growth, with the two World Wars' evident impact. This century was the time when the need to understand the knowledge of luxury consumption arose.

German psychologist Werner Sombart in *Luxus and Kapitalismus* (1913) explained luxury through the lens of the pleasure involved in the consumption process. This is an essential factor. Luxury started to be linked to personal pleasure, besides luxury as a form of social status.

Professor Stana Nenadic suggests that the "Romanticism movement" of the nineteenth century shaped future consumerism by stimulating the role of personal pleasure or hedonism.[20] Romanticism was focused on emotions, which was the opposite of the Enlightenment movement, which was more

The concept of luxury

focused on rationalism. In this regard, Professor Nenadic suggests romanticism became the initial support of consumerism as it dealt with "unfocused dissatisfaction". The role of consumerism was to fulfill an emotional void. And it was the emotional connotations of products the primary rationale behind their consumption (as they satisfied the feeling of these voids). Therefore, this new hedonistic self-consciousness stimulated consumerism. And, consequently, the powerful emotional connotations of luxury products enabled the expansion of the luxury market.

There is another factor that helps understand the rise of the luxury market. One of the most notable contributions to understand luxury and its consumption pattern was provided by Thorstein Bunde Veblen. His idea of "conspicuous consumption" has been traditionally one of the most frequently used concepts when discussing luxury consumption. In his *The Theory of the Leisure Class* (1899), Veblen explains how the process of consumption is shaped by two factors: utility and waste (ostentation).[21]

For Veblen, wealth accumulation develops the "leisure class" in function and structure, and there arises a differentiation within the class.[22] Thus, the new wealthy population differentiates among themselves through consumption that the rest of their community can see. Hence, the idea of conspicuous consumption represents the concept that others must observe consumption to support this social differentiation. In this way, Veblen considers that conspicuous consumption is "a means of representability of the gentleman of leisure".[23]

But not only is conspicuous consumption a form of social differentiation among wealthy individuals, but it is also a mirror for the rest of society. Veblen considered that the leisure class's manner of life and standards afforded the community's norm of reputability.[24] This is the fundamental idea behind what we call "status". Luxury possession has always marked social hierarchy; what Veblen stated is how this now shapes consumer buying behavior.

The rise of luxury consumption, and the consequent growth of the luxury market, is triggered by two main factors. One factor is the emotional satisfaction that luxury products can provide. And the second factor is the expressive attributes that luxury consumption offers its buyers.

In most recent times, luxury has continued to evolve. Its continuous adaptation to the way society evolves has impacted the meaning and the consumption of luxury. A clear example of how luxury mirrors society was witnessed in the 1980s and 1990s, when the luxury market grew significantly with

Concept of luxury. Past, present & future

expressive attitudes. After the 2008 financial crisis, however, luxury evolved again to become more personal and intimate. Chapter 8 covers in more detail future drivers of change, like the digital transformation of luxury firms.

Lessons from the concept of luxury. What the luxury manager needs to know

Learning about the concept of luxury and its past evolution might be an interesting introductory consideration. The stories and historical events behind the idea can also provide some interesting anecdotes. However, it is normal to wonder, *Is this of any importance for a manager of a luxury firm today?*

Inadequate knowledge of luxury as a concept can lead to poor managerial decision-making. Here, we explore the fundamental lessons that the anthropological perspective provides for the management practice.

Luxury as constant change. The challenge of defining luxury

Adapting to the evolving shape of luxury is problematic for luxury managers. The difficulties many firms faced over the first decade of the century to understand the impact of digital change can serve as an example.

Luxury is very complex to assess, given that this is a concept shaped by evolving social perceptions, as the previous section unveiled. Consequently, luxury managers can face problems when "defining" luxury. Many debates have been centered on the key variables that define luxury. However, this approach aims to define luxury as a static concept and fails to assess its dynamic nature.

Teaching experience with students and executives suggests that rather than formulating a definition to be shared, it is more meaningful to observe the historical evolution of luxury. This helps luxury managers differentiate the core idea of luxury from its continually evolving facade. As the previous anthropological approach showed, luxury in its core represents how societies relate to their organizational systems. Luxury also shows how different societies faced the constant dilemma between necessary and unnecessary needs (or also phrased as needs vs. desires).

Some concepts are better understood than defined. Consider concepts like love or friendship, which are hardly encapsulated into a closed definition.

The concept of luxury

Explaining these concepts proves to be a very tricky job. When shared in the classroom, it isn't easy to find consensus. Especially in relation to a multicultural audience, many are the different attributes and characteristics to be considered to agree on one single definition. Interestingly enough, everybody in the classroom gets the concept of love or friendship when we talk about it. It is the same with luxury.

The main lesson a luxury manager can get from the anthropological perspective is that while luxury continually changes its format, these tensions remain and shape its evolution. Hence, luxury should not be understood in absolute terms. The problem with providing a closed definition of luxury is that it could be constrained and limited in scope, and we could forget its dynamic component.

Considering luxury as a static phenomenon might only show its meaning at a given time. And this is precisely the opposite of the very essence of luxury as change.

Luxury as relativity. A mirror of society

Luxury is a mirror of society. We highlight here that we use the word society and not culture. There are noticeable cultural differences that impact how people interact and appreciate luxury. However, here the intention is broader. Society is defined by its time and age, accepting the natural differences we might find in different regions.

Luxury has to be observed through the lens of the time being considered. Its meaning is relative to the society we are considering. It is then tough to extrapolate luxury or assess its future evolution if we do not observe society's development adequately. In the same way, looking back a few years to understand luxury is a mistake as well. That is what we said earlier about the misconception of luxury as being classic. Such type of assessment creates stereotypes rather than understanding.

There is an important lesson here. It is not for companies to dictate what is or what is not luxury; it is the society that defines luxury. Indeed, big companies might have some influence, especially on their form and shape. But companies are only to understand and capture value from the societal changes.

Capsule 1.1 shows the example of Sneakers as an example of social change. Sneakers are not only bought by young generations. People in their 50s feel younger and consume products more in line with their beliefs and lifestyle.

Concept of luxury. Past, present & future

Capsule 1.1. Can sneakers be luxury?

Consider for a moment sneakers. None considered this product category a luxury category until very recently. And yet, today, it is a fundamental category where all major players have launched a collection of sneakers.

It was kind of a choke when Chanel launched their sneaker collection back in 2014 as a part of their haute couture collection. This was perhaps a turning point in the evolution of sneakers as a luxury category. Chanel was not convincing their consumers that sneakers were a luxury product; instead, they made a great (and brave) move by realizing that social attitudes to luxury were evolving and took the lead of that change. Today, most luxury fashion and accessories companies produce sneakers. Not only that, but sneakers have also become an iconic, even best-selling, product. How does a product category (sport shoes), generally considered non-luxury, become a luxury icon?

The answer lies in the fact that luxury is a mirror of society, as mentioned earlier. Chanel's early move on sneakers shows how to read social signals and bet on them. Luxury firms must accept that they do not decide what is or what is not luxury. It is for the society to determine what is or is not luxury. It is for firms to compete meaningfully to achieve business success, but not to define luxury.

The acceptance of sneakers is based on three aspects. One, the young generation likes them. Two, we have more affluent young consumers than before. And three, all consumers buy them since they feel more youthful. And that is a crucial point. It is not that all consumers mirror the consumption of younger generations. Our society feels more youthful than before. And sneakers are perhaps the best representation of this fact.

An anecdote can be self-explanatory. On an executive session with several CEOs, one of them happened to say, "You know what some say ... the 40s are the 30s". Rapidly an executive jumped and said, "And 50s are the new 40s!" Our society feels younger. Thus, the sneaker popularity reflects the more youthful and more casual lifestyle of our society today. This has not been decided by any board or any

> company. This is society as a whole changing. And it makes sense, considering that we have the means to live longer, and tight social norms are relaxing. Sneakers are just a representation of the society we live in and what we value.

The underlying idea is that today we feel younger. This is a strong feeling that encapsulates our society today. Today, one feels younger than someone of the same age some 10, 15 or 20 years ago. In Spain, for instance, life expectancy is about 82 years old, while it was 60 years old in the 1950s. These days, we have the technology and the science to live longer and enjoy life more, so feeling "younger" is a natural consequence. In the end, it is society as a broader entity, and not the consumer as a segmented mindset, that dictates the luxury industry.

Need versus desires, or basic versus sophisticated needs

The concept of luxury has always revolved around the relationship between the notion of need and desire. Regardless of whether we consider need versus desire, natural versus unnatural, raw versus refined/sophisticated, luxury is a stimulus that pushes boundaries, a human drive of going beyond. And this is something that is in our nature, regardless of the time and society we want to consider.

This is a crucial lesson for luxury managers. It might be very difficult (or even impossible) to find the line between what is basic and desire. But what the luxury manager should not forget is that we are always trying to explore, reach and cross that limit. This is the idea luxury managers should get when we say that luxury satisfies sophisticated needs (or desires).

Luxury as a threat. The negative perceptions

Luxury was perceived as a threat to early societies. Even in the eighteenth century, there was an intense debate between luxury as a threat and economic and development factors. This debate teaches us the importance of how meaning is built.

Luxury managers should be aware of the foundation behind the negative and the positive perceptions. Being aware of these perceptions, and knowing about the times in history when they were created, would prove

Concept of luxury. Past, present & future

helpful to luxury managers; we might forget the origins of meaning given the fast pace at which the market and consumers change. This awareness might prove very valuable when assessing corporate decisions. And it also helps us tear down some myths, as we will see in the next section.

The notion of quantity versus quality

Luxury originally meant ostentation and wealth. The idea of refinement appeared sometime later. This shows that, in general terms, quantity preceded quality. We initially associated luxury with ownership, and it took some time for us to appreciate a specific characteristic (refinement) involved in that ownership.

In the early years of the last century, owning a car was a luxury. Today, owning a car can still be a luxury, but only a specific car like a Ferrari or a Pagani. This process can be observed more easily when technology is relevant, as the example of the car highlights. Changes in social habits are a bit harder to watch, but they are equally relevant. The way we consume and our appreciation of value is also continually evolving. There is no better way to observe this dynamic evolution of luxury than with the sneakers example in Capsule 1.1.

This helps us observe how luxury has evolved from ownership (quantitative) to refinement (qualitative). This balance between quantitative and qualitative is a critical consideration when assessing luxury.

Refinement and appreciation. The link with art

The fact that there is a path from quantity to quality in luxury leads us to the role of art. Art is how we can assess and appreciate quality, or better said, how we can evaluate and appreciate value.

What art has represented to societies from the Renaissance is the pursuit of beauty and excellence in the making. It might be worth reminding that art is a form of expression where a given skill is required. And this is key to luxury since luxury managers, oftentimes, do not need to find a unique solution to problems; instead, what they need to do is unveil the multiple options available and choose one among them.

As a way of expression, art helps luxury managers better understand the fundamental dilemma of building something valuable on their terms. This is the main idea behind creation or creativity.

Every luxury manager should learn about art. Art helps us develop the needed sensitivity to appreciate details, understand that form and shape

25

The concept of luxury

matter, and above all, that there are different meaningful ways of doing things. It is all about finding yours.

A second valuable lesson is the role of an artist. The Renaissance introduced the distinction between artist and artisan. Today, luxury firms can be relevant through a creative artist, like creative directors in fashion, watch designers in watchmaking, or *chef de caves* in winemaking.

Managers who come from FMCG to luxury usually face a similar problem. It takes them from six months to one year to understand the business. Why does a successful manager with years of experience needs months to understand a new firm? The reason is the role of art. As we will see in more detail in Part 2, value creation is more of a choice than a solution. And choices are ultimately based on artistic conceptions. This could lead to a mental crash for many managers holding a problem-solution type of thinking. This is why managers with the sensitivity to appreciate art and the artistic mindset learn faster how luxury firms operate.

Luxury as a development force before being an industry

Luxury has become, over the last two centuries, a force behind social development. Artisans have become companies for a wider audience. And as a result, today, luxury is a market.

Luxury managers should never forget what luxury was before it evolved into a market. The fact that firms satisfy consumers should not undermine the real meaning of luxury as a social agent. It existed long before there was a (modern) market of luxury, and this is because the concept of luxury goes beyond the limits of the relationship between clients and companies. Luxury exists as it is a social factor that influences how societies are organized, and it affects the way human beings observe their self-identity. A luxury manager can be no stranger to these very important luxury notions before heading to the marketplace to compete.

Table 1.1 summarizes the main lessons discussed in this section.

Breaking the stereotypes, the road to analysis

The previous section's lessons are of utmost importance for luxury managers as they support a better understanding of luxury as a phenomenon. This might be precious support in their decision-making. Likewise, the study of

Concept of luxury. Past, present & future

Table 1.1 Lessons of the anthropological perspective on luxury

Key aspect	Lessons
Luxury as change	– Luxury is a dynamic concept. It is continually evolving. – What remains is the human nature of going beyond limits.
Mirror of society	– Luxury is defined by society, not by firms. – Luxury evolves as society does.
Basic (need) versus sophisticated (desire)	– The human drive to go beyond boundaries
Luxury as a threat	– Luxury represents a threat to social organization and hence has received negative connotations.
Quantity versus quality	– Quantity defines luxury as access. – Quality defines luxury as (a later) sophistication (refinement) of certain characteristics.
Link to art	– Art is a way to appreciate sophisticated attributes. – Artisanship deals with skills, while artists deal with creation. – Art represents a different mindset. Creation based on self-expression through skills
An economic force	– Luxury as an economic force is only the modern perspective of luxury.

the history of luxury might also help tear down some myths and stereotypes that can bias luxury managers.

Luxury stereotypes are the enemy of luxury managers. Falling into prejudices goes against sound analytical skills and insightful decision-making. There are several stereotypes associated with the concept of luxury. We will evaluate a few of the most common here to bring some perspective to the lessons learned in the previous section.

Luxury as superficiality

The classic debate that luxury brings forth is the discussion between needs and desires or basic needs and refined needs.

From an anthropological perspective, it is clear these negative connotations on social consumption of luxury were the outcome of a thorough social debate. But a luxury manager cannot assume that luxury is superficial. That

The concept of luxury

would be neglecting the other side of the discussion—the part that deals with refinement in the arts, with the sophistication of needs and with the role of social development or self-identity. Thus, considering that luxury is superficial is just a simplification of a much more profound debate.

The second important aspect here is to differentiate the concept of luxury from individual consumer behavior. A classical stereotype is to consider that luxury is nothing else than rich people burning their excess cash. Luxury is a more complex phenomenon than individual consumer patterns, regardless of their motivations.

Luxury as unfairness or inequality

The classic debate on luxury is also about social organization. It is about the idea of justice and social well-being. And luxury has been the enemy of these as it stimulates corruption and selfishness. In the eyes of many, consumption of luxury is unethical and signals a product with no real value whatsoever.

But the Enlightenment debate shows us how this is only one side of the story. One should also consider the role of refinement in the arts, social development, and economic growth. Powerful ideas and positive social transformation are derived from the pursuit of beauty, from the efforts behind refinement of basic needs or from the passion for crossing the limits. This is also at the very heart of luxury. Art, music and engineering (like cars or watches) have improved and pushed our society further.

The luxury manager should pay close attention to this debate to differentiate meaning from prejudice. Luxury managers mustn't be ashamed of what they do. There is nothing wrong with managing a luxury firm; on the contrary, luxury can have a positive influence on society.

It is not the author's intention to provide a moral argument here, but rather to illustrate the broad and rich meaning of luxury as a phenomenon. Societies are imperfect and luxury can, indeed, signal unfairness. But luxury is part of human nature.

Luxury as classic or everlasting

Another common misunderstanding comes from the idea of luxury as being classic. Luxury is frequently related to some solid values anchored in the past. And to a certain extent, it makes sense, as luxury products have not

Concept of luxury. Past, present & future

changed much over the past decades. The reason is that luxury firms have experienced a tremendous expansion over the past three decades. They have been growing organically, trying to reach more number of countries with a similar proposition. As a result, the goal has been not to evolve the product, but instead to make it accessible to more people. Over the past decades, luxury has been "conquering" new territories in countries like the United States, Japan and, more recently, China.

That said, we might tend to observe luxury today as what we have seen over the past decades. Firms have been protecting their (old) iconic products with their beautiful communication and their nice stores. This can create the false perception that luxury is about classical and everlasting values. Many times, what we call a classic was a kind of revolution in their own time. Capsule 1.2 provides the example of the Royal Oak and the steel sports watch segment.

If there is one consistent thing about luxury, it is change. The evolution we are witnessing today is nothing more than one more development. Luxury managers should embrace change, not fight it. And it is, indeed, very complex to face change, but it is inevitable. Not long ago, there was a dilemma whether or not to display prices online. The reason was the strong link between luxury and previous classical values.

Capsule 1.2. The origins of "iconic" designs

When Gerald Genta designed the Royal Oak for Audemars Piguet, it was kind of a revolutionary watch. It was the first sports watch in steel—and something not very well received back in the 1970s.

Today, many companies have followed that path and the steel bracelet watch is a fundamental watch segment. Since the original was conceived in the 1970s, we might refer to it as a "classic watch" or/and "iconic design"—something to be protected and not to be changed. However, we hardly recognize that this was a revolutionary product that required a brave approach to break the then status quo. What we call "iconic" or "classic" today does usually represent an original creative approach. That creative approach is to be protected, rather than the design per se.

The concept of luxury

Luxury as craftsmanship means it is opposed to technology

Luxury is frequently observed as a synonym of craftsmanship. However, this often conveys the idea of being opposed to technology, but this is a stereotype.

What we have discussed in the previous sections illustrates how mistaken can it be to consider luxury being opposed to technology. In the Renaissance, there was a fine line between art and engineering. We have to look at Leonardo Da Vinci and his multiple creations and inventions to realize the limitation of splitting art from science. The Enlightenment debate on luxury also considered that the appreciation of luxury might not be confined to one perspective. Considering luxury being opposed to technology only limits the luxury manager's ability to embrace change and creativity. It is a barrier that must be broken.

Summary

This chapter provides an introduction to the concept of luxury. This is a needed requirement to gain a better perspective on the evolution of luxury, but primarily to gain a sound knowledge of luxury as a phenomenon.

The historical introduction highlights how comprehending luxury through the lens of different areas of expertise like sociology, anthropology and economics is essential. Only in this way can one appreciate the ongoing relationship between luxury and society. This approach unveils luxury as a human pulse to go beyond—a pulse that has always impacted social organization and human relationships. This section also shows how luxury can be better understood by observing the different debates about the concept of need and the way societies are organized. This study also unveils how luxury is a dynamic concept in constant evolution, mirroring society's development.

The chapter also provides some valuable managerial lessons derived from the anthropological study of luxury. This would help the luxury manager gain a more profound understanding of luxury than a narrow definition, which would ultimately refer to luxury at a given moment in history. The different types of needs, the dynamic component of luxury and its link to art and refinement are clear examples of how valuable a solid anthropological perspective on luxury can be for a luxury manager.

The chapter concludes with some final remarks on stereotypes that frequently accompany the concept of luxury. Considering luxury as everlasting is of particular relevance here—something that challenges the view of luxury as dynamic and being apace with social developments. This is why these stereotypes are also barriers to a sound analysis of the luxury firms discussed in the following chapters.

Self-study questions

1. *What differences do you observe in the concept of luxury during the different historical ages described in the chapter?*
2. *Why defining luxury with generic notions like exclusivity, status or quality might not provide a comprehensive understanding of the phenomenon of luxury?*
3. *Why has luxury traditionally had such negative perceptions?*
4. *Does luxury contradict rationality? What is the foundation for this apparent contradiction?*
5. *How can the appreciation of more refined (or sophisticated) needs be linked to the arts?*
6. *Identify a luxury stereotype and argue why this might be a limiting factor for managerial decisions of luxury managers.*

Notes

1 Lipovetsky G. and Roux E. *Le luxe éternel. De l'âge du sacré au temps des marques.* Gallimard, 2003.

2 Berry, C.J. *The Idea of Luxury.* Cambridge University Press, 1994.

3 Vasari, G. *The Lives of the Most Excellent Painters, Sculptors, and Architects.* 1568.

4 With gratitude to Professor Amaya Alzaga. For her advice and kindness in sharing with me her great expertise in the history of art.

5 Gallego J. *El pintor de artesa a artista.* Universidad de Granada, Departamento de Historia del Arte, 1976.

6 Berg, M. and Eger, E. *Luxury in the Eighteenth Century.* Palgrave Macmillan, 2003.

7 Berg and Eger, page 7.

8 Hont I, Chapter 13 from "The Cambridge History of Eighteenth-Century Political Thought", edited by Goldie, M. and Wokler, R..

The concept of luxury

9 See Hont, page 383, with references to Fénelon's "Les aventures de Télémaque, fils d'Ulysse", 1699.

10 See Hont, page 387.

11 Berg, M., "In Pursuit of Luxury: Global History and British Consumers Goods in the Eighteenth Century", *Past & Present*, Vol. 182 (2004), pp. 85–142.

12 See Berg, page 86.

13 Erlin, M. *Necessary Luxuries: Books, Literature, and the Culture of Consumption in Germany, 1770–1815*. Cornell University Press, 2014.

14 Berg and Eger, page 18.

15 See Hont, page 389.

16 See Berg and Eger, page 20.

17 See Berg and Eger, page 22.

18 "Consumers and Luxury: Consumer Culture in Europe, 1650–1850", edited by Berg, M. and Clifford, H. 1999.

19 Ffoulkes, F. Chapter 9 from "Consumers and Luxury: Consumer Culture in Europe, 1650–1850", edited by Berg, M. and Clifford, H. 1999.

20 Nenadic, S. Chapter 10 from "Consumers and Luxury: Consumer Culture in Europe, 1650–1850", edited by Berg, M. and Clifford, H. 1999.

21 Veblen, T. *The Theory of the Leisure Class*, 1899. See page 69 of the Oxford University Press edition, 2009.

22 See Veblen, page 54.

23 See Veblen, page 53.

24 See Veblen, page 59.

PART 2

Principles of luxury value creation. The *essence* of luxury

2 The need of a managerial approach. Luxury and strategy

Introduction and objectives

This book has a fundamental premise, the general lessons on marketing and strategy might not be enough to analyze a luxury firm. This chapter explores and justifies this necessity—the potential of current knowledge in strategy and marketing to deal with the most common luxury management problems is limited. This chapter explores the limitations or the need to adjust some assumptions behind the main managerial tools. In this way, we will argue the necessity of luxury-specific knowledge.

Most of the analytical tools we know usually are linked to a specific problem they aimed to solve and (or) to a particular moment in time. Therefore, one should be careful when applying analytical tools. We should always carefully consider what the framework was initially conceived for and which are its assumptions. This is the main reason why managerial frameworks can have difficulties when applied to luxury. It is merely the fact that they were not originally designed to deal with these sorts of problems. Likewise, it could be the case that the assumptions of core managerial tools enter into conflict with the core idea of luxury.

This is then the first step in our journey to a luxury strategy—the justification of luxury-specific organizational tools. This is not aimed to contradict existing knowledge but to complement it to better understand the strategy of luxury firms.

DOI: 10.4324/9781003015321-5

Principles of luxury value creation

> By the time you have completed this chapter, you will be able to:
>
> - Identify the main managerial problems (challenges) that most luxury firms face in their business success path.
> - Learn the difference between client-centric and artistic-based approaches to the market and their impact on the management discipline. These are the so-called traditional paradigm and luxury paradigm.
> - Understanding the management problems that arise when companies are driven by creativity or artistic conceptions is paramount.
> - Identify the limitations of marketing and strategic analytical tools.
> - Reason about generic managerial tools' principles and assumptions to identify the necessity to adjust them to luxury-specific requirements.
> - Justify the need for a specific managerial approach for luxury firms.

Luxury and its managerial challenges

One fundamental question any book on strategic management is intended to discuss is, "Why are some firms more successful than others?" The answer to this question, or a better understanding of this question, unveils the market competition's complexity.

In this section, we will show the main areas of complexity that luxury firms face. This is the first step to assess how traditional principles on marketing and strategy respond to luxury firms' managerial issues. At this point, we will consider a generic approach, and we will refer to luxury as one entity. Competing in the mega-yacht industry differs from the fashion industry. Nevertheless, this introduction aims to argue the need for a proper managerial approach to luxury. This specific managerial approach to luxury, if needed, can be later on transferred to the particular requirements of each luxury industry.

In Chapter 1, we discussed how luxury became a global market. But until very recently, the luxury market was tiny compared to other industries. Perhaps, this is why traditionally, luxury did not capture much of the attention of management research.

The luxury market has grown significantly over the past 40 years, and so it has increased its exposure to media. We are now more familiarized with luxury firms, their success, and their failures. In the 1970s, luxury was a relatively small market. Luxury firms had a relatively small size despite their popularity. Today luxury has become a market where everyone is invited. Few can afford an haute-couture dress, but many can afford lipstick or a tie from a luxury house. And so, what once were small workshops have become multibillion corporations.

The competitive challenges and the way to achieve business success have also changed. Managing luxury implies the understanding of the main choices that any firm faces in its path to success. Today, it is arguably more complex to sustain luxury firms as they engage with a more diverse set of clients. Their activities have extraordinarily expanded, and their global reach poses severe organizational difficulties.

One of my original researches in luxury was intended to identify the main conflict areas in luxury firms. The idea was to compare luxury management conflicts with, let's say, generic management conflicts. In this way, we could unveil to what extent managing luxury firms differed from management practice as we know it. In other words, to reveal to what extent the current knowledge in strategy and marketing was useful to deal with luxury-specific problems.

After some years (and a few hundreds of interviews with luxury executives and luxury experts), I learned that fundamentally there are four main areas of conflict specific to luxury management.[1]

- The creativity challenge. The tension between management and creators.
- The growth challenge. The tension between mass and exclusivity.
- The change challenge. The time dilemma.
- The control challenge. The issues to sustain value on creativity-driven firms.

These four areas will be referred to as luxury managerial challenges. The challenges are not a comprehensive list of firm problems. Of course, firms face a wide array of issues that go beyond this set of four. These challenges suggest the specific areas where the practice of management in luxury encounters severe difficulties. Therefore any framework should consider these challenges to assess the luxury strategy. In other words, the luxury challenges are a checklist of critical requirements that any managerial tool or framework should address specifically.

Principles of luxury value creation

The creativity challenge. The tension between management and creator

One fundamental aspect that sets apart the management of luxury firms from other types of firms is the role of creativity. This is not to say that creativity, innovation or design is not essential in other industries. But their role is not the same as in luxury. When we speak of creativity, as briefly introduced in Chapter 1, we do not aim to discuss innovation or design, which is vital across many industries. It is the role of the whole creation that differs slightly from other sectors. Frequently, this role is done by a single individual (like a fashion designer), but it also entails a comprehensive set of firm abilities.

We usually consider the CEO the most essential "employee" of the firm and the person accountable for its leadership and future evolution. In luxury, we might need to fine-tune this perception.

The Gucci turnaround in the late 1990s is a very well-known example. Under the leadership of (creative director) Tom Ford, Gucci reconquered its position as a synonym of avant-garde fashion. But fewer people know the role of Domenico de Sole, CEO of the firm at the time. Under Mr. De Sole's leadership, the firm redesigned its supply chain to ensure product quality while increasing efficiency and flexibility. Something similar in nature happened at Louis Vuitton in the 1990s. Marc Jacobs was the creative force behind the modernization of its visual imaginary. But few know the role of Yves Carcelle, who, as CEO, transformed the firm and its operational excellence. Fashion is perhaps the clearest example of the tension between management and creativity. But certainly, this is not a fashion issue. We can say similar things in other industries like *chef de cave* versus CEO in the wine industry, or the role of designers versus CEO in any other sectors like the yacht, automobile or mechanical watchmaking industries.

Are creative directors more important than CEOs? It is likely that students in a business school answer no. And students in a school of design will answer yes. What happens when a business student, who becomes a CEO, meets a student of art, who has become Creative Director under the same roof? They most likely think that they have accomplished their life goals. And it is likely they both consider themselves the "most important person" in the organization.

However, this is hardly the question. There is no need to make a ranking on who is more important. The key here is to understand the relationship between the managerial and the creative components in luxury firms. We

Need of a managerial approach

will address the management of creativity in Part 2 in more detail. So far, we only want to identify its importance.

Interestingly enough, these two examples of Gucci and Louis Vuitton have something in common. In both cases, there was a well-defined task differentiation between the CEO and the Creative Directors. There was mutual recognition of the other's talent. More than the competition, this is about internal cooperation between two critical components—a puzzle more than a pyramid.

The previous question comparing the CEO with the creative designer is fascinating for the students of luxury management. Are you (student of luxury management) ready to accept the leadership of an artist-driven personality? And how do we decide when we encounter differences between the "analytical" and the "artistic" perspectives? Management studies lead us to think that it is the CEO, senior managers, and their analytical skills the firm's main asset. But we link analysis with rationality. And this is a limitation for luxury, as we unveiled in the previous Chapter 1. Therefore managing a firm where artistic thinking is critical should be less "analytical" if we think that analysis means rationality. And this is an explicit limitation for many analytical tools.

My personal experience with luxury executives showed a persistent feeling. The manager's previous (non-luxury) expertise is hardly applicable to a new luxury position. It is quite frequent to hear things like, "at the beginning, I didn't understand anything", "I thought the company was mistaken, nothing of what I knew before was applicable here", "but where do I apply my know-how now?" "I needed to learn everything like I was new". Luxury managers need to accept the fact that managerial and artistic skills must co-exist. It is then in the best interest of luxury managers to develop their creative talents. Not to become a designer, but to understand, appreciate, and work meaningfully with artistic-driven personalities.

Consequently, any managerial tool to support decision-making in the luxury arena should consider the dichotomy between management and creativity.

The growth challenge. The tension between mass and exclusivity

Another specific managerial characteristic of luxury firms is the notion of growth. The strategy of a firm is responsible for ensuring valuable growth. In general terms, growth is a positive aspiration. Only when growth is the

Principles of luxury value creation

outcome of a strategy, we avoid the perils of too aggressive or off-target growth. However, in luxury firms is a bit trickier. Most of the managerial tools we know are designed based on the assumption that growth or business size is not a problem.

Luxury firms face a significant controversy in developing their business. The perception of exclusivity is inversely proportional to the volume of production or sales. In simple words, the more one sells, the less exclusive it becomes. This is even more dangerous when growth can only be achieved from lower-priced goods or categories. This is frequently called the mass versus exclusivity dilemma. The idea is that luxury firms can only grow by expanding to other, lower-priced categories when their core market is already satisfied.

Sometimes growth is a necessity. The launch of the Porsche Boxster in the 1990s is a clear example. The automotive industry is very capital intensive, and economies of scale play a dominant role. Consequently, it is quite tricky that one company can remain profitable selling one model only. This was the situation Porsche was facing. Their iconic 911 model was not enough to sustain the engineering, R&D, and manufacturing of an entire automotive firm. That was one of the main reasons to launch the Porsche Boxster, a two-seater sportscar priced below the 911. With this new model, Porsche got enough scale to balance their cost and profits.

Therefore opening the door to more consumers in the lower spectrum (what frequently is known as becoming more mass-oriented) is only one side of this challenge. Many are the potential areas of conflict as the luxury firm grows, like developing the distribution systems, the diversification of the product portfolio (in lower end categories or other categories), or the international expansion. Therefore we might need to fine-tune our concepts and tools to respond to this reality.

The development of luxury firms entails a tricky balance to ensure the ability to deliver value. In luxury, value creation is a complex equilibrium where the firm's different areas need to enhance each other consistently. Chapter 3 will discuss in-depth this value creation process. Luxury firms must always consider the potential adverse effect of their business development and growth carefully.

The change challenge. The time dilemma

A related aspect issue with growth is to sustain over time. There has been a miss-perception that luxury is about lasting values, and luxury firms should

Need of a managerial approach

be reluctant to change in luxury. This wrong perception was discussed in Chapter 1.

However, dealing with change is a tricky aspect of luxury. Two contradictory forces might need to be balanced. On the one hand, satisfying the needs of current consumers, and on the other hand, securing the arrival of new consumers to sustain future growth. It is frequent to encounter this tension between conservative or more mature clients with superior consumption power against younger clients with lower consumption power. This is a typical situation, but it is not always the case. Therefore the luxury manager should not stereotype age (young) with income (lower).

In luxury, there is tension between the short-term and the future development. Serving the business today (like core clients with superior income) might need to be balanced with engaging with prospective consumers (launching a different set of products, for instance). It becomes a tricky balance when satisfying the current demand might bring some trade-offs to stimulate future demand. In short, core clients might not welcome the activities designed for new clients, for instance, launching new products with lower price points.

However, not evolving the business over time is also risky. Core clients might not sustain the business in the long run, and new consumers might never enter. The luxury firm might become an "old company", making it not attractive to new consumers. They might consume in other firms, and the firm might put its future at risk. When Mercedes-Benz was perceived by new consumers as not very attractive, this created a significant problem for the firm. The future sales of their most valuable models are to a certain extent based on the ability to welcome clients in their entry-level models so they can grow with them. The firm redesigned very successfully its A-class line to be more attractive. The firm also embarked on different communication activities, like sponsoring fashion shows to show the new approach. As a result, the company evolved with the times, become more attractive to new consumers, and prepared the company for future success on the rest of its portfolio. Similarly, Gucci and Louis Vuitton's examples seen above also represent an example of change over time. The arrival of new designers proved to be a way to attract new consumers and refresh the company without hurting its core values.

The time dilemma represents the need for a change of luxury firms and the trade-offs between current and future activities (especially regarding client acquisition). Luxury firms need to change over time while protecting their core activities in the short term.

Principles of luxury value creation

The control challenge. The issues to sustain value on creativity-driven firms

The last specific characteristic of luxury management is the need for control. This might sound strange, as all firms should be concerned with it. So, why is control crucial in the management of luxury? The answer here is less evident than in the previous challenges, and it requires some notion of the way luxury creates value.

In Chapter 3, we will discuss in more detail the luxury value creation process. In simple terms, control is needed since luxury value creation is fundamentally constructed over emotional attributes. The characteristic of emotional is that unlike functional attributes, they are difficult to explain. It is precisely the same difficulties we face in defining our feelings, for instance. In the case of luxury firms, the relevance of emotional benefits in their value creation process makes it challenging to communicate who they are and share what they do. Therefore consumers face difficulties in ascertaining the firm and its value. This is very specific for luxury, and hence it requires specific managerial tools. We will come back to this with more detail in Chapter 3.

The control of the point of sale is the best example to argue why the need for control is a specific luxury challenge. When Louis Vuitton expanded its business in the 1980s in Japan, it opted for a controversial approach. Instead of licensing, the most frequent method, the firm created a subsidiary to secure strict control. This is perhaps the origin of the retail business model that fueled luxury growth. For the first time, a luxury firm decided to integrate distribution and run their stores. This is what is frequently called a Direct Operated Store (DOS). Common sense suggested that this approach was too expensive for a "niche" market like luxury. However, this approach proved to be very successful, and it was rapidly imitated. But why this expensive approach was needed?

The control of the point of sale has been a cornerstone behind the successful expansion of luxury firms. Controlling operations is complex and costly. It requires owning many activities that could be easily licensed. Likewise, it forces the firm to undertake continuous training programs and operational improvements. The traditional strategic logic suggests that international expansion should first control the risk and limit the initial investment.

However, there is a fundamental problem in luxury. Partner companies, like licensees or distributors, might have a hard time communicating why a consumer should pay a price premium for a luxury good. It is complicated enough for a firm to understand its competitive advantage. It is a miracle that a third company can: (a) understand it equally as the firm, (b) communicate it clearly, and (c) run its operations efficiently. The solution to this dilemma is to do it yourself. The rationale is clear. It is expensive, but that is the only way to deliver the critical message effectively. And that is a priority in luxury. As said, the assessment of value is complex in luxury. So understanding first the value increases the likelihood of luxury consumption. This is why the Louis Vuitton approach proved remarkably successful.

There are, however, more reasons that justify the need for control in luxury. Third parties can misrepresent the interest of the firm. Both licensors (buyer side) or subcontractors (supply side) can engage in unwanted activities like discounts (buyer side) or serve the black market (supply-side). Therefore luxury requires strict control of all activities as the value proposition is complex (based on emotions) to build.

In 2010, Burberry produced a local collection in Spain. At that time, the company was trying to win back its reputation as a luxury brand player under Angela Ahrendts and Christopher Bailey's leadership. The facilities in Spain did prove too costly for a local collection. Moreover, and more importantly, in Spain, a sub-brand named "Thomas Burberry" has gained popularity in the Spanish market. This sub-brand was positioned as a premium ready-to-wear collection in the price point of Polo or Lacoste. What made the move of Thomas Burberry not consistent with the global goals for Burberry.

Consequently, the firm decided to cancel both the local collection and the sub-brand to win back a sense of common perception as a luxury. Burberry could do it as they had full control of the subsidiary. Many were the firms, particularly in the 1980s and 1990s, like Gucci in the United States, that had to cut on licensors and buyback subsidiaries to regain control of operations and align the global strategy.

To conclude this section, Table 2.1 summarizes the specificity of the luxury challenges. These are vital aspects to be considered for any managerial tool aimed to help luxury managers and their decision-making.

Luxury from the lenses of the consumer: traditional marketing and its limitations

Luxury has been studied frequently through the lenses of marketing or branding. This approach provides priority to explain business success to how the client perceives luxury and how it interacts with the firm. Consequently, a

Principles of luxury value creation

Table 2.1 The luxury challenges

	Creativity challenge	Growth challenge	Change challenge	Control challenge
What is ...?	Conflict Management versus Creativity • Managing luxury requires two senior decision-making roles. • Management and Creation might face confronting objectives or different managerial attitudes.	Conflict Mass versus Exclusivity • Growth (in term of sales, client reach or output) enters into conflict with the perception of luxury as limited (such as niche segment, reduced output or exclusivity). • Growth (oftentimes) can only be pursued in lower categories. High and low categories do, oftentimes, pose conflicts.	Time Dilemma • Change over time is needed to sustain the luxury business. • Too much focus on short-term activities or core clients, might enter into conflict with the future development of the firm.	• Control to effectively deliver emotional values • Luxury firm based their competitive advantage on emotional attributes. These are complex to explain and communicate • Control is the way to limit potential conflicts in lack of clarity or misrepresentation.
Why is luxury specific?	The leading role in an organization can actually be composed of 2 individuals.	Growth needs to be managed, but always is perceived as positive. In luxury it is not.	Change introduces trade-offs to secure new clients acquisition.	Luxury firms need a superior control than other industries. They need to ensure the delivery of a complex to explain emotional argumentation.

Need of a managerial approach

principal research area has been the way the luxury consumption process differs from other mass consumption processes. Another common area of research has been the categorization of luxury and its brand attributes. Most of the work trying to explain success has emerged from these principles. And it makes perfect sense since these are well-developed tools and their application certainly provided insightful lessons.

The approach of this book does not aim to contradict or challenge this view but to complement it. Why should the marketing perspective on luxury be complemented? Do we need specific knowledge tailored to deal with the luxury challenges? Part of this justification comes from the lessons seen in Chapter 1. The difficulties in defining luxury and the need to hold a broad perspective suggest the need for a broader managerial perspective.

One of the main areas of improvement comes from the identification of luxury as a creative process. Chapter 1 showed luxury as a concept under constant evolution and shaped by commerce's arrival and shaped by the arts. The value that emerges from a luxury product or service is linked to that good to appeal to human emotions. Hence, this value creation process is more related to the firm's ability to create than to the ability of the client to perceive it. If we only look at how consumers perceive value, we might not fully appreciate the firm's ability to create in its terms. This is why luxury firms have to remain, to a certain extent, independent from the client demand to stimulate a natural creative process.

This is similar to the difference between artisan and artist discussed in Chapter 1. An artisan delivers excellent work based on the client's dictate. Artists "create" in their terms and, while the client can undoubtedly have an influence, the value is intimately linked to the artist's skills and view. The conclusion is not that luxury firms should be insensitive to their client base. We concluded in the last chapter that luxury as a concept is mostly defined by society, so observing the client is certainly not irrelevant. But firms must also understand (protect and develop) that their fundamental way to be valuable is through their ability to create. This is why luxury firms are so similar to artists.

To enhance the artistic view of luxury, it is useful to consider two distinctive business approaches. They will be defined as two different paradigms: the classic paradigm and the luxury paradigm. Hence, the confrontation of those two paradigms aims to illustrate the way luxury firms can approach their market meaningfully. This is a mental map intended to emphasize the role of luxury as an artistic conception.

45

The classic paradigm

The classic paradigm (Figure 2.1) is the traditional mental map that usually businesses consider to approach market competition. It is based on the idea that market competition starts by asking (or understanding) what consumers want and then offer them exactly that in a better way than the rest of the competitors. If we accept this rationale, what we need to do is to (a) understand very well what consumers want and (b) defeat our rivals. Therefore companies are being prompted to become better than others in relevant areas. To do so, efficiency becomes paramount as there will be fierce competition where all players are trying to satisfy consumer needs.

It is true that this is a simplification. It is not the scope of this book to deep dive into this way of thinking. The classic paradigm's main point is that this way of thinking stimulates that client understanding, and client satisfaction is the cornerstones of a firm's competitiveness.

This classic paradigm emerged in the 1970s. The first half of the twentieth century was turbulent with two global war periods. However, the second half, sadly in some regions of the world only, started to enjoy unprecedented well-being. This was so noteworthy that the (US) generation born in the 1950s was called the "baby-boomers". They were the sons of the economic boom.

As a consequence, more and more companies joined the market. In the 1970s, the marketplace became more crowded and hence more complex. What was originally a job based on planning and distributing in the 1950s became a matter of differentiation from the rest in the 1970s.[2] It is not a coincidence that the concept of positioning emerged in the late 1970s as a tool to help companies face this new reality.[3]

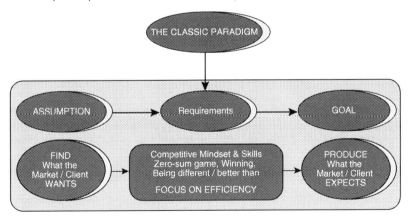

Figure 2.1 The classic paradigm.

Need of a managerial approach

The classic paradigm, however, poses fundamentally two limitations to help luxury firms analyze their specific challenges. These limitations are the consideration of value as driven by the consumer and the type of competitive mindset. These two aspects are discussed next.

Limitations of the "value driven by consumers" view

The classic paradigm is a mindset that assumes that value is created as a response to the client's need. Therefore it is critical to research how the client perceives and behaves. But what if it is the firm that defines what value is? Where is the role of creativity if the client determines why the product is valuable?

In the luxury arena, success may depend more on the firm ability to create rather than its ability to satisfy. Art can be a great example to understand this principle. Let's considered a Picasso painting. Its value does not reside on how the artist understood their clients or the market in general terms to sell his "product." It is ultimately an expression of the artist. Similarly, for luxury firms, the guiding principle should be to deliver a proactive view.

As a result, an excessive emphasis on the client, or the buyer side, can enter into conflict with the firm's ability to create. This is why the appreciation of art is so relevant for luxury managers. We need to realize that value can also reside on the maker's skills and view rather than on the receiver's expectations. What art teaches managers is that there are millions of different alternatives to do things. In simple terms, art is a form of expression (a way of doing). So rather than finding the best way to do something, luxury firms need to be sensitive in finding their way to express how to do it.

There is a limitation associated with the idea of client satisfaction. It is perceived that in business, we provide solutions to consumers' problems. Initially, there is nothing wrong with that. Here we embrace a, let's say, scientific thinking based on a problem-solution. However, this might force us to believe that we need to find "one" solution to "one" problem. But in business, there are multiple ways to understand the problem and deliver a meaningful solution (so there are numerous ways to fail too).

Luxury is not a zero-sum game

The classic paradigm does also assume a comparative type of competition. Companies need to defeat their rivals since the consumer will choose between them. If a consumer decides to buy from a company, it also implies that she/he does not buy from the rest.

Game theory defines this as a zero-sum game. In simple words, this means that for one player to win, another has necessarily to lose. Therefore two players can never win, just like in any tournament's final game. One finalist gets to be the champion at the expense of the other player losing. In business competition, we would say that when one firm gets to sell its product, its rival firm loses that sell. This stimulates the thinking that companies steal sales from each other. Either we sell, or we lose sales. As a result, firms embrace an aggressive and face-to-face kind of competition.

Likewise, a zero-sum game mentality also stimulates benchmarks. It is rational to pay close attention to someone stealing your sales. Benchmark is just the result of being concerned with what the others are doing. However, the more concerned we are with what someone else is doing, the less we think about the way we want things to be, precisely what creativity is all about.

This is why luxury is not a zero-sum game to start. A luxury consumer can decide to buy one or several products for different reasons. The same if one consider luxury services. But assuredly, the purchase of luxury goods does not necessarily imply that other luxury firms lose anything.

The luxury paradigm

The luxury paradigm (Figure 2.2) describes how luxury firms create value to avoid the limitations discussed above.

An artistic conception always starts with the way the creator sees or interprets the situation. This is a fundamental role of creators. Therefore the artistic skills to make this into reality are needed. Then the firm is ready to deliver on something the client is not expecting, at least to a certain extent. Unlike the idea of innovation, there is no need to consider an artistic expression as a totally new or radically new product.

The luxury paradigm is a mental map to stimulate the creative mindset within the firm. It is visual support to help managers realize how luxury firms should approach the market and face market rivalry. However, it is not a framework to stimulate creative work within the firm or leverage creativity skills. Nor is its intention.

Need of a managerial approach

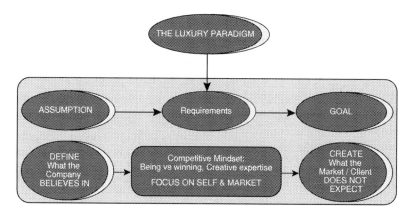

Figure 2.2 The luxury paradigm.

Another aspect of the luxury parading is to stimulate the competitive mindset of the firm as an entity. In this book, we will typically refer to luxury firms and not to luxury brands. This is because we will try to analyze luxury competition from decision-making and its link to business success.

It is true that the most relevant asset a luxury firm can own is the meaning and set of attributes (frequently also referred to as associations) they hold in the market and the mind of the consumer. In other words, their brand. In this way, we consider the firm as the whole entity and the brand a fundamental asset to be managed. The fact that firms "manage their brands" is the best example of how brands are linked to the firm's managerial ability and decision-making.

An intriguing question that arises at this point is: can luxury firms with powerful brands go bankrupt? Or, in other words, is it enough proper brand management to ensure business success? Even powerful brands can face competitive difficulties. Rather than being stand-alone entities or an end in itself, brands are the consequence of the firm's managerial decisions. This is why the lessons of brand management provide suitable lessons, but we might need to consider the strategic decision-making process for a more comprehensive view.

The analysis of such a decision-making process is a crucial lesson to learn with this book. These lessons are not intended to contradict the existing knowledge of marketing, brand management, or luxury client perception. They are aimed to complement it by leveraging the role of management decision-making.

Principles of luxury value creation

Traditional competitive strategy and its limitations for luxury

The other main area of expertise where executives could look for support is strategy. Traditional strategy analysis does not respond entirely to the specific challenges of luxury firms. Hence we will not challenge this kind of study, but instead, we will argue the need for a complementary view or an adjustment of some principles.

The strategic analysis aims to unveil the rationale behind the firm's performance and decision-making. These are the underlying reasons why some firms perform better than others. Therefore there is no need to mention that luxury firms need a strategy. The main principles of Strategy as Positioning (this is the way a firm competes in the market) and Strategy as Direction (this is the firm's specific set of values and the way the firm sees future competition) are valuable and will be considered here.[4] Usually, the action of defining the strategy as positioning and as direction is called strategy formulation.

Our aim here is to provide the analytical tools that help managers design a luxury strategy. So the question we aim to address in this section is: does the traditional strategic analytical tools and frameworks respond to the specific challenges of luxury firms? Or in other words, if a manager of a luxury firm relies on conventional strategic analysis, would she or he be well prepared to design its strategy meaningfully? We will explore here the main limitations.

The competitive mindset

One of the main competitive strategy principles is the analysis of and the quest for a Competitive Advantage. Following Michael Porter's approach,[5] a firm owns a competitive advantage in the market the moment can do one of these two things: (a) provide a rationale to justify a price premium or (b) acquire a superior cost structure. The first is called differentiation advantage, and the second is called cost advantage (sometimes also referred to as cost leadership).

Luxury companies cannot be primarily based on a superior cost structure to achieve business success. Even more, a mistaken price policy can also damage the perception consumers own about the firm.

50

Need of a managerial approach

A remark is needed here. One should not confuse a cost advantage with cost discipline. Of course, luxury firms must be efficient in their cost management. Cost advantage implies that the cost structure is the main driver behind the business's success. Chapters 6 and 7 will provide more details on this matter and how luxury firms face rivalry. Here our focus, however, is to observe the limitations of the traditional strategy analysis.

Differentiation is a meaningful approach as it helps firms understand the need for differentiated value and its rationale. But is it enough for a luxury manager? The problem with this approach is that it does not provide specific tools to appreciate how luxury firms create value and how they sustain competition.

As mentioned above, the concept of positioning as an analytical tool is a consequence of the exact moment when it was conceived. The theory of competitive advantage is not an exemption. It emerged in the 1980s as an answer to the competitive issues of that moment. Indeed, the quest for differentiation advantage is significantly related to the idea of marketing. Most strategy textbooks assume that when a firm aims to own a competitive advantage through differentiation, marketing skills become paramount. We already discussed in the previous section how a generic approach to marketing needs to be complemented to deal with luxury-specific challenges.

Later on, in the 1990s, Professor Jay Barneys complemented the competitive advantage concept and its approach to assessing resources and capabilities and the so-called resource-based view (RBV).[6] This theory helped companies understand that a more competitive landscape required the acquisition of critical resources and capabilities accountable for value creation.

In the case of luxury, the idea of competitive advantage needs to be adjusted. If not, it might force us to consider that companies need to differentiate from each other by offering unique valuable features that justify a price premium.

Why is this an issue? Because it establishes a comparative type of thinking. Considering competition as a confrontation against your rival is a limitation. The problem arises when this mindset makes us forget about the core idea of creation on our own. It is perhaps not the core idea of the framework, but the reality is that many companies, when crafting their strategies, accept this feeling of being "better than" or "winning." That is what we call a competitive mindset. The moment one aims to be better than someone else or defeat someone else, we are placing "unconsciously" someone else at the center. Luxury firms must take care of their "own" way to create to be valuable, and they are at the center, not someone else.

Was Picasso a "better" painter than Matisse? That's not even the problem; it is not about being better. Both can be great artists, but both needed to be great creators on their own. And of course, there can be competition among artists. The rivalry between Picasso and Matisse is a great example. But this should be a competition inspiring individual creation.

The point is not to neglect that companies engage in rivalry; the fact is that comparison, benchmarks, or confrontation should not primarily drive them. We should complement our analysis to consider our creative terms. We will come to luxury rivalry in Chapter 6. The bottom line here is that luxury firms do not aim to outperform each other in the way other industries do.

The economic logic

The idea of price premium can also be misleading for a luxury manager. In luxury, it is imperative to break a stereotype: price and cost are not necessarily related. When someone considers the idea of a price premium, it might be unconsciously accepting the fact that there should be a relationship between price and cost.

Pricing starts typically with a cost analysis. For obvious reasons, we can't price a good or service below cost. But cost serves as well as a reference to explore how far we can go with our price. There is a common belief that price has to hold a rational relationship with cost. The way we assess the value of a good is intimately related to its cost. The moment price goes too high, consumers will perceive the good as "unfair" or "not competitive." If this happens, consumers reduce their willingness to pay. This situation becomes more complicated as we have more players in the marketplace. More competition equals a higher challenge to claim a price premium successfully.

Considering that willingness to pay is shaped by cost is a limitation. Under such an assumption, we can charge a price premium only under certain "logic limits." The idea of the price premium is to justify how far we can go with this logic limit.

The assumption that price is rationally related to cost is what we call economic logic. We don't say this is always the case. However, there is a tendency to consider that the perception of cost shapes the ability to decide the price. Which ultimately influences the positioning of the firm.

In luxury, there is no economic logic. Luxury is sometimes negatively perceived as irrational precisely for this reason. It might be challenging to find a rationale or logic behind price and cost. But there is no need for an economic logic for the good to be valuable. Unlike other businesses, we assess its value differently, as we will explain in more detail in Chapter 3.

The idea of price premium works very well when the competition is based on a roughly homogenous supply. Here, we can discuss the way to break "slightly" this homogeneity. But in luxury, we don't speak about 10% or 20% price markup. We are considering a price that multiples by "n" the price of the non-luxury products. So basically, we are talking about something else. This notion is miles away from the idea of a price premium. We can't justify the price of a luxury good with the concept of a price premium.

Again we can refer to art to explain this. What is the price of a modern art painting? In Capsule 2.1, we can see a great example of the clash of approaches that the economic logic represents. A painting price is complex

Capsule 2.1. Untouchable and the modern art gallery visit. Price premium, the economic logic and the assessment of value

In the inspiring French movie "The Intouchables", directed in 2011 by Olivier Nakache and Éric Toledano, a scene shows the dilemma behind the economic logic. On a visit to a modern art gallery, one character (details are avoided to prevent spoilers) decides to buys a contemporary painting. After revealing the painting price, his friend screams how come modern art could be so costly. Not only that, his friends argue that he could paint a similar composition himself for way less money. This discussion starts with a short conversation on the value of art and hence the different reasons why people pay for it.

This situation nicely illustrates the different approaches to value creation. In this scene, one character assesses price primarily as an emotional purchase, while the other does by focusing on its making (cost). The critical aspect here is that different people evaluate their value for various reasons. Art is a perfect example of how cost or functionality is not the primary driver of value creation. Hence we might expect differences in the way consumers assess its value and thus perceive its price. The moment we can't find a rationale to evaluate the price, we face ambiguity in determining the good value. This is precisely the meaning of the economic logic means. But the fact that we can't relate price with cost does not necessarily imply that the good is any less valuable.

Principles of luxury value creation

to decide. It is based on multiple factors that exceed our scope. But one thing we can learn from it. The price decision is undoubtedly not related to its manufacturing cost. So value creation is not always linked to cost. There is no need for an economic logic between price and cost for a good to be valuable.

The assessment of value

Traditional strategic analysis might also need revision in the relationship between value and emotion. We understand why firms sell their products and become successful at the moment; we can assess the value they deliver. This creates a tendency to focus on the reasons behind value creation. Most of the successful companies are built around a "better", "more reliable", "superior", ... value. But what if value creation is not so easy to understand? What if value creation is based on emotions, or even worse, subjectivity?

In many industries, we can assess value creation by understanding the benefits provided by the product or the way companies fix consumer's problems/expectations. Then it is for companies to fight and deliver better than competitors. In this way, companies explain the way they create value in a way that is clear to understand and credible.

Luxury is a different entity. We need specific tools to understand the fundamental emotional component of value creation, as also shown in Capsule 2.1. The traditional strategic analysis was not conceived to explain value creation when emotional aspects are paramount. The reason is that value is frequently observed through the lenses of functionality. But the moment the rationale behind the product's acceptance is emotional, we rely on basic notions of consumer choice. But this does not help much to ascertain a leading luxury player. This is not to say that value assessment is more difficult in luxury. The main point here is that value assessment is slightly different.

Strategy analysis helps us understand that there are reasons behind the success. But it does not help is much when those reasons challenge our functionality-oriented logic. But what is the rationality behind a product which has very little, if any, functionality? What is the purchase logic of a superfluous, excessive, or irrational product? We know that consumers buy luxury, but how do we ascertain the "winning firm" when logic does not seem to be much valuable?

The traditional external analysis

The last aspect we will briefly review is the idea of industry analysis. Following Michael Porter's approach, traditional external analysis is aimed to understand the drivers of profitability or the activities that determine value.

Again, this is a mindset that emphasizes efficiency and rationale. Chapter 5 will unveil in detail the different types of business environments highlighting the main characteristics of creative markets. So far, we want to acknowledge that creativity is not the main focus of management frameworks.

The traditional mindset suggests thinking that efficiency and differentiation from competitors are paramount. However, in luxury, the role of artistic partners is also equally relevant.

The need of a luxury strategy

Luxury firms compete in the marketplace. And, indeed, some do perform better than others. And this happens for a reason. The role of luxury management is to unveil those reasons and help the firm navigate business decision-making's tricky waters. To do so, we need tools and concepts that guide this decision-making process to make more meaningful and competitive choices in its path to business success.

It is no big news that management tools evolve. As new problems arise, we need new tools to face them. Barney's focus on resources and capabilities (RBV) resulted from a more sophisticated competition in the 1990s. And the arrival of concepts like Platform Markets was needed to explain the success of a new pleiad of leading companies that emerged in the early years of this century, the likes of Apple, Google and Facebook, to name a few. Management evolves to explain how companies compete and achieve success. The aim of this book is to shape those concepts to better respond to luxury firms' core managerial problems.

The concepts we know today nicely explain the success of leading companies in other industries. The likes of Starbucks in the 1990s or Google in the new century are very well understood. But how can we explain the unparalleled success at Chanel or Patek Philippe? As Maximilian Büsser, founder of MB&F, once said, "my company is a textbook failure." Yet he has built relatively in few years one of the most prestigious mechanical watch brands in the market today, as we will unveil in Chapter 5.

Principles of luxury value creation

For this reason, we will dedicate the next chapters to complement our current knowledge. With its support, we will better prepare to tackle our very core question: Why do some luxury firms perform better than others? Our overview of the main managerial tools has been brief. It is only our intention to suggest the need for adjustment. As we have discussed, aspects like brand management, the competitive mindset, the economic logic, the difficulties in assessment value, and the industry conception need some revision. We might need to introduce new principles more in line with the way luxury firms create value and the way they compete. This is why we need a luxury-specific managerial view. This is what we call luxury strategy.

Case study. Maggie Henríquez arrives to Krug Champagne

In January 2009, Maggie Henríquez took over as President and CEO of Krug. Her previous successes in complex restructuring processes paved her way. She had previously saved the fortunes of the biscuit company Nabisco in Mexico. Under her direction, the company, with over 3,000 employees, had gone from hanging by a thread to certain bankruptcy to utterly transforming the biscuit market. By identifying consumer needs and focusing on a unique selling proposition, new, smaller and better quality formats were introduced. This reverberated in the recovery of the business and greater cost-effectiveness. Thus, while offering greater quality to the client, jobs were also maintained.

With this in mind, Maggie's plan was to apply this knowledge to the restructuring of the small house in Reims. With only 60 employees and much simpler operations, Krug appeared to be a less daunting challenge. The common thread would be maintained—identify the problem, channel operations and retake competitive messaging with clients.

However, after a year, sales fell by another 35%. In only two years, the company had lost over 64% of its volume and 95% of its results. Maggie was facing the first failure in her career.

56

Need of a managerial approach

I underestimated the problem. I thought it would be simple, because it was a small house and I thought operations would also be simple. To think this would be easy was my first error, because nothing that truly matters is ever easy. The problem was not channelling operations or identifying a unique selling proposition for the client. This works well, but in mass consumption.

Thus, a more in-depth search was launched in order to unearth the real root of the problem. The LVMH group offered training synergies for the luxury sector and the opportunity to share experience with other experts within the group. This allowed Maggie to delve into the world of the luxury sector. At one of these events, the president of another house of the group mentioned something to Maggie that began to show her the real scale of the challenge she faced. "Forget trying to turn this situation around in six months, as you would in mass consumption. Luxury is another universe. Your brand has not been developed and this will take three or four years. Because luxury is time."

In the same way, Yves Carcelle, previous CEO of Louis Vuitton and widely credited as the architect of this brand's renewed fortunes in the 1990s, provided Maggie with another piece of advice which would further shape her understanding of this market. Maggie asked him which one word encompassed luxury, and his answer was surprising: "The word which best encompasses luxury is coherence." How come Maggie, with such a successful track in management turnarounds, face difficulties when she arrived to Krug?

Adapted from Millán, D., "Krug Champagne. The savoir-faire of a luxury turnaround". IE Publishing, DE1–230-I.

Summary

Chapter 1 provided a comprehensive view of the concept of luxury and its historical evolution. Chapter 2 places the focus on the practice of management. This chapter justifies the need for luxury-specific tools.

The section on luxury managerial challenges explains that the management issue that luxury firms face differ to some extent. As argued in this chapter, luxury firms have specific problems that suggest the need for tailored

Principles of luxury value creation

managerial tools. The tension between mass and exclusivity, the role of creativity in management, and the need for control are examples of uncommon situations that most traditional managerial tools are not designed to address.

As luxury firms face different competitive challenges, we might need to adapt the analytical tools we employ to take the fundamental strategic choices. While not in-depth, this chapter has shown some of the most typical aspects where traditional knowledge on marketing and strategy are not very much in line with the luxury challenges identified. Therefore this chapter does not offer many answers. On the contrary, it serves as a guide to focus the questions we will address in the next chapters.

Self-study questions

1. *Identify a luxury firm that has gone bankrupt. To what extent the reason behind the bankruptcy is poor management? To what extent the reason behind the bankruptcy is poor creative talent or brand recognition?*
2. *What can be different priorities that managers and creator own? Why is this sometimes a conflict of interest to manage a luxury firm?*
3. *Why art is so important for the practice of luxury management?*
4. *What can a student of management learn from the way art is conceived and marketed?*
5. *What is economic logic? What is its role in shaping the price of a luxury good?*
6. *From the perspective of a luxury manager, what is the difference between a luxury brand and a luxury firm?*
7. *Which is the difference between the classic and the luxury paradigms?*

Notes

1 This is based on an exploratory qualitative research with more than 100 luxury executives (Global CEO or Country manager level) and experts (luxury professors and media) to identify the key problems involved in managing a luxury firm. Additional confirmatory research was conducted with the selected three challenges, with successful results. The luxury sectors researched include the personal luxury (fashion, accessories, hard and soft luxury), the yacht industry, the automobile industry and hospitality. While based on research, the four challenges are not aimed to convey an empirical finding. They are aimed to show the lessons gained by the author based on research, observation and personal experience.

2 See for instance Grant, R. *Contemporary Strategy Analysis*. Wiley. Chapter 1 provides an overview of the concept of strategy. 9th edition, 2016.

3 Ries, A. and Trout, J. *Positioning: The Battle for Your Mind*. McGraw Hill, 1980.

4 Grant, R. *Contemporary Strategy Analysis*. Wiley. Chapter 1. 9th edition, 2016.

5 Porter, M.E. *Competitive Advantage*. New York Free Press, 1985.

6 Barney, J. "Firm Resources and Sustained Competitive Advantage", *Journal of Management*, Vol. 17 (1991), pp. 99–120.

The *essence* of luxury. Unveiling the luxury value creation process

Introduction and objectives

The previous two chapters have introduced the challenges and specific requirements to define a luxury firm's strategy. Chapter 1 helped us to appreciate the concept of luxury better with an anthropological perspective. And Chapter 2 argued the need for luxury-specific managerial tools.

This chapter places the attention in a critical area of interest for any luxury firm—the way luxury creates value. This chapter will hence set the ground for the competitive discussion of luxury as it unveils the fundamental principles that explain a luxury firm's ability to compete meaningfully in the market place.

The first part looks into the relationship between value creation and luxury. Two alternative forms to conceive value creation will be discussed. Each of them represents a distinctive way to understand market rivalry: *normal* competition and *excess* competition. The second part is explicitly dedicated to the complex analysis of extraordinariness, as a form of *excess*, and the complexity involved in achieving it.

To conclude, the last section of the chapter provides the guidelines to ascertain the boundaries of luxury competition. Here we will pay special attention to the definition of the luxury firm's entry-level offering.

By the time you have completed this chapter, you will be able to:

- Distinguish the two primary types of value creation process: the *normal* and the *excess*.

Essence of luxury

- Appreciate the difference between the *normal* and the *excess* universes and identify their different characteristics.
- Understand the process of value creation applied to luxury and its relationship with the types of benefits.
- Apply the *excess* framework to ascertain value creation on a luxury firm and assess the complexity in placing the boundaries of luxury competition.
- Identify the role of consistency as a way to ensure luxury competition.
- Learn the complexities involved in managing the firm's entry-level offering.
- Appreciate the potential for competitive advantage that the excess framework offers. This is called the *essence* of luxury.
- Identifying the different alternatives to achieve excellence and its relationship with luxury competitiveness.

Luxury and value creation. Is luxury valuable?

The previous chapters introduced the concept and managerial complexity of luxury. These chapters provided some valuable, but generic information. In this chapter, we will focus our attention to the process of managing luxury. In this way, we approach a more specific territory where the analysis revolves around the fundamental decisions to be made to run a luxury firm.

The first aspect we will review is the value creation process. Any firm's ultimate reason for existence is the creation of value to consumers. The way this value is built in luxury will hence become a fundamental tool in the conception and design of a luxury strategy. Therefore, this section provides some light into the very first question behind any luxury strategy: Is luxury valuable?

We have seen how luxury has been historically perceived as a threat to social order or as superficial (non-basic) type of consumption. These negative perceptions, have installed the idea that luxury does not create "real" value. Chapter 1 explained that this is a misperception of the concept of luxury. Here, we will complement this view by bringing more clarity on the way luxury creates value.

Principles of luxury value creation

Type of benefits

In general terms, the idea of value creation is quite simple; it is a positive balance between benefits and cost. From the lenses of the consumer, what is, oftentimes, called consumer surplus, value is created whenever the consumer's willingness to pay for a good surpass its acquisition cost. By cost of acquisition we imply mainly the price, but in certain occasions it can be influenced by other considerations like transport to the point of sale or needed information.

In the same way, value creation from the lenses of the firm, the firm's surplus, is the balance between the firm's output and input. In other words, the ability of the firm to transform its inputs into a more valuable output. This is the underlying idea behind the fact that price is higher than the total cost of making the good. The total value created in the acquisition of a good will be the sum of the consumer and firm surpluses.

Value creation can be the basis of a more in depth discussion, like the role of stakeholders for instance. However, our aim is to unveil the ability of the firm to create value for the consumer. This is the cornerstone behind the ability of the firm to be relevant in the market and hence the basis of any strategy formulation. Therefore, we will place our attention mainly in the trade-offs that consumers and firms face.

One way to evaluate the consumer willingness to pay is based on the firm's ability to provide benefits. So we can also say that value creation takes place whenever the benefits provided by the firm's offering surpass the cost of acquisition. Therefore, the understanding of the benefit side becomes paramount to ascertain the ability of the firm to create value.

Following David A. Aaker and Erich Joachimsthaler's approach,[1] there are three main types of benefits to define a value proposition or value offering: functional, emotional and expressive. These types of benefits are not mutually exclusive.

- Functional are those intrinsic benefits the offering provide. These are the benefit obtained by its function or functionality—in simple terms, "what the offering can do".
- Emotional are those benefits which refer to the emotions the offering can provide—in simple terms, "what the offering can make me feel".
- Expressive. Benefits refer to the message I want to say with the offering. This is a communication act, an expression—in simple terms, "What the offering says about me or helps me saying".

Essence of luxury

Let's see the difference with a simple example. A consumer can decide to acquire a pen for different reasons or expected benefits. All of the reasons of course are subjective since this is the consumer's individual choice. Functional benefits might include a certain level of quality, of finishing, durability, easiness to use and so on.

Likewise the consumer might pursue certain emotions like the feeling of being educated, a childhood memory, the product origins remind a beautiful time in that country, the happiness to possess it or the excitement of shelf achievement, among many others.

Last but not least, the consumer might also expect from the pen certain expressive benefits. These benefits are related to the message the consumers aims to send. Aspects like shape and form can help convey attitudes toward design, origins might help convey savviness or expertise on the category, and, of course, the consumer might want to convey lifestyle, economic or social "status". As introduced in Chapter 1, the latter is, oftentimes, referred to as conspicuous consumption, Veblen consumption or simply status-driven consumption (Veblen, 1899).

Consider that status-driven consumption is just one kind of the broader category of expressive benefits. We enjoy a benefit by sharing with others our status (lifestyle or economic situation), but expressive benefits goes beyond status. As stated above, I can choose to buy a pencil to show my status, but also to show my attitude toward design for instance.

Expressive benefits are also related to emotions, so they are in way a particular kind of emotional benefit. However, it is important to notice the difference. Emotional benefits are what the buyer feels, so it is a self-consideration. With expressive benefits we are aiming to convey a message. So it is a self-consideration plus a (social) interaction, in other words, an expression.

The idea of expression is very important in many purchase evaluations. By placing clearly the firm logo in our t-shirt we provide "free advertising" to firms. It looks like a very good business to enjoy consumers that on top of their purchase they provide us with free advertising. Why we do it? Because it helps us saying something about us, that we want to say. This is what ofttimes is encapsulated under the umbrella of brand values. A brand is fundamentally a relationship between any firm facet and its meaning. If managed properly, companies can successfully build relevant meanings to help them compete. What consumer do is to share the meaning they perceive from the firm to help them express themselves.

Principles of luxury value creation

Consider for instance a firm that has created a meaning of being avant-garde around its firm. So one brand value of the firm is avant-garde. If this is successfully done in the market, consumers willing to express its avant-garde attitude toward fashion (or life), might be happy "expressing" themselves by showing that logo. So, do consumers provide free advertisement to the firm? Well, actually is not for free, the firm is helping us saying something we want to say.

Here we are only considering the assessment of value of the firm's offering through the benefits it can provide. We are not considering at this moment the buying process as a whole. Hence, we do not consider, at this point, the relevant aspects of the buying process like distribution, easiness to find or communication.

These types of benefits are not mutually exclusive. Following the pen example, a consumer might evaluate the pen's offering as a combination of different types of benefits, say, a combination of functional (usage, comfortable handling), emotional (enjoy the feeling of being well educated) and expressive (convey the consumer passion for design) benefits.

These types of benefits resemble the three technical means of persuasion of Aristotle's *Rhetoric*. Aristotle considered that the art of persuading an audience (which is not that far away from the notion of persuading a firm's clientele) could be achieved in three different ways: the ethos, the pathos and the logos.

The ethos refers to the "character" of the speaker that faces the audience. Persuasion is achieved through the credibility and trust in the speaker. The pathos was referred to as the ability of the speaker to persuade through an emotional engagement with the audience or empathy. And the logos, where persuasion occurs thanks to the logic, rationality or intellect of the audience. Here we observe a similar distinction between logic, credibility and emotions.

The functionality trap

The previous section suggest that value can arise from a diverse set of benefits. Therefore, it is a limitation whenever we associate benefits with only one type of benefit. Just like there is no single way to persuade an audience, a speaker can effectively rely on a combination of the three methods (ethos, pathos and logos). In a similar way, there is no single type of benefits to create value and relying on only one is a limitation. In business, we, oftentimes,

Essence of luxury

associate value with functional benefits. We refer to this limitation as the "functionality trap".

In general terms, we limit our ability to assess value the moment we only consider one type of benefit. Focusing on a single type of benefits leave opportunities that might arise from the combination of the other different types of benefits. It is the same mistake as placing science and art in different spaces. When we think of science we might think in terms of rationality and logic. Whereas when we think of art we conceive it in terms of emotions. But we never think of the combination of both. However, it is the combination that unleashes more value. There are many examples of the positive combination of science and art. It is perhaps Galileo Galilei the best example that science and art are not worlds apart, but complementary skills. Later on, we will see a very good example with Horacio Pagani (Capsule 3.2). And it is very well known the relationship between Steve Jobs and Jonathan Ivy at Apple where technical and artistic skills were behind the conception of successful products.

But the most frequent problem is to simplify benefits by functions. Is as simple as this: not everything in life has to have a functional purpose to be valuable. And here, art can be a magnificent guiding light. We already used art in Chapter 2 to help us understand that the approach to market can also be understood by a creative proposal (luxury paradigm) and not as a reaction to consumer expectations (classical paradigm). Here consider the value of art. Certainly art can be assessed though functionality, for instance through the evolution of superior painting techniques as it might fulfill better the purpose of representing objects. But it is most likely its emotional or expressive benefits what better describe its ability to create value. Capsule 3.1 provides a very good example of how even a simple offering (a product in this case) can provide significantly more value than anticipated when we leverage wisely the different types of benefits.

Normal competition

The previous sections have unveiled the idea that luxury creates value in a different way than other goods. This is to acknowledge the fact that in luxury the set of benefits and principles behind its consumption are simply a bit different. Therefore, it might make sense to distinguish between two different "competitive spaces", each of them characterized by a different way of value

Principles of luxury value creation

> ## Capsule 3.1. New York City Garbage. Emotional and expressive benefits on a "non-valuable" product
>
> New York City Garbage or NYC Garbage (nycgarbage.com) is a company founded in 2004 by Justin Gignac (*). It is a company built around exactly what its name says: garbage of New York City. Its product is a selection of non-organic garbage items packaged on a transparent methacrylate cube (see image below). The firm was originally conceived to prove the importance of packaging. Justin aimed to "find something that no one would ever buy, and package is to sell" (**).
>
> This is an excellent example of the *functionality trap*. The fact that we can find something nobody would buy means that the expected benefits that shape value are perceived to be non-existent. This is why we throw items into the trash can; they are not worth it anymore. Indeed, there is some residual value in recycling, but to achieve that we must throw away the product. So recycling takes place when the actual product has lost its original value.
>
> But why anybody would buy something "no one would ever buy"? The answer lies in the difference between assessing value considering functionality as the only type of benefit and assessing value considering the three types of benefits. If one assess value by focusing only on functionality (which is intimately linked to rationality and logic), the products in the trash can have already lost its value and the only thing we can do is to recycle. Therefore, as functionality is inexistent, no one would ever buy it.
>
> However, if one considers emotional and expressive benefits there is additional room for value creation and hence a reason for consumption. A consumer might want to purchase an NYC Garbage cube for several reasons, or better said, expecting several benefits. Whatever the reason we might consider would normally fall into the emotional or expressive benefits categories. For instance, emotional benefits might include a trip memory, the feeling of being provocative, the happiness of owning or decorating a home or any other feeling related to the acquisition. Expressive benefits are also found in this example as consumers might want to share attitudes toward design,

Essence of luxury

discovery, travel lifestyle, breaking stereotypes, underdog, rebellion and so on.

As a consequence, consumers might appreciate benefits on a firm's offering, even without functionality. So value creation can take place even if the product has no specific function to perform. This normally challenges our common sense and logic. How can value creation occur without a function? The beauty of this example lies in the way NYC Garbage stimulate purely emotional and expressive benefits.

The assessment of Benefits (or Value) is not performed in absolute terms

Where some people find a benefit other simple do not. The proposal of NYC Garbage is not to persuade everyone, but to resonate with whoever might appreciate its offering. NYC Garbage is not a leftover; it is an artistic expression. This is very typical of emotional or expressive benefits.

Oftentimes, functionality is related to rationality, problem-solving or logic. The more we think in terms of functionality, the easier is to find ways to measure value in absolute terms as subjectivity is less important. However, emotional and expressive befts are more related to choices. And choices are intrinsically linked subjectivity. So the assessment of value when emotional or expressive benefits are relevant is more relative than when functional benefits predominate.

Luxury semantics to convey emotional and expressive benefits

NYC Garbage is "100% authentic" and "Hand-picked from the fertile streets of NY, NY". One can observe the semantics of luxury here with the idea of quality ("authentic"), craftsmanship ("hand-picked") and creativity ("fertile streets").

As seen in Chapter 2, the classic paradigm is a mindset that starts on the consumer need (or problem). This type of thinking tends to prioritize a problem solving mindset to unveil and satisfy that consumer's problem. On the contrary, the luxury paradigm starts with the creative approach of the firm. This type of thinking is more oriented to make

Principles of luxury value creation

choices than to solve problems. The semantics to convey the benefits of NYC Garbage support the choices and beliefs of the founder hence delivering a proposition based on an artistic approach.

Going even further

Functionality leads to improvement. Where does emotional and expressive benefits lead? Here we have more alternatives to create value. We see this potential with the example of the "limited edition" cubes. (Yes, garbage packaged in limited editions!). NYC Garbage offers limited edition cubes based on special events or locations.

If we follow our logic, this is a contradiction. How come a garbage-based product be considered as "limited"? The only way to break this contradiction is to embrace emotional and expressive benefits to break our functionality-driven mindset. If NYC Garbage is an artistic expression, it makes perfect sense to consider the potential of limited editions. Even more, as any cube is based on a unique combination of garbage items, any cube is unique. Therefore, we can also think in terms of "scarcity". This open the door to collect them or hunt cubes with singular items.

Lessons from NYC Garbage

Indeed, NYC Garbage can hardly be considered as a luxury product. But it is an excellent example to tear down one of the luxury myths we unveiled in Chapter 1: luxury products are not valuable. Most of the time, we think something is not valuable because we are considering only its functional benefits (and this would include logic or rationality, what we, many times, call common sense). This is exactly the functionality trap.

However, as we see with NYC Garbage, even with low or inexistent functionality we can create value. The moment we consider value creation as a process that emerges from a combination of different types of benefits we are in a better position to consider more creatively our value offering and unveil unexpected alternatives for value creation. There is an excellent quote from Justin on its website: "if Justin can sell garbage you can sell anything". And, indeed, Justin Gignac has

Essence of luxury

> provided us with a great example of the limitless possibilities of emotional and expressive benefits and how to break the functionality trap.
>
> (*) Hereby it is my gratitude to my former Professor Kate Elis, from Schulich School of Business in Toronto, for unveiling to me the example of NYC Garbage.
> (**) Source: http://nycgarbage.com/about, images can also be seen on this web page.

NORMAL	EXCESS

Figure 3.1 The 2 competitive spaces. Normal and excess competition.

creation. By competitive space we refer to the situation where a market transaction occurs between a consumer and set of competing companies.

We will name one competitive space as *normal* competition. This is a situation where luxury value creation is not existent and consumption occurs through the common value creation process. We will name the second competitive space as the *excess* competition (*Figure 3.1*). This is a situation where luxury consumption takes place and hence luxury creates value. The reason to call it *excess* is due to the etymology of luxury. The word "luxury" comes from *luxus*, which ultimately means *excess*.

Let's start with the *normal* competition. The word "normal" is not aimed to convey any negative, pejorative, simple or basic connotation. It is just a name to refer the most common, or normal, form of value creation. We touched on that in Chapter 2. We now aim to provide a more structured approach.

The main characteristics of the *normal* competition are (see summary given in Table 3.1) as follows.

Functionality is key. In a *normal* competitive space consumption occurs when the identification and satisfaction of a consumer need (problem) is highly dependent on functional benefits. The "normal" way for companies to compete

69

Principles of luxury value creation

Table 3.1 The characteristics of a normal competition

Normal competition	
Functionality is key	– Functional benefits are fundamental and dominate the assessment of value.
Normal does not mean basic	– The product or service is not necessarily simple or basic. It represents any kind of offering, including sophisticated and innovative ones. – Normal refers to value creation and does not describe the product or service.
Emotional and expressive benefits are relevant, but not dominant.	– Emotional and expressive benefits are present, but not dominant in the assessment of value.
"Common sense": the importance of logic and rationality	– Together with the importance of functional benefits, we find the importance of logic and rationality.
Competition sets normality.	– Competition takes place the among many players providing a similar value offering where supply meets demand. – Differentiation is complex to achieve. This refers to the "normality" of the segment/market.
Breaking normality: price premium & economic logic.	– Breaking "normality" is complex. As companies try to differentiate the functionality tights prevent price from escaping (significantly) normality. – Premiums refer to the normality conditions (or average price). The limitation to increase price is influenced by the economic logic (price and cost must be related).

in any marketplace is to solve a consumer problem (we might also say indistinctly: to satisfy a consumer need). So the "function" of products and services is to satisfy the problem. This way of consumption is by definition linked to a functionality. This is what we called in Chapter 2 the classic paradigm.

Normal does not mean basic. The *normal* competition is not a description of a product or service. It describes how companies face competition and how value creation takes place in the transaction between the consumer and the firm. Therefore, the word "normal" does not refer to simple or basic offerings. It also includes the consumption of sophisticated goods or very innovative offerings as well.

Emotional and expressive benefits are relevant, but not dominant. While functional benefits might be dominant, still emotional or expressive benefits are present and relevant. The assessment of value is always the result of a

Essence of luxury

combination of the three types of benefits. In any market companies try to enhance their value offering through emotional and expressive benefits to the best of their abilities. This helps them differentiate their offering and increase the willingness to pay of the consumer. However, these emotional and expressive benefits does normally support the core functional aspects.

For instance, if we want to sell toothpaste we can invigorate our offering with additional functional benefits (better flavor, better ingredients, superior results, etc.), we can also stimulate emotional benefits (like environmental friendliness that makes the consumer feel better) or even expressive benefits (like packaging to help to convey any message about the consumer lifestyle). But we can never forget that the assessment of value is significantly shaped by the original consumption problem, which is the ability to clean. We can put things on top of functionality, but we are linked to that type of benefit as this the one that triggers its consumption. And the reason why differentiation is, oftentimes, so difficult to achieve.

"Common sense": the importance of logic and rationality. Normal competition means that the assessment of value is, to a certain extent, influenced by logic and rationality. A *normal* consumption happens when things make sense. And things make sense when our logic and our rationality support our decision-making based on functional benefits.

But what does really mean that something makes sense? When most of the times we say that something does not make sense, it is simply because it unveils a conflict between value and function. The moment value and function are not clearly related we assume it to be irrational or illogical. Why pay $1000 for a writing instrument when you can get a good one for $50? Well, this idea of getting "a good one" is an example of prioritizing function. Good enough, or value for money are simply functional driven considerations. We unveiled this consideration in Chapter 1, when we said that luxury challenges common sense.

Competition sets normality. Any market is determined by the conjunction between supply (firms) and demand (consumers). A typical characteristic of any market is its organization into different segments. These segments represent a refinement of the core consumer needs (or problems) and it is, oftentimes, represented by specific functions (quality, usage, features, etc.).

A fundamental challenge firms face in any segment or market is to differentiate themselves from competitors. And this is the consequence of the difficulty in providing a distinctive functional benefit, as most of the players can offer a similar one. As said earlier companies can support it with

Principles of luxury value creation

additional type of benefits, but functional benefits are the core. This similarity in the value offering ends in an equilibrium situation, where supply meets demand and an average price is determined as a consequence. This is what we, oftentimes, refer to as "normality". So in other words, it is difficult for companies to go beyond normality as they need to justify an improvement over competitors (note the word improvement is a functional consideration either). And even if they do, it is always an incremental improvement referring to normality, not a modification of the normality.

Breaking normality: price premium and economic logic. As said earlier *normal* competition defines an equilibrium that companies try to break. Therefore, *normal* competition is characterized by certain limits. Companies might break the limits of the equilibrium, but they can't go very far away. A price premium is nothing else than the justification that this normality and its limits do exists.

A price premium always refers to an average price. As we said, there is a normality where most companies can provide a similar offering, so we might expect an average price linked to that equilibrium. A price premium is nothing else than a relative increment over the average price justified with a superior benefit. So a price premium is a justification that normality exist and companies try to slightly break it.

Price premiums also suggest that there is price limit. A price premiums is a percentage over an average price. So the price premium always refers to the average price. But why we can't break this limit? Why can't we go beyond without the reference of the average price? *Normal* competition means that functionality driven benefits, logic and rationality prevail. Whenever this happens, whenever the assessment of value is significantly influenced by functional benefits, consumer might expect a "reasonable" relationship between price and cost. This is what we called the economic logic in Chapter 2. Therefore, the existence of the economic logic is the consequence of a situation where prices (and hence competition) have a limit. And breaking it is challenging.

Let's build up on the previous example of toothpaste. Why we don't pay $1000 for a toothpaste bar? Based on what we have said, functionality, logic and rationality might prevail. This will generate that many companies can provide a compelling offerings at a price significantly lower, let's say, $5. Does it "make sense" (whenever we say make sense we refer to logic and rationality) to pay more? Can emotional or expressive benefits justify it? The economic logic suggest that toothpaste has a certain price limit as price can never scape a certain relationship with cost. Therefore, whenever functionality prevails there is a price limit where most consumers will never

72

Essence of luxury

NORMAL	EXCESS
Logic / Rationality Functionality Segments & Differentation Price limit Economic Logic	

Figure 3.2 Main assumption of normal competition.

be willing to pay for. Some companies would be able to increase the willingness to pay above $5. But none of those companies will ever reach the $1,000 price tag—at least following the assumptions of *normal* competition.

In short, *normal* competition is a set of assumptions that rule any market competitive dynamics (see *Figure 3.2*). Under such assumptions, companies compete against each other, they try to differentiate themselves and they try to create as much value as possible.

Going beyond normality: excess competition

The second way we can consider business rivalry is *excess* competition. This is the competitive situation where luxury creates value. *Excess* and *normal* competition are related but the assumptions are different. *Excess* takes places whenever we exceed normality. As said in Chapter 1, luxury is a way to go beyond certain boundaries. So *excess* is the representation of a situation where we go beyond normality. The key idea is the notion of going beyond. Therefore, *excess* is not a way to "improve" normality but to "go beyond" normality.

Excess competition is a situation where the assumptions of *normal* competition simply do not apply. But at the same time we need to ensure value creation. Otherwise we cannot talk about market rivalry and consumption. Therefore, we will refer to *excess* competition the moment we ensure that at the same time:

a) We can go beyond normality by breaking the assumptions of *normal* competition.
b) There is value creation.

Principles of luxury value creation

Table 3.2 The characteristics of an excess competition

Excess competition		
	How do we exceed (go beyond) normality?	Does it create value?
Breaking functionality	Unneeded, stupid e.g. Why go beyond basic-core function	Not necessarily
Breaking logic— rationality	Illogic, irrational, crazy, extravagant, exaggeration. e.g. Add diamonds, Gold toilet WC	Not necessarily
Breaking social order	Unfair, superficial e.g. Superfluous consumption	Not necessarily
Achieve extraordinariness	Through a combination of Benefits: where Emotional, Expressive benefits are dominant e.g. Luxury goods	Potentially yes

With this in mind, we will explore how we can go beyond *normal* competition and what determines *excess* competition (Table 3.2).

Breaking Functionality. The main aspect to break the assumptions of *normal* competition is to break the functionality driver of consumption. We can consider a scenario of *excess* competition the moment functional benefits are not dominant.

Luxury is a perceived conflict between function and value. We oftentimes cannot understand why something that is not "needed" can provide any value. Note that "needed" here means a basic need associated with function, so functional benefits. But in reality this is not a conflict but a simplification. Not all consumption must be justified by functional benefits.

As introduced in Chapter 1, value and hence the benefits behind a good consumption can happen without function. Emotional or expressive benefits can the dominant benefits behind value creation. This is what we, oftentimes, encapsulate under the statement that luxury satisfies desires while non-luxury (*normal*) consumption satisfies needs. The latter statement is very common as we tend to associate needs with functional benefits and desires with emotional or expressive benefits. However, in our approach, we will only differentiate type of benefits that justify consumption. We do not aim to make any connotation to differentiate needs from desires.

The quintessential critic to luxury is that luxury is not needed. Luxury is hence perceived as unneeded, superfluous or even stupid. This belief is anchored on the assumption that value must be linked to function. It is

Essence of luxury

function (or functional benefits) that drives the satisfaction of needs. However, this is but only one of the ways to satisfy needs, we can also satisfy them through emotional or expressive benefits. Therefore, luxury is valuable. It is simply a satisfaction through different types of benefits.

But breaking functionality does not guaranty value creation. There are multiples ways to break functionality. Some can be valuable some others not.

We all have in our minds examples of situations where braking function is not necessarily valuable. If we only break functionality without ensuring another set of benefits we can certainly observe products and services that are unneeded or superfluous. In our previous toothpaste example we raised the question: Does it make sense to pay more, when you can get the same for less? Can we increase the benefits of a toothpaste based on emotional aspects and claim a price of $1000? Here, breaking functionality does not necessarily lead to value.

Another meaningful example is smartphones. Different have been the efforts to offer a luxury smartphone. However, this category is mainly driven by functional benefits like technology or the operating system. The latter is ruled by network externalities, this means that the more users an operating system have the more valuable it become for all its user (for instance more Apps and better features can be expected). It is normal to find difficulties in breaking normality in a product whose main benefits are related to annual improved technological features and value linked to volumes of users.

Breaking Logic (Rationality). The assumptions of *normal* competition can also be broken by challenging the limits of logic and rationality. As argued before our logic and rationale is a way to express our orientation toward function.

But breaking logic alone does not necessarily lead to value. We all have in our minds examples of situations where braking the logic or rationality behind consumption can only lead to extravagance or exaggeration. Does it make sense (or is it of any logic) to put diamonds on our toothpaste bar? And a gold WC for our bathroom?

It is tempting to move from *normal* to *excess* by adding gold or diamonds. Indeed, we can try to go beyond normality through extravagance and exaggeration. Many companies actually do. But this is, oftentimes, a very poor approach to luxury value creation. While a subjective perception of emotional or expressive benefits can be found in breaking logic in this way, there is a very fine line where value is created here. We will simply not hold this

Principles of luxury value creation

approach as they it does not represent a meaningful way to sustain a luxury firm's strategy.

Breaking Social Order. Another common way to understand *excess* is through inequality. In this way, normality is linked to social order and *excess* is linked to inequality. A typical critique to luxury is that it is not of any value. Through these lenses luxury it is simply a way to burn rich people's excess cash. As a result, luxury can be perceived as "superficiality" or "rich consumption".

While breaking social order can be a way to understand *excess* (this is going beyond normality), it is a poor business approach. We can increase significantly the price of a good and focus on consumers with a high income power to acquire it. But this does not ensure value creation. Here we are not talking about specific benefits provided. Breaking social order alone is a random consumption of a good just because it is expensive.

We do not believe this to be a meaningful path to value and hence a sound approach to strategy. Still, this might work for some companies, but the most likely scenario is that breaking social order will be a short-lived approach.

Extraordinariness. The key aspect of *excess* competition is to achieve extraordinariness. We exceed normality by being "extra-ordinary". While the ordinary (or normality) is defined by functionality and logic, the extraordinary is defined by breaking the dominance of functional benefits and replace them by emotional or expressive ones. It is a change in the type of benefits that ensure value.

And why is it valuable? In the previous examples of *excess* we argued how breaking functionality, logic or social order does not equal to value creation. On the contrary, here, we have emotional and expressive benefits supporting the creation of value. Therefore, the only way we can consider to exceed normality and create value is through extraordinariness.

Luxury consumption occurs whenever emotional or expressive benefits are dominant. Luxury cars are not bought for transport, luxury watches are not bought for telling time, luxury bags are not bought for storage or luxury wines are not bought for quenching thirst. In all these examples, we might have tough of other benefits like lifestyle, appreciation of refinement or personal enjoyment. All examples of emotional or expressive benefits.

It is of utmost importance to be clear when we refer to extraordinary. We might want to avoid simplistic notions of what extraordinary is. This is

Essence of luxury

perhaps the most complex notion to understand and master. And hence it will be covered in depth in the next sections.

The assessment of functionality is somehow easier. When functional benefits prevail we can always find "reasons" for value. We can "convince" our consumer how our offering is better, superior, faster, lighter and so on. There is a logic on it. We can add some emotional/expressive benefits to enrich it and differentiate from competitors. And consumer can understand it.

However, emotional and expressive are far more complex to understand and explain. On the first hand they do not represent a specific problem to be solved. And on top of that there is not necessarily any logic to support its satisfaction. This is why luxury is, oftentimes, not very well understood. It is, indeed, a complex phenomenon. Therefore, the assessment of extraordinariness is by all means not a simple task. But it is the way we can understand the market reality of luxury consumption.

In summary, the analysis of difference between the *normal* and *excess* competition has helped us understand better how luxury works and creates value. This will be a fundamental pillar in the formulation of any luxury strategy. This section has unveiled what we will refer as the *normal* versus *excess* framework. This is a framework to helps us understand why luxury differs from other markets. It also provides the assessment of extraordinariness as a key element behind luxury value creation (*Figure 3.3*).

At the same time, this approach tears down the myths unveiled in Chapter 1. Luxury as a representation of *excess* can be perceived in different ways. And not all of them are valuable. *Excess* can be perceived as unneeded, illogical, rational, superficiality, extravagance, exaggeration or inequality. They are all form of *excess* and ways to break normality. But they

NORMAL	EXCESS
Logic / Rationality	Breaks logic: Ilogic, Carazy Extravagant
Functionality	Breaks Funtion: Unnned, stupid, irrational
Segments & Differentation	Breaks Social order: Unfair
Price limit	Offer Extraoridnariness:
Economic Logic	Through a combination of Benfits Where Emo/Expre are dominant

Figure 3.3 Main assumption of normal and excess competition.

Principles of luxury value creation

do not lead to value creation, or at least, we will not consider them robust enough to sustain a firm's strategy.

Still some questions remained open. How can we analyze extraordinariness to ensure value? Where exactly is the limit between the *normal* and the *excess* kind of competition? The *normal* versus *excess* framework has just placed us in a situation to start our analytical journey to define the fundamental pillars of any luxury strategy.

The *essence* of luxury. *Excess* as extraordinariness to ensure luxury competitiveness

Luxury value creation is then the pursuit of extraordinariness. This notion encapsulates the fact that luxury is the aim to go beyond *normal* competition, but not in any form, as we also avoid less valuable forms of *excess*.

Extraordinariness is quite complex to achieve. Luxury firms can lose at some point their source of extraordinariness; some can pretend to be extraordinary, but fail to deliver on that promise, and others might simply claim to be extraordinary without even trying to be. This section aim to deal with the challenging task of achieving extraordinariness as the basis of a luxury strategy.

We will consider as a requirement for any luxury strategy to own a sound and valuable form of extraordinariness. Therefore, the competitive advantage, as we discussed in Chapter 2, needs to be related to the sources of extraordinariness. Only in this way a luxury firm can create value and hence compete meaningfully in the market.

We will refer to this situation as the firm's *essence*. The *essence* of a luxury firm is then the source of extraordinariness that can be used as their advantage to compete meaningfully in the market. This is a fundamental pillar in any strategy. The *essence* of a luxury firm is quite complex to analyze. It is not a mere statement of generic desires, like excellence, or a combination of abused terms like superior quality, craftsmanship or scarcity. As argued in the previous section, luxury value creation is linked to emotional (and expressive) benefits. And these benefits are difficult to assess and to communicate.

The analysis of the source of extraordinariness will be based on two fundamental aspects. First, how is extraordinariness conceived. And then how do we aim to achieve it. Only in this way we will be in a good position to

Essence of luxury

assess the firm's *essence* or, in other words, the firm's source of extraordinariness that can be leveraged as a competitive advantage.

Conceiving extraordinariness: luxury as a choice

The fundamental idea of extraordinariness is the notion that we go beyond normality (or *normal* competition). But going beyond normality is quite complex to articulate. This is a process that can't be ruled, measured or rationalized, as functionality is not the main driver of value. Therefore, it is not clear to know when or how we go beyond normality. Here, we will provide some guidelines to understand better the sources of extraordinariness.

Extraordinariness is not an improvement and is hardly measured

Excess competition is not driven by functional benefits; then we should not approach it through the lenses of improvement or aiming to be "better than".

Extraordinariness is by definition a different way of satisfying a need, not an improved or better way to satisfy the need. Improvement fit more with *normal* competition as a way to increase the willingness to pay and claim a price premium.

For similar reasons, extraordinariness can hardly be measured. We can measure objectives, and functionalities, but measuring emotion is more complex. So it is very difficult to ensure at what moment we have gone beyond normality. We will deal in the next section with the fine line between normality an extraordinariness.

Mechanical watchmaking is a clear example. A quartz watch is 10.000 times more precise than any mechanical watch, and its cost to produce is tremendously lower. From this perspective a mechanical watch is not an improvement, but an inferior product. So there is no reason to buy a mechanical watch. But consumers do not buy a mechanical watch because they need watch (functional need). There are a wide array of emotional (appreciation of watchmaking, enjoyment of art on its wrist, etc.) and expressive (convey a lifestyle, a status symbol, etc.) benefits that a mechanical watch can deliver.

Extraordinariness is not "only" about quality

Increasing quality is not enough. If we only consider functional aspects being better is just an enhancement of normality. In other words, we expect superior quality (regardless of product or service) in extraordinariness, but superior quality alone is not enough to claim extraordinariness.

Principles of luxury value creation

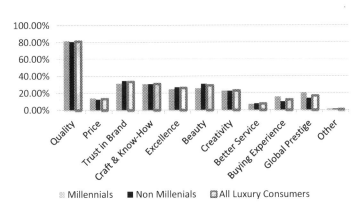

Figure 3.4 Key characteristics to describe luxury.

Still today one of the key characteristic to describe luxury is quality. Our research also suggest that quality is the characteristic mostly used to recognize luxury by consumers,[2] even for younger generations (Figure 3.4).

But superior quality leads to extraordinariness only when emotional or expressive benefits are dominant. Managers that claim extraordinariness by only focusing on the enhancement of core functional aspects will never achieve it. Extraordinariness arises from a different conception that puts emotional/ expressive benefits at the forefront. If we just increase quality without arguing a likely path to those benefits we won't be able to achieve extraordinariness.

In the classroom, oftentimes, the question whether the iPhone is a luxury product resonates. The iPhone is great example of improvement, but in the *normal* universe. It is a (beautifully made) improvement based on design, but above all based on its operating system. This is a clear functional driver. Another clear characteristic is that there is a price premium, so price is related to an equilibrium of demand and supply and cost will play a role in defining it (the economic logic can be found). We don't pay, let's say, 5.000 euros for a smartphone, and it is, in simple terms, because functionality prevails. It is difficult to claim that emotional benefits dominate here. It is difficult to argue this is a luxury product.

Extraordinariness is hard to assess and it requires a learning curve

What is a good wine? What is a good car? What is good leather? These are questions that are not so easy to answer. Some might say that they are subjective, and it is true. And other might say that some learning might be needed to appreciate it. Just like any artistic representation, the assessment

Essence of luxury

of value in extraordinariness is a balance between individual experience and appreciation. And this makes it very hard to be assessed.

It is a common pattern that a consumer might first buy luxury for expressive benefits (status) and then for personal pleasure or appreciation (emotional). In this journey personal experience and a learning curve takes place. Oftentimes, this is called as marked with the difference between status consumer versus the "connoisseur" (knowledgeable) consumer. We will consider, however, that consumers do not need to be experts to appreciate luxury. We do not need to be engineers to enjoy driving a sportscar or appreciating a mechanical watch. Nor we need to be leather artisans to buy a leather bag. However, the moment we increase our knowledge we might appreciate it better.

This knowledge that helps us appreciate luxury is not a technical knowledge (functional benefits) but to learn the values and beliefs behind the extraordinariness. In Capsule 3.2, we see it with champagne. Therefore, the assessment of extraordinariness is through appreciation and not through explanation. Appreciation is about sensorial, about learning, about getting the details. Explanation is about reason and logic.

Capsule 3.2. Examples of extraordinariness as the *essence* of luxury

Pagani. The quest for the ultimate sportscar

Horacio Pagani represents the expertise and one possible journey to what can be an extraordinary car. Fueled by his passion, he move from Argentina to Modena. That young engineer became a visionary of sportscar in terms of new designs, and new composite materials that delivers an ultimate driving experience.

Krug Champagne. The quest for excellence in champagne every year

Joseph Krug founded Krug in 1842. He envisioned that not only was excellent champagne a matter of an excellent year, but it could also be the result of the combination of the different base wines. That allowed him to deliver a revolutionary approach, an excellent champagne every year. That would be the result of the finest blend based on the best possible base wines of the year. For that reason, he mastered the art of the parcel approach to craft every year a large pull of base wines, from which the best flavor of the year would emerge.

Principles of luxury value creation

> **MB&F. The expression of kinetic art**
>
> Maximilian Busser founded MB&F (Maximilian Büsser and Friends) with his personal savings in 2005. His unique approach to watchmaking was based on respecting the best mechanical expertise to transfer his conception of "Kinetik Art" into a reality. By providing a new approach to watchmaking as an art, he pushed the boundaries of what an extraordinary mechanical watch can be.

Companies, like Loewe, use best in class leather. We might appreciate that respecting best materials and working only with them can lead to products whose touch, in the firm's own words "tells the story". There is no better way to assess the extraordinariness of their products other than touching them. But not only is this about high quality, but this is a devoted firm to deliver the best possible softness to express their artistic and characteristic vision of leather. So without it, without complementing the high quality leather component with Loewe's values is more complex to ascertain the firm's source of extraordinariness. In other words, we will never understand why Loewe can claim extraordinariness, without understanding first Loewe.

As there are multiple ways to understand extraordinariness, the learning factor is hence fundamental to ascertain the way any firm has decided to envision their path to extraordinariness.

Extraordinariness requires leadership. The creator effect

Problems lead to a one solution type of thinking, while art leads to infinite possibilities. Getting to extraordinariness is not a one-way road. Therefore, it requires leadership to navigate the infinite possibilities. This is the reason why different luxury companies can claim extraordinariness in the same category without being direct rivals (luxury is not a zero-sum game, as said in Chapter 2).

Most of the luxury firms we know are based on the values and beliefs of their founder, who became the leading factor toward extraordinariness. Without it, we can't understand exactly the extraordinariness of that firm because it is so intimately linked to the visions and values of that personality. There is not one way, but multiple ways to achieve extraordinariness, like there are multiple ways of artistic expression. This leading factor can be named creator or designer, depending on the industry. But the fundamental idea is that the path to ensure extraordinariness is guided.

Essence of luxury

As said in Chapter 1, the role of art is fundamental. We can clearly see why now. Art is a form of expression, not the right way or the best way. Certainly, some paths can be more beautiful and more meaningful, but similarly several can be beautiful and meaningful. Pursuing a singular form of expression can be the basis to go beyond normality and break current understanding. Luxury starts with someone's belief about what normality is and how to break it. It is the belief of breaking what we know, of passing the boundaries, of envisioning something no one has envisioned before. This, of course, is quite complex to do. It requires some extraordinary personality to lead it.

Extraordinariness is a choice not a goal

As a consequence of the previous considerations we can consider extraordinariness as a choice, and not as a goal. A goal it is something we can measure, we clearly know where it is and we can plan how to get there. _Normal_ competition can be better understood by setting goals. This helps us understand the process, the metrics or the benchmarks we might require. But we won't achieve extraordinariness following the rules of normality.

Extraordinariness can be better understood as a choice. A choice embodies the idea of conception, of subjectivity, of leadership, of a way of expression. It also adds the notion of meaning and appreciation as a path to break normality and go beyond it. Just like Capsule 3.2 shows, the path to extraordinariness is better described as a choice.

Learning extraordinariness by examples, not by imitation

Choices are hardly explained or ruled. This is why the understanding of extraordinariness is to a certain extent ambiguous. The best approach to learn how luxury firms conceive extraordinariness is through exploring different examples. This will help us identity the different factors that shape the choices and values luxury firm can consider in their path to extraordinariness. In the Capsule 3.2, we see some real examples of the _essence_ of some luxury firms. Likewise, the case studies and examples provided in this book are also examples of how different luxury firms have conceived their path to extraordinariness.

Achieving extraordinariness: the role of resources and capabilities

After conceiving the path to extraordinariness, luxury firms must make sure they can deliver. It can be quite tempting (and easy) to claim extraordinariness.

Principles of luxury value creation

But then one must deliver on that promise. A typical failure of a luxury strategy is to exaggerate its ability to be extraordinary and overpromise.

To avoid these aspects luxury firms must also pay close attention to the way they achieve extraordinariness. When companies formulate their strategy they must understand that the source of their competitive advantage is based on key organizational capabilities.[3] Luxury firms are not different in this matter. To transfer a conception of extraordinariness into a reality, luxury firms must own key organizational capabilities.

Achieving extraordinariness requires extraordinary organizational capabilities

The assessment of extraordinariness can be ambiguous, as it is based on emotional benefits and individual choices. However, extraordinariness must be realistic, not just an idea or a promise. Luxury firms need to ensure credibility in the achievement of extraordinariness. It is not about claiming to be extraordinary, it is about proving it.

To do so, luxury firms must own organizational capabilities that enable the achievement of extraordinariness. Following Robert Grant's approach,[4] the firm's organizational capabilities are secured by the firm's resources. Therefore, the analysis of organizational capabilities starts with the identification of the firm's resources, which can be divided into tangible, intangible and human resources. Then, the organizational capabilities are identified. And, finally, the potential of those organizational capabilities for value creation is appraised, as shown in Table 3.3.

In luxury we find a similar connection between organizational capabilities and successful competition (or competitive advantage). The analysis of organizational capabilities in luxury must be, however, aligned with its specific way of value creation.

In general terms, this is to say in the *normal* competition, the analysis of organizational capabilities follows a supply chain logic.[5] As we argued in Chapter 2, the classic paradigm is a mindset constructed around the idea of efficiency. It is therefore a meaningful approach to identify all the activities involved that define the value chain. In this way, the value chain help us identify key or superior organizational capabilities that can be leveraged to compete meaningfully in specific activities.

Then the appraisal of key organizational capabilities is done through the VRIO framework.[6] Following this approach a resource or a capability can be the source of a firm's competitive advantage whenever it is *valuable,*

Essence of luxury

Table 3.3 The role of R&C in the achievement of extraordinariness

Essence: conception of self approach to extraordinariness		
Firm resources		
Tangible	Intangible	Human
• Financial. e.g. Cash • Physical. e.g. Man- ufacturing facilities, stores • Raw Material. e.g. Cashmere	• Technology. e.g. Patents • Reputation. e.g. Brand, relationships • Firm Culture	• Skilled Labor force.
⇩		
Organizational capabilities: Identification not based on sequential activities (Value Chain), but on activities linked to self conception of extraordinariness		
– What organizational capabilities support or enable the firm's beliefs? – What organizational capabilities support or enables the firm's creation?		
Extraordinariness through the Making	Extraordinariness through Delivery/Service	Extraordinariness through Talent.
How Tangible resources are applied to achieve extraordinariness.	How Intangible resources are applied to achieve extraordinariness.	How Human resources are applied to achieve extraordinariness.
Manufacturing exper- tise (Watchmaking, winemaking). Financial management. Access or master key components (raw material, manufacturing techniques)	Culture of excellence Service, after-sale expertise Relationship with clients Communication skills	Values and Beliefs about extraordinariness. Leadership Individual talent relevant to source of extraordinariness

rare, inimitable and supported by the *organization*. We might notice here that traditional strategy is also based on the notion of rarity of the key organizational capabilities. So the idea of scarcity per se is not specific to luxury competitiveness.

However, luxury value creation is constructed around the luxury paradigm. There is nothing wrong with the value chain per see. But as noted on Chapter 2, the luxury paradigm suggest competition based on self skills, rather than a competition based on beating others. Hence luxury firms should not be looking capabilities to be "better than others". This would only lead to improve *normal* competition.

85

Principles of luxury value creation

As argued in previous sections, they key idea of *excess* competition is the predominant role of emotional and expressive benefits. In luxury, we are looking for organizational capabilities that support extraordinariness, so key organizational capabilities will be those supporting those type of benefits. As argued in the previous section a luxury firm's *essence* is tightly linked to specific choices and the role of a creator. This is unsurprisingly similar to the Luxury Paradigm, which starts with the firm's values and beliefs, intimately shaped by the firm's founder.

Therefore, the identification of organizational capabilities must be done following the principles of the luxury paradigm and not based on the value chain. The identification of the luxury firm's organizational capabilities must be in line with the firms values and beliefs, and creative approach. Therefore, organizational capabilities must respond to these questions:

What organizational capabilities support or enable the firm's beliefs?
What organizational capabilities support or enable the firm's creation?

Then, and only then, the value chain and the VRIO could be used. It might provide a support to consider the capabilities that enhance extraordinary making, extraordinary delivery and extraordinary talent, as shown in Table 3.3.

For instance, following the value chain we might encounter that superior quality past the VRIO framework and hence can be the basis of the firm's competitive advantage. But to what extent a Pagani is a better car? Or a car with superior quality? Organizational capabilities are not those supporting a competitive skills, but supporting the firm's choices. Like for instance the search and apply of composite materials to deliver extraordinary driving experiences. Similarly Joseph Krug envisioned a great champagne every year. This ambition is beyond a comparative idea, but a quest for plots and wine making skills to ensure that a magnificent blend can be made every year.

Achieving extraordinariness takes time, a lot of time

In the previous sections, we have already unveiled the two reasons why achieving extraordinariness is so time consuming. The first reason is the fact that extraordinariness is linked to emotional/expressive benefits, which are complex to explain. And the second reason is the fact that extraordinariness is appreciated rather than explained. Not only consumers but managers might take time to appreciate the reasons behind the firm's extraordinariness, just like the case study in Chapter 2 discusses.

Therefore, communicating the source of extraordinariness requires more time than usually considered. In a time where our digital world move fast and everything is one click away, speaking of patience and long term might seem like a contradiction, but it is, indeed, needed. We will come to this point in the Part 3, when we will cover with more detail the rivalry aspects of luxury competition.

In the examples provided in Capsule 3.2, Horacio Pagani, Maximilian Büsser and Joseph Krug are both a leader envisioning a way to break normality and a scarce resource in the form of the talent needed to make it a reality. Now we can see how, oftentimes, luxury firms are so intimately linked to their founders.

A reminder on scarcity. Extraordinariness implies scarcity. In order to achieve something extraordinary it must be complex to achieve, otherwise many firms can do it and we enter into *normal* competition. Therefore, the idea of scarcity is intimately linked to extraordinariness.

We, oftentimes, relate luxury with scarcity in terms of raw material (diamonds), know-how or expertise. Consider that these are scarce organizational capabilities that enable extraordinariness and pass at the same time the VRIO framework. Only when we can link scarcity with extraordinariness and when we pass the VRIO framework on organizational capabilities we can speak of luxury. We should not relate luxury directly with scarcity. Not all scarce elements constitute the basis of a competitive advantage in the luxury arena.

A luxury brand is a consequence not a goal. It is in this way interesting to remember that a Brand is a powerful (intangible) resource to own. But it is an organizational capability enabling extraordinariness what creates value. A brand, understood as the link between recognition and meaning, is the consequence that this path to extraordinariness was once achieved. Therefore, a Brand is always the consequence of extraordinariness and not otherwise. So it is the ownership of key organizational capabilities what build great brands.

Being extraordinary versus looking extraordinary. Oftentimes, we confuse luxury with the appearance of luxury. A beautiful store, a great service, a high price or a multibillion dollar promotional campaign (claiming "we are a luxury firm") is just a mask not luxury. Without an honest approach to extraordinariness there is no luxury. In Chapters 6 and 7, we will discuss with more detail luxury rivalry, but one thing must be clear by now: without *essence* there is no way a luxury firm can compete meaningfully.

Principles of luxury value creation

To conclude, not everything can aspire to be extraordinary. Many companies in the *normal* space use the term luxury to "slightly" distinguish themselves. Just go to any supermarket and count the number of times you see the word luxury. However, luxury is not about saying, but about being. Only creative ways to break normality and supported by organizational capabilities to realistically claim the achievement of extraordinariness will be in the path to a successful luxury strategy.

The limits of luxury

We have now two tools to ascertain luxury. First we have the lessons of the concept of luxury in Chapter 1 to help us understand luxury as a social phenomenon. Then we have the *Normal* versus *excess* framework to help us consider extraordinariness as the mechanism of luxury value creation. With these tools, we can, in most cases, ascertain the boundaries of luxury rivalry.

In general terms identifying the *normal* and the *excess* competition is quite evident. If we just pick any category, like bags (the most important good of the accessories category), we will find that the market offers luxury bags and non-luxury bags. Telling apart between the luxury and the non-luxury bags is, in most of the cases, evident.

A firm can be considered as luxury firm the moment it goes beyond *normal* competition and meet the characteristics of *excess* competition. Based on the principles of *excess* competition, luxury bags will be characterized by the satisfaction of sophisticated needs where emotional or expressive benefits are dominant. This will be combined with an offering of extraordinariness. This is how consumers can easily identified luxury.

However, it is sometimes more complex to place the line between the *normal* and the *excess* type of competition. This is what we call the limits of luxury. So, where is the limit between normality and excess?

The role of consistency. The fine line between normality and excess

The line between normality and excess is blurred for two main reasons. As emotional or expressive benefits dominate, there is no metric to measure of extraordinariness and hence it is always a complex assessment to make.

But also the line is blurred as the word luxury is among the most abused terms in marketing and strategy. Everybody wants to be perceived

Essence of luxury

in better terms and there is no better way to do so than "looking luxury". As a consequence, several terms have emerged to suggest the idea of luxury on *normal* competition. Concepts like premium, prestige, masstige, affordable luxury, trading-up and new luxury are just but a few examples.

Our approach will be more simple. Luxury is a social phenomenon and not a product or firm characteristic. As we described in depth in Chapter 1. Therefore, there is no need to add more adjectives to luxury. We only need to understand the phenomena. For instance, there is no need to say "new" luxury. Whenever one understand the dynamic component of luxury, it is obvious that luxury evolves with society so the products and services that represent luxury are constantly changing (as we saw with the sneakers example in Capsule 1.1).

These adjectives mentioned before (the likes of premium) are normally intended to upscale normality. But this analysis goes beyond our reach, as we are not concerned with the analysis of normality. The important point here is that luxury managers should focus on *excess* competition and not being distracted by how normal competitors aims higher.

A typical problem for luxury managers is to be distracted by normal competition and forget about ensuring *excess* competition. *Normal* competition can be interested of luxury managers, as way to explore and understand another way of competition, but not to follow it.

The way to ascertain the fine line between normality and excess is through consistency and not through firm or product characteristics. We follow here a similar approach here than in Chapter 1, when we tried to avoid a closed definition of luxury. Specially we should put attention to avoid defining luxury by price. Price is a consequence of extraordinariness, but not a driver of extraordinariness on its own. In simple terms, increasing the price does never transform an ordinary into an extraordinary product. As discussed in the section before, extraordinariness is way to deliver value not a price reference.

To ascertain the limits of luxury we will always need then ensure consistency between the following aspects, just like Capsule 3.3 shows:

- Consistency with luxury as a phenomena and extraordinariness as way to create value.
- Consistency in all facets of the firm, as inconsistency destroys emotional or expressive benefits.

Capsule 3.3. Is Coach a luxury firm?

Coach's origins date back to 1941 when a small, family-based, leather goods workshop started manufacturing wallets and billfolds in a loft in the garment district of New York City. In 1946, Miles Cahn joined the company and by 1950 he was running it for its owners. In 1961, Mr. Cahn with his wife Lillian Cahn's support bought the company (1). The story of Coach is therefore intimately linked to Mr. and Mrs. Cahn leadership, and frequently they are credited as Coach's founders (2).

1960 was a turning point in the evolution of the company. Based on the distinctive properties of baseball gloves, Mr. Cahn "devised a way of processing leather to make it strong, soft, flexible, and deep-toned in color, as it absorbed dye well" (1). He had engineered the perfect material to craft more durable and higher-quality products. The second key decision was to follow Lilliana's advice to enter the more lucrative woman handbag category. The latter move was done under the new Coach brand.

At that time there were many small workshop in New York City, but thanks to these moves, Coach became a recognizable and successful company. In 1962, the new designer Bonnie Cashin provided an innovative approach to Coach. She introduced new designs that later on became icons of the house like the duffle sac, the bucket bag or the tongue bag. Some analysts and reporters credited Ms. Cashin to take "the American purse from a stiff, impractical, ornamental pocketbook to something that women could use in their daily lives as mothers, workers or travelers" (2).

The Cahns sold Coach in the 1980s to Sara Lee, who envisioned more ambition plans for the firm. Under the managerial leadership of Lew Frankfort and Reed Krakoff as designer, Sara Lee took Coach to another level. The expansion was fueled under different principles though. Coach increased their product portfolio, add new distribution channels and build new manufacturing facilities. Department stores and outlets were added to the core boutique distribution channel. And by the end of the 1990s most of the production was outsourced (2).

Essence of luxury

The transformation was tremendous. The Cahns were very protective and concerned with securing high quality and control of the point of sale. When Sara Lee acquired Coach in 1985 it only had six boutiques, one manufacturing facility in West 34 St. in New York City, and total revenues were $19 million. By the year 2000, the moment Sara Lee divested Coach, sales amounted to nearly $550 million. There is no better description of this transformation than the word "affordable luxury", which is believed to be conceived to describe Coach in this period.

So while Coach increased significantly their size and reach, this did not come without a cost. The firm, ever since has suffered to claim a luxury positioning. So rather than asking whether Coach is or is not a luxury firm. We might better identify whether Coach is consistent with luxury, or as we have said it is consistent with the *excess* competition. The reason why Coach has ever since suffered to claim a luxury stepfoot is most likely their inconsistencies between what the company was originally and the way they have achieved growth. Issues with outlets (discounting), lack of quality control and misalignment of the point of sale have emerged with certain frequency. These are tactics more consistent with the normal space. For an independent company like Coach Inc. (which later became Tapestry in 2017), these issues seem to come back once in a while, as their last change in CEO position seems to convey (3), which hurts again the company's ability to claim their place in the luxury arena.

Today, Coach claims to be the "original American house of leather" in their website. And the company's origins are explained as "to make beautiful, functional items in modern shapes from the finest leathers". It is a pity, however, that their website does not explain Coach's beautiful origins, the role of Mr. and Mrs. Cahn, and their journey to extraordinariness in NYC.

Source (1) http://www.fundinguniverse.com/company-histories/coach-inc-history/
Source (2) https://www.nytimes.com/2017/02/11/business/miles-cahn-dead-coach.html?searchResultPosition=1
Source(3) https://www.cnbc.com/2019/09/04/coach-owner-tapestry-appoints-jide-zeitlin-as-ceo.html

Principles of luxury value creation

Managing the "entry-level" category

One of the most complex aspects to manage in a luxury firm is the entry-level offering. As the line between normality and excess is difficult to ascertain, the entry-level offering can mislead the assessment of value and ruin the perception of extraordinariness. A poorly managed entry-level offering can therefore break all efforts to maintain consistency and ruin the whole luxury strategy.

As stated in Chapter 2, luxury firms need to manage the mass versus exclusivity dilemma. The problem is that growth in lower market segments is at the same tempting and risky. The *normal* versus *excess* framework helps us manage this dilemma. To do so successfully, luxury firms should concentrate only on the *excess* type of competition to ensure value creation. Otherwise luxury firms might be perceived as mass oriented, which is not wrong per se, but just inconsistent with being extraordinary. This occurs the moment we enter in the *normal* competition. The negative perception associated is, oftentimes, referred to as brand dilution. Brand dilution is the lack of consistency that takes places between saying we are luxury (*excess*) and behaving differently (*normal*).

The challenge with the entry-level offering is therefore to sustain extraordinariness while accessing a lower segment—indeed, a tricky balance to keep. The main criterion should always be to protect extraordinariness, rather than exploring growth potential. Growth will not be an issue as long as extraordinariness is protected, just like the case study[7] explores with the launch of the Porsche Macan.

However, if extraordinariness is not protected the luxury firm will suffer. And then the mass versus exclusivity dilemma will shows signals of a mass oriented offering that ruins the perception of luxury. There are plenty of examples that companies not respecting the drivers of extraordinariness in their entry level. In 2001, Jaguar, under the ownership of Ford, launched the Jaguar X-type. It aimed to rival the dominant German players, the likes of BMW 3 series, Audi A4 and Mercedes Benz C-class. However, the Xtype was essentially a Ford Mondeo with a few changes. Similar engines and interiors made difficult to claim that the Xtype represented Jaguar's way of envisioning extraordinariness; on the contrary, it was more similar to Ford's normality.

Similarly, Aston Martin launched a small urban car, the Cygnet, in 2011. This was basically a Toyota iQ with Aston Martin interiors. Any assessment of extraordinariness that one can make about Aston Martin is hard to find on an urban car. Even if the market space for upscale urban cars exists (consumer need), that doesn't mean a luxury company must do it. Unlike in the *normal* space, *excess* deals with the ability of the firm to provide extraordinariness (Luxury paradigm). The fact that there is business potential does not mean that the luxury firm must take it. We need to ensure first consistency with our own source of extraordinariness. If not, it is a business opportunity, but it is not "our" business opportunity. These two examples also put into perspective what we unveil in Chapter 1. It takes time to appreciate luxury. Managers experienced in *normal* competition might not appreciate the need to protect exclusivity over growth.

If the assessment of value is properly made, luxury firms can only offer entry offering that shows their extraordinariness. Perhaps it can show a simple or an introductory version of extraordinariness. But always there is clear connection with the source of extraordinariness. This is a combination of a flavor of your skills in an entry format. The management of pricing is essential here. The entry-level offering (a time only watch) of Patek Philippe can be in the realm of $17.000, while the entry-level offering of Rolex can be around $4500. Price shows the level of extraordinariness that you will get from each company. As we will cover with more detail in Chapter 8, price is the firm's best communication tool. So we better use it wisely to convey our level of extraordinariness and to show consistency.

There is no magic rule to define the entry level. Again, it is a quest for consistency between what the company can offer and their honest approach to extraordinariness. Therefore, if the firm does not perform an honest and profound assessment of their *essence*, it is unlikely they can understand where can be the limits for their entry-level offering.

Case study. Porsche Macan, beyond the limits of luxury?

The end of 2013 was a very exciting period in the long and successful history of Dr. Ing. Ferdinand Porsche AG (Porsche), the German luxury carmaker. In September of that year the Porsche 918 was presented, an extreme sports car with a hybrid engine of more than 800 horse power (HP) and a price of more than €750,000. In November, Porsche

Principles of luxury value creation

introduced the new Macan with an expected entry price of €60,000; it was positioned as one of Porsche's entry offerings.

The new models showed the wide product offering Porsche had achieved in just a decade. In the late 1990s Porsche mainly manufactured the iconic 911, but by 2014, the German manufacturer had six different models on offer: Boxster/Cayman, 911, Panamera, Cayenne, Macan and 918.

Porsche had already achieved extraordinary success with its latest launches, such as the Porsche Cayenne and the Porsche Panamera. By continuously adding new models, Porsche had also showed its capacity to access a wider client base. However, the two new models could also bring additional complexity.

Porsche's new models showed the potential of expanding its current portfolio. The Macan would provide an entry-level car from which clients were able to "taste" the Porsche feeling and later move up toward the Cayenne, Panamera or 911. Initially, Porsche launched the Macan with the most powerful engine (Exhibit 1) in order to provide more exclusivity image30. This growth opportunity also seemed to address increased demand for luxury cars from clients in emerging markets.

Porsche had already been successful in doubling its size. However, doing it again was not a simple task and not only from a manufacturing perspective. Porsche was targeting new customers and as its portfolio of cars grew, some new issues came into play.

Till then, all Porsche models represented a success story and the company had proved that it was able to fulfill the demand from luxury clients. However, some questions remained. Was Porsche able to capitalize on its previous successful launches? Was it risky to launch two models in such different segments of the market? What implications would it have for the company? And above all, what was the limit, if any, for a manufacturer of luxury cars?

Adapted from Millán, D., "Porsche AG. The limits of luxury". IE Publishing, DE1-204.

Essence of luxury

Summary

This chapter provides the fundamental analytical tools to evaluate the challenges and potential for competitiveness of luxury firms.

The first section of the chapter explores the *normal* versus *excess* framework as a way to ascertain luxury value creation. To do so, *normal* competition is differentiated from *excess* competition. Normal competition is the most common competitive form and it is characterized by a dominant role of functional benefits, the considerations of logic and rationality linked to functionality, the supply-demand equilibrium (normality) from which companies fight to differentiate and the notion of premium pricing which refers to an average price.

Unlike normal competition, *excess* competition explains how luxury can be valuable through the key idea of going beyond normality. The dominant role of emotional or expressive benefits explains the misconception of value linked to a function. And it also explains a different competitive form where companies do not try to break or improve normality but to go beyond it. But not all forms of *excess* leads to value creation, and only extraordinariness is the way to ensure at the same time going beyond normality and value creation.

The second section of the chapter provides a more detailed analysis of Extraordinariness. This is a fundamental tools to understand how luxury firms can create value, which ultimately explains how successful a luxury firm can be in the market. However, this analysis is complex and ambiguous as extraordinariness is heavily dependent of meaningful individual choices guiding the path to go beyond normality rather than being based on an analytical processes to evaluate market competition. It also adds complexity the fact that extraordinariness is hardly a specific goal that can be measured

A second critical aspect is the ownership of key organizational resources. Unlike in Normal competition, organizational capabilities must not respond to key activities of the value chain, but more importantly they must support to the fundamental choices made behind the conception of extraordinariness. This constitutes another different in the way competitive advantage should be analyzed for luxury firms.

To conclude, the chapter provides in its last section a discussion on the fine line that sometimes exist between normality and excess, especially when firms define their entry-level offering. This is one of the typical problems to ascertain luxury. The role of consistency with the path to extraordinariness and in all facets of the firm is explained as fundamental.

Self-study questions

1. *A value offering can be better understood as a combination of different types of benefits. Can you identify a value offering (product or service) where functional benefits are predominant, And another one where emotional or expressive benefits are predominant?*
2. *What is the managerial limitation that the functionality trap is aimed to highlight?*
3. *Luxury cannot be described as normal competition; what best describes normal competition? Can you identify an industry where normal competition clearly explains how companies compete?*
4. *Based on what you have read in the chapter, what difficulties do companies face when in the conception of extraordinariness?*
5. *Why consistency can be a sound approach to ascertain the fine line between normality and extraordinariness?*
6. *Why entry-level offering can be a threat to a luxury firm's strategy?*
7. *Can you find a current example of a luxury firm with a successful entry-level offering? And an example of a firm that fails to offer a meaningful entry-level offering?*

Notes

1 Aaker, D. and Joachimsthaler E. "Brand Leadership", The Free Press, 2000. The value proposition, page 49.

2 Millán, D. "Luxury Surrenders to Internet. The Role of Millennials", IE & Mastercard Premium and Prestige Observatory, February 2017. Accessible at https://observatoriodelmercadopremium.ie.edu/en/.

3 Grant, R. *Contemporary Strategy Analysis*, 9th edition 2016. Wiley, page 118.

4 Grant, page 119. 9th edition, 2016.

5 Grant, See for instance Chapter 5, page 123. 9th edition, 2016.

6 Barney, J. B., "Looking Inside for Competitive Advantage", *Academy of Management Executive*, Vol. 9 (1995), pp. 49–61.

7 Adapted from Millán, D. *Porsche AG, Beyond the Limits of Luxury*. IE Publishing, 2013.

PART 3

Principles of creativity-driven industries. The *nature* of luxury

The luxury firm and the role of creativity

Introduction and objectives

The previous Chapter 3 introduced the notion of extraordinariness to ensure both competing in the realm of excess while ensuring value creation. This chapter complements this analysis by adding the role of creativity in the analysis of the firm.

The first part of the chapter explores the firm analysis and argues that creativity is a much-needed aspect to achieve extraordinariness. Creativity is the form through which extraordinariness can be expressed. It is a critical component in any luxury strategy, as the examples of different creative processes in various industries will show.

Then the concept of creativity will be explored. This will provide a better understanding of the idea itself and tear down typical misunderstandings and stereotypes. Notably, this section aims to explain how creativity is not just a superficial aspect but also linked to value creation. The differences between art, fashion, and technology will be highlighted. And then, particular interest will be provided to describe the role of creators as a fundamental piece of the luxury firm's creative capability.

The last part of the chapter will center the focus on the interplay between creativity and the firm strategy. The fundamental principles to manage creativity for luxury firms will be provided. We will see how creativity shapes the firm's ability to compete meaningfully and their value creation process, which is frequently called the Strategy as Positioning. We will also study the role of creativity in shaping the firm's

DOI: 10.4324/9781003015321-8

Principles of creativity-driven industries

own set of values and beliefs, commonly called Strategy as Direction, following the same approach.[1] Creativity is then, when properly managed, a mighty tool for any luxury strategy.

By the time you have completed this chapter, you will be able to:

- Assess accurately the concept of creativity and how it should be evaluated for luxury value creation.
- Identify the most typical myths and misperceptions associated with the notion of creativity.
- Assess the differences between the concepts of creativity, design, fashion, and innovation. With a particular interest in their application to luxury firms.
- Gain practical knowledge on the fundamental managerial aspects to be considered when applying creativity to luxury firms.
- Understand creativity from the firm perspective, and assess how it goes beyond the product characteristics or the individual talents.
- Appreciate the role of the creator in a luxury firm and evaluate its potential conflict of interest.
- Differentiate between the classic and modern approaches to luxury.
- Understand the dynamic component of luxury firms and identify the perils of static companies.

Why is creativity key for the firm analysis?

In Chapter 1, we saw how luxury is a mirror of society, and its evolution accompanies social change. Then, we introduced the Luxury paradigm in Chapter 2 to suggest that luxury firms can be better understood when their ability to create value is conceived within the firm. This is opposed to non-luxury firms (classic paradigm) characterized by the ability to identify value potential in the market. Finally, the previous Chapter 3 showed the notion of extraordinariness to help us argue how luxury firms can create value in a way that exceeds normality.

Chapter 3 also showed that the path to extraordinariness can be identified with certain easiness once created. However it is much more difficult to conceive extraordinariness from the ground up. The explanation relied fundamentally on the idea that luxury firms provide value based on the

Luxury firm and the role of creativity

aggregation of several complex variables which are in nature complex to assess, for instance, emotional benefits. The complexity in conceiving luxury is, in short, based on the combination of:

a) The need to exceed normality.
b) The focus on emotional or expressive benefits, which are, in nature, complex to ascertain.
c) The role of leadership to conceived it on the firm's own terms.

This was captured with the notion of luxury being ultimately a choice.

Therefore, the link with creativity is a natural consequence of the analysis described in the previous chapters. Creativity is a fundamental skill that can help companies sustain this approach to value creation based on emotional or expressive benefits and stimulated by self-approach choices.

This chapter provides further clarity to manage creativity for luxury firms. We already anticipated the role of creativity in Chapter 2, when we discussed the tension between management and creativity. We noted as well in Chapter 3 that business competition requires the ownership of key organizational capabilities. Therefore, in luxury, organizational capabilities will need to be related to creativity.

At some point, all luxury firms are or have been creative. It is inherited in the notion of luxury to be creative. A luxury firm cannot claim to be extraordinary unless it can claim a self approach to go beyond normality, which is intimately linked to being able to create on its own. We could say that creativity is hence the guiding path toward extraordinariness.

The bottom line, creativity is an essential characteristic of a luxury firm. And this is a good thing for managers and strategists. There are no single, but multiple (infinite one would argue) paths to extraordinariness and this opens many possibilities to compete meaningfully in the marketplace.

There are two fundamental aspects that we will consider in our approach to creativity. Creativity must fulfill the two requirements of extraordinariness:

- Going beyond normality. The idea of going beyond normality shapes novelty. Novelty is a crucial characteristic of creativity, but stand-alone is not enough. We need to ensure that creativity is linked to this notion of going beyond normality to connect creativity with luxury property.
- Ensure value creation. Not any novelty that aims to go beyond normality would be enough either. Value creation must also be achieved. As stated

Principles of creativity-driven industries

in the previous chapter, extraordinariness is going beyond normality while being valuable, so it must be valuable excess.

We will only speak of creativity for luxury firms the moment we can ensure these two critical components. We want to avoid naive or partial views of creativity. Otherwise, luxury managers might be tempted to use (or even abuse) the word creativity for its obvious positive connotations. Therefore, creativity is a must-have organizational capability for any luxury firm, and it shapes the firm's path to business success. The following sections will explain the concept of creativity in detail and offer principles to manage it properly.

A conceptualization of creativity for luxury firms

So far, we have considered creativity in absolute terms, with minor clarification. However, the concept of creativity is a complex notion that is not only referred to as individual skills. As far as it is concerned with business, creativity is a concept that can be widely applied to different purposes, and this makes its analysis quite complicated, indeed.

It is not the scope, nor the ambition, of this text to cover a comprehensive review of the concept. This section aims to provide some clarity on the main aspects that characterizes it. This section will also serve as a needed introduction to some of the fundamental principles that we will use to analyze the interplay between creativity and the firm strategy in the following section.

The concept of creativity

The concept of creativity is broad. Like we did with the notion of luxury in Chapter 1, other disciplines, here psychology and sociology, provide very relevant insights to appreciate the concept better. The work of Professor Teresa Amabile is perhaps one of the crucial references in this area. The first approaches to creativity differentiated between the creative process, the creative person, and the creative product. Professor Amabile offered in 1982 a consensual definition of creativity, which was one of the first attempts to include the three approaches into a definition:[2]

102

Luxury firm and the role of creativity

A product or response is creative to the extent that appropriate observers independently agree it is creative. Appropriate observers are those familiar with the domain in which the product was created or the response articulated. Thus, creativity can be regarded as the quality of products or responses judged to be creative by appropriate observers, and it can also be regarded as the process by which something so judged is produced.

This heavily relied on the eyes of the observer and its expertise to assess the creative output. While not a comprehensive view, this definition introduces an interesting aspect: the observer's expertise to appreciate the creative output. We discussed in Chapter 3 how luxury is instead appreciated, and this frequently requires a particular sensitivity of the buyer.

Her later conceptual definition of creativity was more comprehensive, and for years it has become widely observed a reference to define creativity. Professor Amabile conceptual definition of creativity is:[3]

A product or response will be judged as creative to the extent that (a) it is both a novel and appropriate, useful, correct, or valuable response to the task at hand and (b) the task is heuristic rather than algorithmic.

This conceptual definition is more in line with our field of study as it tries to explain the role of the creative output and its relevancy. In summary, for a given output to be creative, we need it to be novel and valuable.

It is noteworthy to observe as well the second part of the definition. The difference between the algorithmic and the heuristic approach is equally relevant. The classic approach considers[4] that an algorithmic task is where the path to the output (solution) is clear, so an algorithm to the outcome exists. A heuristic task is different in nature, as there is no clear path to the output, and an algorithm must be developed.

We did cover in Chapter 3 the vital role of leadership (founder or creator) in conceiving extraordinariness. The path to exceed normality was ultimately defined as a choice based on a self approach, rather than a search on external sources (like clients). That is precisely an example of a heuristic task, where the path to the output is not clear, and it has to be made. Just like we discussed for the case of extraordinariness in luxury firms, for creative output to emerge, not only the output itself, but the process to get to it must signal novelty. In this way, we can also relate normality with an algorithm approach, while luxury with a heuristic approach. This is why we do not speak of creativity only when the form or shape is new or different (even when valuable), but also when the conception of it shows a novel approach (heuristic).

Professor Amabile also suggested that the assessment of the creative performance is divided into the:[5]

a) Domain-relevant skills (referred to the cognitive aspects),
b) Creativity-relevant skills (related to personal characteristics), and
c) Task motivation (applied to both personal attitudes and social environment).

It is interesting to see that creative performance is linked not only to the skills (cognitive and personal) but also to the social environment. Following this approach, the analysis of creativity for luxury must entail a review of the firm (performed in Chapter 3 as organizational skills) and the social context (shown in Chapter 1 with the idea of luxury).

Furthermore, we can drive intriguing parallelism with the evolution of luxury and the difference between artisans and artists, as seen in Chapter 1. We argued how the transformation from artisan to artist in the Renaissance was based on the personal approach. While an artisan replicates a work based on learned know-how (cognitive skills), an artist does so based on its own way (personal skills). Thus creativity in business must be analyzed as a combination of the skills to perform the outcome but also on the self-conception of the outcome.

The latter suggests a final exciting aspect, the role of social change. In Chapter 1, we observed luxury as a mirror to society. In line with this perspective, the notion of creativity from the lenses of sociology can be seen as:[6]

An intentional configuration of material and cultural elements that is unexpected for a given audience.

While psychologists and sociologists do not frequently agree on their approach to defining creativity,[7] it is impressive how both take into consideration the role of environment and social context. Therefore, the analysis of creativity for luxury firms should also pay close attention to the social context and its evolution.

It is interesting to notice that we do not observe a valuable consideration in this later definition, as the creative outcome does not need to be beneficial for the audience. In our approach, we will need to consider the role

Luxury firm and the role of creativity

of a valuable output to recognize its market potential. And in the case of luxury, we need to find a valuable output as a requirement for extraordinariness, as noted in the previous section. Here the notion of value, defined in Chapter 3, still applies. Value is not only a function of functionality. So when we say valuable, we do not only mean functionality.

Companies that observe value creation in broader terms are more creative. The reason is that they break the boundaries of functionality, and they can find novelty by exploring new areas for value. A clear example is a Portuguese firm Renova and its approach to commodities. A commodity is a clear example of a product where little can be done beyond their core function, so firms end up competing in prices. Renova is an example that creativity can be applied even to a commodity. Their core market is toilet paper. However, rather than considering themselves as a commodity producer, they see themselves as a wellbeing company (self approach). But this is no tagline; it is a belief that shapes their decision making. For instance, their colorful lines are an example of what creativity can achieve when properly applied as a way to conceive value beyond functionality.

Shapes of creativity: art and fashion

Another source of confusion in the analysis of creativity is the wide array of concepts that are frequently used to substitute or complement the notion of creativity. Here we just aim to provide some light to clarify the (perhaps) most frequent ones: art and fashion.

We have stated several times in the previous chapters the positive influence of art in enhancing the ability of the luxury firm to compete (Chapter 3), to understand the luxury paradigm (Chapter 2) and to appreciate the concept of luxury (Chapter 1).

Based on the previous section it is somehow evident the relationship between art and creativity. The moment we consider creativity as a self approach, or a heuristic task, where something new and valuable is generated, then we can easily see how art is an example of it.

The key differences hence between creativity and art are therefore the boundaries of the outcome. While creativity can be widely applied, art is mostly concerned with certain type of outcome. In its definition, art is,[8]

The expression or application of human creative skill and imagination, typically in a visual form such as painting or sculpture,

Principles of creativity-driven industries

producing works to be appreciated primarily for their beauty or emotional power.

So, basically, art is one form of creativity applied to human expression or human creativity. Traditionally, the fine arts have been painting, sculpture, architecture, literature, music and dance (or performing). With film making being a more modern addition, and popularly known as the seventh art. In the definition of art it is also inherited the idea of capability, skill or ability to do something. Art it is not a mere form of expression, it is a form of expression where a certain skills or ability is needed. So according to the set of skills we consider we can consider artisans when we have only domain-relevant skills and artist when we add personal skills.

As we said in Chapter 2, considering art ultimately as a form of expression. It makes all sense to use artistic creativity to support another form of creativity, business creativity. And here we speak of business creativity and not only luxury, as the influence of art in solving business problems creatively is significant,[9] just like we mentioned before with Renova. But this, of course, goes beyond the boundaries of our study.

Another area of confusion in the understanding of creativity is the notion of fashion. We, oftentimes, hear indistinctly concepts like creativity and fashion. And while related, they are not the same and it makes sense to clarify their difference. Specially to break the stereotype that creativity is only relevant in the fashion industry, but not so important in other luxury industries.

Professors Patrick Aspers and Frédéric Godart make a fantastic case explaining the concept of fashion from other related concepts like style or innovation.[10] Fashion etymologically comes for the French word *façon*, which means ways of making and sing things. It is also related to the Latin term *modus*, which also implies the idea of multiple ways of doing things or diversity of practices. The word "fashion" in Spanish, *moda*, or in French, mode, still marks the link to its Latin origins. The key idea is that no single solution rather alternatives can be found to conceive an outcome. In general term we consider Fashion as the creativity applied to a specific outcome, clothing.

Here we observe similarities between fashion and art, as they both are ways of expression and implying multiple ways of conceiving the outcome. Both, in summary, heuristics tasks applied to specific fields. However creativity is far more a broader concept. Therefore, we should never restrict

106

Luxury firm and the role of creativity

creativity to be a matter or a skill of a given discipline or type of outcome. Creativity can be found in any luxury industry. Just like the case study of this chapter explores with MB&F.

Role of innovation and technology

On many occasions, creativity and innovation are used indistinctively. While the two concepts are related, they are not the same. However, most of the time, it is not very clear the difference. Indeed, there is a relationship between the concepts of innovation, technology and creativity. But it might be useful to clarify the distinction for a better understanding of creativity.

One likely reason behind this confusion is the low importance that the management discipline has devoted, unfortunately, to creativity.[11] In management, it is frequent to speak in terms of innovation. One gets the idea of value in innovation, where there is the notion of improvement and lasting influence in social practice.[12] However finding the link between creativity and value is more complex. This might be the reason why traditionally creativity has been considered as less important for managers, and oftentimes used as a synonym of subjectivity and aesthetics. And this is due mainly to the difficulties in assessing value through emotional and expressive benefits (Chapter 3).

Another critical component of innovation is the economic return. We speak of innovation when there is a financial return, while the original idea is denoted as creativity. So in simple terms, creativity is often conceived as the generation of the idea, while innovation is associated with successful business implementation.[13] This is why creativity is typically used to describe individuals while innovation to companies.

Nevertheless, in our study, we will always refer to creativity. The definition of creativity implies value creation, so there is no need to degrade the word to a less critical role. It might make more sense (perhaps) to note the difference between innovation and creativity in other areas beyond our study. However, in luxury, creativity is a crucial aspect to discuss extraordinariness and to achieve it. Hence, it is not needed to deviate from the core notion of creativity.

The same happens with technology. For many years it has been considered that luxury and technology were worlds apart, even a contradiction. We already noted that in Chapter 1, the mistake to consider luxury as opposed to technology.

When Mr. Breguet invented the tourbillon, he provided a cutting-edge advance to mechanical watchmaking. The internal combustion engine

Principles of creativity-driven industries

allowed new and more powerful cars to be accessible last century. And today, advanced engineering generates recycled fabrics. Technology has always been very present in luxury, and it makes total sense as going beyond normality might require a broad set of skills, technology being one. But there is not always a need for technology to break normality. Creativity can base its novelty by breaking certain principles or assumptions.

Art is, once more, can serve as an example. Any new creative movement, like the impressionist, signals a new way to conceive and express painting, without actually modifying the painting technique. It is more about a new conception than a new technique or technology. Art pioneers are fundamentally individuals who push or redesign the boundaries to understand art. Let's see this with one example.

The Spanish painter Diego Velazquez became famous in the sixteenth century for his outstanding painting skills. He became the painter of king Felipe IV and became a reference in Spain. However, little was known about him internationally. When Claude Monet went to Madrid in the mid Nineteenth century, he studied Velazquez defined him as the greatest painters of all. Why Velazquez was such a great painter goes beyond our scope.[14] But among his many attributes, one finds his pioneer and breakthrough vision on art. He started to do and conceive art in a way none had done before. He transformed some of the previous (classical) approaches and began to play with new elements, like combining religious scenes in a still life painting. He also fostered the importance of the portrait. But perhaps his most significant contribution is the notion of monumental art. His work showed a new dimension in terms of size to display art. He was not only a great artist, but he transformed and contributed to the evolution of art.

In short, there is no need to conceive a given technology to transform and push the limits of our conceptions. A pioneer can be understood as a change in the assumptions and principles considered; not only is it a matter of a given (technical) improvement. This idea of artistic pioneer can be ultimately converted into business pioneers. Considering the impact of Coco Chanel, one would quickly transfer these lessons into the business of luxury.

Role of creators: founders and designers

The last aspect to consider in the analysis of creativity is the role of the creator. If creativity is a heuristic task where a path to the outcome has to be

Luxury firm and the role of creativity

created, then the creator is responsible for conceiving, setting, or defining the path to the outcome in their own terms.

This is why creativity is by definition unique. The moment one person leads it, it is unique, as unique is that person. Then the challenge is to ensure value. Like in any recruitment process, any candidate is scarce by definition, as there is only one in the world. The challenge is to transfer that uniqueness and scarcity into value for the recruiting firm in this case.

Individual skills shape creativity. This is not to say that creativity is only about the creative person, or as noted here, the creator. The social background shapes creativity, either. The firm can influence creativity by influencing the creator, as Professor Amabile note as the work environment.[15] We can often observe that in business is the collaboration within the company that stimulates a far better creative approach than the one from one or a few individuals.

This suggests that creative firms are a matter of internal collaboration, rather than only an individual talent. This might explain, for instance, why some firms, or even some regions, are more successful than others. Why France has a dominant position in luxury while Spain not? One likely factor explaining this fact is that in Spain, unlike in France (or even Italy), creativity is widely understood as individual talent. While in France, luxury firms seem to have embraced a more meaningful combination between personal creativity and internal collaboration. The orientation toward Arts et Métiers shows the approach to different skills beyond individual talent. While here, we speak of country cultures, which is very open to debate, and very sensitive as well. The lessons are that collaborative firms have the potential to be more creative than companies based only on individual talent.[16] The case study of this section on MB&F is another supporting example of this statement.

As a result, the way the firm is organized, and its shared values influence its ability to be creative. And here, it is a fundamental difference with art. In art, we can think of the creative person, the artist, as the fundamental driver of value. The artist is, of course, influenced by social background. However, this is hardly the case in business where we should consider the role of teams, processes, and shared values, frequently referred to, and firm culture. As noted in Chapter 2, this is what is often denotes as the Strategy as Direction.

But not all aspects are positive with the role of the creator; there are some risks too. We could consider a situation where the creative person, let's say a fashion designer, is an employee but not the owner or founder. Who is

Principles of creativity-driven industries

more important, the firm or the designer? This question is not aimed to be addressed by the client based on what consumers prefer. This is a crucial strategic consideration to be made by the firm, just as Capsule 4.3 shows.

The fundamental aspects covered in this section are summarized in Table 4.1.

The assessment of creativity for the luxury firm. Lessons for managers

The previous section has provided the foundations for a better appreciation of the concept of creativity in general terms, and luxury specifically. However, little was mentioned about how this conceptualization can be transferred to the management practice. This section will take those lessons as a starting point to build specific managerial insights. In this way, this section will focus on the key aspects that luxury managers should consider when formulating their strategy.

Luxury managers should carefully assess how a firm approaches creativity. As can be inferred from the previous section, the role of creativity must be a fundamental piece in any luxury strategy. On the one hand, creativity can shape the luxury firm's ability to compete meaningfully and their value creation process, which we noted as Strategy as Positioning in Chapter 2. And on the other hand, creativity is also a representation of the firm's own set of values and beliefs, what we noted as Strategy as Direction, in Chapter 2.

Of course, it is not our intention to transform the manager into an artist but to stimulate the skills to manage a luxury firm. The appreciation of creativity might encourage the development, and eventually motivate a personal journey of self-discovery, toward a more creative mindset. Hopefully, this reading will stimulate this path.

Embracing creativity requires will and adaptation

The first aspect that a luxury firm should consider about creativity is to take it seriously. There is a temptation to use creativity only to attract consumer attention through advertising or to differentiate the design of the product, the so-called product refreshments. Creativity must be embraced seriously and with the will to deal with its trade-offs. This is

Luxury firm and the role of creativity

Table 4.1 The concept of creativity and its implications for luxury

Concept and value (business) approach.	– Creativity is ultimately about novelty and value – Importance to realize that creativity is valuable (other non-business considerations might not need the valuable part) – Importance of heuristic versus arithmetic approach. – The heuristic approach is associated with creativity. The path to the outcome has to be created. In luxury, this speaks of the importance of firm values and self-conception.
Boundaries of the outcome: art and fashion.	– Creativity is a general and broad notion that embraces other concepts like art and fashion. – Art and fashion are applied when specific outcomes are considered, while creativity is more widespread notion. – In luxury, one should speak in terms of creativity, as it exists in all luxury markets. – It is a stereotype to consider creativity only in fashion-driven industries, as creativity is not only concerned with the shape and alteration of the outcome.
Innovation and technology.	– Innovation is generally linked to business success (economic return), while creativity is more linked to the ideas behind it. – Innovation is linked with technology, while creativity with art. – This is a stereotype, as creativity is also meant to be valuable and not related only to the shape of the outcome. – Art pioneers are a source of inspiration to luxury (business in general as well) managers. They bring novelty by a new conception of the outcome (associated with emotional benefit) rather than an improvement of the outcome (associated with functionality).
The creator.	– A fundamental role, following the notion of creativity as a heuristic approach, leadership is needed for conceiving the path to the outcome. – The creator is a key driver of the required skills in terms of knowledge and expertise (cognitive skills), but also his personal view (personal skills). – But the social background (society and firm) complement or influence the set of skills needed for creativity. – The notion of creativity as a set of collaborative aspects around the creators might explain differences in the business approach to creativity.

111

Principles of creativity-driven industries

what Maximilian Büsser (see the chapter's case study) encapsulates as the enemies of a creative firm:

- Shareholder value that force firms to focus on the short term.
- Traditional marketing that focus firms to be concerned with minor differential improvements.
- Middle management that makes firms risk-averse.

There is not a better way to simplify the role and impact of creativity for firms. Creativity is not a minor, aesthetic touch to stay relevant. On the contrary, it is a choice that requires commitment and shapes the whole idea of what the firm is all about. A firm decides to be creative as an entire entity. The role of creativity is not a mere tactical aspect, regardless of if the product design or a new communication theme.

And of course, the firm must be ready to stimulate and sustain the risks that will offer. Is the firm prepared to accept lower sales if that fosters the creative process? Is the firm willing to take the longer times needed in the development of valuable novelty? Is the firm ready to perform an internal analysis to have a clear idea of their inner vision rather than rapidly copy-pasting what's hot in the market? These are fundamental questions that suggest that creativity implies commitment, effort and time. Otherwise, the luxury firm can become more market depending and loosing then its creative approach.

For that reason, luxury managers need to accept the challenges and benefits of being creative. Being a creative firm is a belief to be shared among the firm's managers. And this force managers to adapt to the principles identified in the previous chapter.

Firm creativity has multiple forms beyond design

Fashion companies rely on creativity to stay relevant. However, product design is not the only form to stimulate creativity within the firm. Creativity must lie in the core competitive principles of the firm. To remain competitive, luxury firms should not consider creativity as a matter of shape and form, but as a way to shape their overall way of competing.

Capsule 4.1 shows the creative approach at Krug, which is a clear example of the power of creativity beyond the modification of the product, what we usually refer to as design.

Capsule 4.1. Creativity at KRUG. Creativity beyond design

At Krug, creativity is at its heart. Unlike any other champagne house, Krug offers a new edition every year, which is the outcome of their approach to prestige champagne and know-how. Rather than looking for a consistent quality standard to be kept annually, the company plays with the best wines of the years to achieve a blend that fully expresses the richness of the year. That is the crucial concept of the Krug Grande Cuvèe.

This is a pioneer conception that challenged traditional champagne-making, based on the vintage approach. The vintage method is based primarily on the idea that prestige champagne must be produced only on excellent climatic years. But Joseph Krug, back in 1842, had the idea that every year can be the basis of a great champagne. To do so, Joseph Krug became a master of the plot parcel approach. Every plot is transformed into wine. Then a palette of many wines, including some from previous years, serves as components of the blend. Joseph Krug became an expert in blending himself, and today this complex and explorative process is led by the Chef de Cave.

There is no better way to conceive a creative approach than self-creation on an annual basis. Here we see how creativity is a combination of best ingredients but also the expertise to blend them properly to get the most of the year's potential. Krug is therefore known as a master of the blend. And this is, at the same valuable and proprietary. Krug is a creative expression of the full potential of the year. This places them as an extraordinary product not only for the highest quality of their products but for the unique proposal. Only Krug can offer the highest expression of champagne every year.

Therefore, Krug is an excellent example that creativity lies in the firm's core competitive approach, and this is what makes them valuable. It is also an example that creativity adequately understood is a far more powerful concept than a mere selection of product aesthetics or catchy communication taglines. Creativity at Krug is a matter of principles and choices that shape their path to extraordinariness.

Principles of creativity-driven industries

Creativity lies in the conception of the set of values and beliefs that define explicitly the firm. So it is challenging to understand creative firms without understanding the persons and values behind them. Another example in a different industry is provided with Capsule 4.2, which explores the role of creativity at Mugaritz.

Capsule 4.2. Creativity at Mugaritz. The conception of the business

Mugaritz is a restaurant located in Errenteria, a little town on the outskirts of San Sebastian (Spain). Mugaritz is the culinary expression of Andoni Aduriz. It has been the only restaurant systematically ranked (ever since 2009) as one of the top 10 restaurants in the world by the prestigious *Restaurant* magazine awards. The underlying reason for such great recognition is Andoni Aduriz's unique creative philosophy toward gastronomy.

If Mugaritz were a restaurant, it would be focused on delivering high-quality food, scarce ingredients, or secret recipes. Mugaritz is not about quality or even consistent quality. Mugaritz goes beyond the notion of a restaurant; it is a creative culinary expression. It is at the same time a laboratory to explore the limits of gastronomy, and a restaurant to show its outcome. "Mugaritz explores the limits of gastronomy with art, the limits of the culinary world with science", claims their site. It is then a fantastic combination of different culinary and non-culinary skills like art, to push the boundaries of what gastronomy can become.

Mugaritz is a clear example that creativity requires will and commitment, and it is not a mere tagline. The restaurant is closed to clients for three months. This is a period to concentrate on experimentation and research. In this period, the new season is defined after several rounds of literally thousands of possible plates. It might be impossible to do so while running a restaurant at the same time. If one wants to be creative, it needs to dedicate time and effort. So Mugaritz is committed to that, and they close their doors. From the lenses of a rational business

Luxury firm and the role of creativity

mindset, closing the doors is not a very good idea as revenues decline. But creativity is complex to be achieved, and at Mugaritz, they are fully aware of it.

Every season Mugaritz prepares a selection of 150 plates from which the firm chooses to do its service. This allows them to modify throughout the year the offering. Guests at Mugaritz do not choose, but they are offered (with individual consideration based on tastes and health conditions like intolerances). So two visits to Mugaritz, even in the same season, can provide different culinary experiences.

Some might guess that it is recurrent for restaurants to claim to offer experiences and that their menu is a culinary journey. But many only say it or pretend to be. Creativity is about choosing not about claiming. When Mugaritz speaks of creativity, they have the legitimacy to talk about it, they experience it and put the resources to practice it. It is the fundamental driver behind their crucial decisions and their reason for being. Mugaritz is a place for constant exploration, a true passion for what can be new, and finding what can push the boundaries of what we know.

Firm creativity is not only about individual talent (Firm versus Creator)

A fundamental lesson that the analysis of creativity derives for luxury managers is the management of the different elements accountable for creativity. It is of particular interest the role of creator and its relationship with the firm. As discussed earlier, creativity is better appreciated as a combination between the creator and the firm's environment. In non-luxury industries this is also relevant.

As we said in Chapter 3, a natural consequence of this is the relationship between the founder (or creator) and the luxury firm. Extraordinariness is a creative path, not a scientific path. And this requires the role of a creator. That is why luxury firms are so intimately linked to its founders.

Therefore, a pivotal lesson to consider is how the management of creativity can unleash more value when both creator and firm environment work consistently. If the creator and firm do not work in the same direction, the

Principles of creativity-driven industries

firm will create less value, and even create a conflict of interest between the two. When the creator is at the same the founder, one could observe a lower potential conflict of interest (although still could exist). However, this becomes more relevant when the creator is not anymore the founder, as Capsule 4.3 shows.

Therefore, when we say value, it is meant to be the firm's value creation, which is the combination of the creator and firm environment. Indeed,

---

Capsule 4.3. Creator versus Firm. A potential conflict

Over the past years, some luxury firms, mainly in fashion, have changed their visual identity and logos, firms like Celine, Saint Lauren, Balenciaga, Burberry, Balmain, Berluti, Rimowa or Diane von Furstenberg. These changes have something in common; they represent a change in creative leadership. The underlying rationale might not be the same for all companies. Still, they share certain principles like the need to revitalize the brand, become more attractive to a younger audience, make the visual identity to work better online, or signal a new brand attribute of the firm.

Interestingly enough, these changes have something else in common; the new logos are surprisingly similar. Fashion analysts and specialized media started to wonder why luxury logos were suddenly so related. These similarities might suggest that certain forms or aesthetics are better to signal modernity, but still surprising in an industry where creativity is critical.

But this also raises a very intriguing dilemma. The creative director is a driving force on a luxury firm to claim extraordinariness. His artistic conception, imagination, and skills can bring the needed components, making perfect sense to follow his vision. And here we have the dilemma: who is more important then? The designer or the firm? So there is a complex balance here, as we might want to respect and change the firm at the same time.

The moment a luxury firm is the mirror of his creator only, consumers would wonder what is the role of the firm anyway and associate all benefits to the designer. And what when a new designer comes? The

Luxury firm and the role of creativity

new designer will most likely have his imaginary, so eventually, he will change the previous one. Does it mean a new change in the logo? Therefore, the balance between firm and designer is a complex one.

The way to deal with this managerial tension is through proper management of the firm principles. Only then can we ensure liberty for the creator. So there is liberty, but there are also boundaries to respect. The firm must ensure what values and principles define the extraordinariness of the firm. And this is for the firm to decide. Then the designer can be given the freedom to play with the rest. When Marc Jacobs refreshed the Louis Vuitton brand in the 1990s, he brought a fresh newly Louis Vuitton, with their logos in color, for instance, He did not bring not a fresh new Marc Jacobs. A second valuable component is a mutual respect for the decision areas between the creative director and the CEO. When Tom Ford reinvigorated Gucci in the 1990s, the CEO, Domenico de Sole, was clearly defined, and the relationship between the two was trustworthy and respectful. We could see similarities too in turnaround between Angela Ahrendts as CEO and Christopher Bailey as the creative director did for Burberry in the early years of this century. Interestingly, in these very successful stories of creative leadership, none, Gucci, Louis Vuitton or Burberry, changed (significantly) their logo.[17]

creators are both a scarce resource and an essential resource to achieve extraordinariness. And this leads to power and influence within an organization. But always this will be the resource of the firm, and hence subject to be managed.

Management and creativity are complementary skills

A consequence of the previous point is that management and creativity are complementary skills of luxury firms. This explains why excellent creators could have difficulties in launching their firm. One of the most recognized watch designers was Gerald Genta. He designed some of the most iconic and successful watches, like the Royal Oak for Audemars Piguet and the Nautilus for Patek Philippe. However, when Gerald Genta opened his own firm in the '80s, he never achieved significant success. Similarly, it is not

Principles of creativity-driven industries

unusual to see fashion firms to have awareness and attention based on their creative skills, but then suffer financially based on poor management skills.

It is common to observe in very successful luxury firms a collaboration between a CEO and Creative Director. Among the most notable examples, we find how Domenico de Sole and Tom Ford turned around a troubled Gucci in the late 1990s, as Professors David Yoffie and Mary Kwak describe in an excellent case study.[18] And we also find Yves Carcelle and Marc Jacobs transforming Louis Vuitton into a global leader. But this is not only a matter of fashion. In watchmaking, jewelry, perfume, automobile, wine, or restoration, we observe the needed combination between management and creativity similarly.

The balance between creativity and management is not equal across the different luxury industries. In Table 4.2, we show a selection of luxury industries and their creative role. But this will only be a successful firm, the moment those creative skills are adequately managed within the boundaries of a firm, as we can observe in the table. Some luxury industries the role of creativity a bit lower, and this is because extraordinariness can be achieved by access. So, there is no need to break normality as the simple access to it denotes extraordinariness.

Table 4.2 Selected luxury industries and their creative roles

Luxury industry	Creative role
Fashion	Designer
Accessories	Designer
Jewelry	Designer
Watchmaking	Watch designer, watchmaker
Perfume	Perfumist
Cosmetics	Driven by scientific results.
Automobile	Designer, engineer
Yacht	Designer
Wine	*Chef de cave*
Gourmet—Restaurant	Chef
Hospitality	Designer, architect
Gourmet—Food	Driven by quality of raw material.
Aviation	Driven by access. Complemented by design
Diamond	Driven by quality of raw material

Luxury firm and the role of creativity

In Chapter 3, we discussed how a bag could be normal or an extraordinary good. In the case of luxury hence the path to extraordinariness must be conceived, and for that, we need creativity. However, a private jet today is extraordinary by access. So while companies might compete against each other to sell, the role of creativity will be less critical in ensuring extraordinariness. Some other luxury industries are scarce by nature, diamonds being the clearest example. So the role of creativity is vital in jewelry. This also applies to certain gastronomic items that are scarce by nature or extraordinary by origin. Here we could also observe a lower effect of creativity, as the access to it without any significant transformation is already what denotes mainly extraordinariness, and only a particular process to protect flavor is expected, like, for instance, olive oil or caviar. Here the driver of extraordinariness is commonly perceived as the purity of the raw material, unlike the case of a restaurant where the role of the chef is paramount.

In general terms, in luxury, we observe a significant role of creativity and a need for sound management. So we could say that both components are needed, and whenever one fails, the strategy will suffer. As a result of the previous discussion, we could say that:

Creativity without management derives into bankruptcy, and
Management without creativity derives into irrelevance.

Classic versus modern style is not a problem; it's a choice

The typical misunderstanding between creativity and fashion makes luxury managers have problems with the firm's approach or what we could say their style.

Here we observe the notion of style as a long-lasting reference that is easy to be identified. So a firm's style is a consistent and recognizable approach.[19] Even in the fashion industry, some firms are more prompted to change and hence perceived as modern or fashion-driven. On the contrary, some other firms choose to rely on less mutable aesthetics changes and therefore being recognized as more classic. This happens in other industries as well, where we see a difference between classic and modern styles.

For many years it has been perceived that luxury is about classical and everlasting values. That was a way to grow the business. Keeping the company under competitive immutable values supported consistency for international expansion. It simply made sense. As you grow, there is no need to

Principles of creativity-driven industries

change: it is more interesting to do the same in more places. So the idea of being classic, referring to glorious past events, was a competitive one. However, as discussed in Chapter 1, luxury is not only a matter of being classic or everlasting. It is neither a matter of fashion or avant-garde.

This misunderstanding of defining luxury as classic or everlasting endurance is even among us today. Companies had new territories to conquer, namely the USA, Japan, and then China, and a lot of growth potential. So they did not need to create anything new; they sold more of the same in more locations. This approach worked well, and there was, let's say, a lower necessity to be creative.

However, the moment this growth potential came to an end, companies need to go back to their creative roots as extraordinary firms. They need to go back again to what they made them extraordinary in the first place and the way to reinvigorate it today. And to do so, the role of creativity becomes paramount.

Luxury managers need to know that the firm can freely choose their style. In simple terms, Patek Philippe is a magnificent watchmaker with a classic style, while MB&F is a splendid company with a modern style. As said in Chapter 3, luxury is a choice, and this choice includes style. A natural consequence of the concept of creativity is a personal choice.

Companies can choose their path to extraordinariness, and they can do so through different styles. Being classic or modern is by no means a problem, it's a creative choice. Of course, choosing a style will not directly make the firm to succeed or fail as the achievement of extraordinariness is far more complicated than the selection of a style, as Chapter 3 explained.

Static versus dynamics companies. That's the problem

Another lesson of creativity is the need for constant change. This is what we will refer to as a dynamic firm. It is at the very notion of extraordinariness to create something new, but the value of this novelty does not last forever.

If the source of extraordinariness is not renewed at some point, then it becomes normal. This is the natural effect of market rivalry. Competitors can catch up to what was once extraordinary, and consumers can get used to it too. This usually is very easy to see with technology. A car was a luxury 100 years ago, now a specific type of car can be luxury. So what once was extraordinary can lose its relevancy. And this is a dilemma for firms. On the one hand, there is a need for change to update and remain extraordinary.

120

Luxury firm and the role of creativity

But on the other hand, focus on specific constant values might be better suited for growth and recognition.

This is a vital issue for a luxury manager. Selecting the style is a choice, but being a dynamic firm is not a choice, it is a requirement. What luxury firms cannot afford is to remain static. And here, static is referred to as a constant approach characterized by the lack of creativity. So if we keep on repeating something, even though it was extraordinary and thriving in the past, we end up losing our extraordinariness.

Being a static company is a problem in luxury. When analyst raised concerns on Prada's financial situation, the critical aspects to be blamed for the underperforming financial results was the lack of creativity. A strong focus on market penetration, such as increasing retail space, was combined with a static creative work.[20] As a result, the firm was perceived as more of the same, which damaged their source of extraordinariness. As a consequence, consumption and perception were hit. This is of particular relevance in the fashion industry, which is more dynamic than other luxury firms, but this problem is not exclusive to fashion.

This was referred to as the time dilemma in Chapter 2. If a firm becomes static, soon enough, it will not be attractive to new consumers entering the market, as the source of extraordinariness is only relevant to previous consumers. Maintaining the source of extraordinariness up to date, while being connected to younger consumers is challenging. For this, novelty must be in line with the source of extraordinariness, just like the case study in Chapter 3 explored.

We can now add the lessons of the previous section, on the choice between classic and modern styles. We tend to believe that static is the same as classic, while modern is similar to dynamic. And this is an assumption luxury manager must never hold. Classic is a style choice, while static is the lack of creativity regardless of the style.

In other words, a firm with a classic style can be very dynamic. And here, we can refer to the same example stated before. Patek Philippe is a company with a classic style that annually improves the quality and technology of their movements. It launches new editions as a result of their creative approach suggesting new combinations of complications. They protect their style, but they are a very dynamic company either.

Similarly, MB&F is a very dynamic firm with a modern style. In Prada, we observed the contrary for some years. We have a firm with a modern style in fashion, which relied on the same or very similar creative approach

Principles of creativity-driven industries

annually, hence a modern static firm. It is perhaps not a coincidence that Prada reacted to this situation with a renewal of their creative role to reinvigorate their stand as an extraordinary firm.

In summary, choosing the style is an alternative, but not necessarily a problem. But the absence of a creative approach, being static, is a problem for luxury firms. The Moncler Genius approach is an excellent example of how to maintain the role of creativity to support the path to extraordinariness, shown in Capsule 4.4.

Capsule 4.4. Creator versus Firm. Moncler Genius. Setting the ground of a dynamic company

Any firm can increase its reach and scale by being creative. But what if the starting point is a niche category? And even worse, what if that category is not even close to the need for creativity? Moncler is the example that even in adverse conditions, the role of creativity is mighty.

Moncler was born in Monestier-de-Clermont, near Grenoble (France), in 1952. The firm was focused on quality and durable ski jackets. In 2003, under the control and leadership of Remo Ruffini, the company expanded its offering beyond its limited ski jacket segment space. The firm brilliantly builds upon its reputation as a ski jacket firm to expand to other markets and audiences. What was a small, focused ski jacket company, transformed itself into a desirable and fashion-driven garment company.

Moncler is an excellent example of how creativity can play with apparent contradictions and remain valuable. A winter jacket is meant to be durable, warm and comfortable, or made with technical fibers. All of these are functional benefits. Design and fashion on a category mainly driven by the function of protection could seem initially a contraction or a less valuable feature. Moncler's transformation is an example of value creation emerging from potential contradictions. Just the way we discussed value from contradictions in the conception of Garbage of NYC.

This repositioning was a clear example of how creativity can push forward firms. But this is not the only smart point of their strategy.

Moncler has never stopped showing the limitless potential of creativity, and their Genius strategy is perhaps the most explicit example. The Genius strategy is an annual collaboration with artists and designers to create a capsule (limited in time) collections. Every year under the Genius umbrella, different collections are offered, representing a limited edition collaboration with one artist. As the firm says, it is one house with multiple voices.

One critical problem with fashion companies is the need to offer something new annually while dealing with a tremendous supply chain complexity. The operations and distribution of limited collections are quite complicated, indeed. However, the results are outstanding. Why the Moncler Genius approach is so meaningful from the strategic lenses?

Fundamentally The Genius strategy shows fundamental lessons of creativity adequately applied. A recognizable style is not a synonym of a repetitive offering. Moncler explores every year though different collections of how various collaborators see the firm. So the firm stays relevant, with a continually changing offering.

A common approach to protect style is to repeat a similar offering with minor changes, so recognition is protected. The Moncler Genius approach is a way to show the limitless possibilities of a particular style. So few codes are enough to develop endless options. This is what being a dynamic firm is all about—a few clear principles and freedom for creative work. Like in Sport, all teams respect the rules, but none play in the same way. This idea of playing while respecting the rules is very similar to design. While respecting specific rules (the house codes), the outcome can always be changing and open to exploration.

In summary, Moncler is an excellent example of a dynamic firm. As Moncler shows, firms can stay relevant by exploring potential contradictions in the type of benefits that lead to value. Furthermore, dynamics firms are also the ones that do not protect their style with a constant or repetitive offering. Still, they play with particular clearly define codes to play and explore its limitless potential.

Principles of creativity-driven industries

Technology is not a conflict with creativity

The appreciation of creativity provides another lesson for luxury managers. Technology is an ally of creativity, not its antithesis. The path to extraordinariness is carved with multiple obstacles, and creativity combined with technology can frequently solve. We have already mentioned some examples, like the role of composite materials at Pagani to deliver an ultimate driving experience, Mr. Breguet's invention of the tourbillon to achieve greater precision, or Krug redesign of metallic barrels to enhance the wine's freshness.

Creativity is not only a matter of product aesthetics; what we usually refer to as design. It is a guiding line to conceive and achieve extraordinariness. For that, technology is frequently a powerful ally. We should never stereotype that technology is or is not a luxury in absolute terms. If the central role of luxury is to provide something extraordinary, then all possible paths are equally relevant.

In summary, this section has shown different misperceptions and short-cuts in the appreciation of creativity, such as the simplification of creativity as design or the conception that creativity is only relevant for fashion firms.

Likewise, the challenges of managing creative firms have been identified, like the difference between style (classic or modern) and creativity (dynamic vs. static), the role of technology, or the multiple forms through which creativity can shape a business.

Finally, the issues related to the interaction creator and firm have been discussed, such as the complementary roles of management and creativity, the part of creators in firms, and the boundaries of creativity beyond individual talent.

The proper management of the previous aspects can significantly influence the firm and transform its appreciation of what luxury is and what their real challenges are. As a consequence of this analytic process, the firm can define a more sound strategy.

Case study. Creativity at MB&F (Part 1)

Maximilian Büsser (Max), decided to create his own company, Maximilian Busser and Friends (MB&F), in 2005 after a successful management career in the industry. In a short period, the firm secured a position

124

Luxury firm and the role of creativity

in the high-end mechanical watch industry, becoming a synonym of creativity and design. In 2016, MB&F received the award for the best calendar watch of the year at the "Grand Prix d'Horlogerie de Genève" (GPHG). For a company founded about a decade prior, this seemed like an extraordinary milestone, given that the GPHG awards were the most well renowned in the high-end mechanical watch industry. However, this was not the first GPHG award for MB&F. The firm had already won the Best Men's Watch (2012), the Public Prize (2012) and the Best Concept and Design Watch (2010).

Max was initially oriented toward a marketing career with a Swiss multinational, but changed his mind on a meeting that actually ended up changing his life. Mr. Henry-John Belmont, Jaeger-LeCoultre's CEO, tempted him with a very attractive proposition, asking him a question that would always resonate on his mind: "What type of professional do you want to be? One among the thousands working for a multinational, or the one that will help me turn this company around?" This is how Max joined Jaeger-LeCoultre. After some years with their management team, the firm successfully turned the situation around.

In 2005, Max decided to shift the path of his career. He wanted to fulfill a very personal goal: to create his own company.

> I had the impulse to create something by myself. Something I could say is nothing but my vision. Something to be proud of so that when I grow old and I look back at my life I can say: I have been able to create this.

Max had a very personal perspective of the industry:

> After the quartz revolution of the 80's, a mechanical watch is no longer about mechanical accuracy. A quartz watch is 10,000 times more precise than the best mechanical watch. Most of the players in the industry are focused on precision. I simply am not.

Perhaps the role of creativity was what better defined what MB&F was all about. Max was interested in working to create his own products with

Principles of creativity-driven industries

his own rules. A clear illustration of this philosophy was the way he named his products. Max believed that the term Horological Machine (HM) better described MB&F's emphasis on art and creativity.

> Behind my company, there is a philosophy of working, a way of doing engineering. I have a concept which goes beyond a simple product design or aesthetics. It was very important to me to signal that this is not a watch anymore. It is true that it will tell you the time, but that is not even its core value. I define a Horological Machine as a piece of kinetic art, which also tells time.

Unlike many other businesses, the idea of client need was not a central one at MB&F. The goal was not to understand what the market or the customer wanted but to surprise them with something unexpected. Max was convinced in this: "You never innovate by asking the market or someone what they want." He described the creative process as a purely selfish and egocentric one. He remembered his years at Jaeger-LeCoultre and how Mr. Günter Blümlein used to say to him, "Mr. Büsser, creativity is not a democratic process!" In fact, creativity seemed to play a fundamental role not only in the products but also in the values of MB&F. And that was not an easy job to achieve since creativity brings significant trade-offs to a firm. Max used to phrase the challenges that creativity brings to a company by identifying the three enemies of a creativity-based company:

> I believe creativity has three main enemies. The first is shareholder value. This is a problem because it forces companies to shift the attention towards the short term. It is impossible to be innovative while you try to achieve double-digit growth every trimester. The second is marketing or, better said, traditional marketing, which is associated with being a little bit better or a little bit different from our competitors. This might work, but this is not true for innovation. And the third one is middle management. Innovation requires risk, and middle management is usually risk averse since they are focused on efficiency. These enemies create a block in an organization that aims to be creative.

Max used to phrase his approach to business in very simple terms. First, he had some crazy ideas about what the product should be about. He was then guided by his directors to distinguish between what could or could not be achieved. Finally, he had full responsibility for the decision: "I listen and I decide. It is like an enlightened dictatorship."

Every Horological Machine designed to date started from a very different conception. They did not hold any logic or relationship to each other whatsoever. There was a proactive intention not to build on any similarity. In a way, this went against the traditional lessons on building a brand's DNA, where the intention is to identify the link between product and firm.

Despite these efforts, Maximilian was surprised by comments like, "That's clearly an MB&F piece" or "So consistent with the previous models". He had mixed feelings about it: "How can people see similarities in something we create differently?" Max considered that perhaps the brand's DNA was himself. "I felt like the only relationship between the pieces was me. They represented the way I see things and like them to be done. I guess people see some common vision in that."

The concept of kinetic art went beyond the Horological Machines. A second collection, named Legacy Machines (LM), represented MB&F's vision of traditional watch making, or "the pieces that MB&F would have created 100 years ago". The firm also cocreated limited editions with other renowned brands and craft artists beyond the wristwatch product category. On top of that, MB&F had also opened the Mechanical Art Devices (MAD) Gallery in Geneva. The gallery was a place where MB&F could show their vision as well as establish a closer relationship with other creators such as mechanical or kinetic artists.

Over the years, MB&F had gathered more and more attention. Nevertheless, some questions remained open. Entering the market had proved successful, but the firm now faced the issue of consolidation in the market. Was MB&F a fashionable product that would be only successful for a few years? Or on the contrary, had MB&F built the necessary competitive skills to sustain its position in the complex, high-

Principles of creativity-driven industries

end segment of the *horlogerie* world? And if so, what steps should be taken in the future?
Adapted from. Millán, D., "MB&F. The management of creativity". IE Publishing, DE1–219

Summary

This chapter provides the key principles to manage creativity in luxury firms to stimulate value creation.

The first section argues the relationship between creativity and extraordinariness, hence providing the evidences to consider creativity the cornerstone of any luxury strategy. The characteristics of extraordinariness, like the need to break normal competition or the need of a self vision, justify the important role of creativity for value creation.

The second section provides a conceptualization of the concept of creativity. This is meant to tear down some of the most common stereotypes. For instance, creativity is, oftentimes, considered as a less valuable role related to the search distinctive aesthetics or ideas. It is also considered that creativity is important in fashion, or that technology can be the opposite of creativity. Much on the this section provides the argumentation to consider creativity as a key strategic pillar. The section defines the boundaries where creativity can be apply and defines creativity as both novelty and valuable.

Likewise also the heuristic approach has been denoted as relevant. Understanding the heuristic approach as a conception supports the role of the creator as the person or persons, able to conceive the way novelty can be achieved.

The third and last section provides the key principles that luxury managers should consider. Creativity is more of a commitment and a belief of the organization, rather than a commercial tactic to increase sales or raise awareness. Luxury managers need to embrace the idea that the firs is creative, not only its products. Whenever a manager embraces creativity poorly, like a synonym of design, the chances to be creative drastically decline.

Unlike widely perceived creativity is more of combination of skills, rather than the appreciation of individual skills. Certainly a luxury firm must need to rely on certain talents, the creator being the most important one. However creative is more powerful when conceived as the outcome of internal collaboration. This could even become a conflict of interest between the role of the creator and the role of the firm. The section discussed how a right balance between management and creativity can be the way to overcome this potential conflict.

To conclude, the section also offers a rationale to consider technology an ally of luxury. Finally the section justifies the need to be a dynamic firm. This serves as clarification of a typical misunderstanding. The selection of a firm's style as classic or modern is nothing else than managerial or creative choice. The tendency to consider luxury as classic even exists today. However, once creativity is understood, what luxury firms cannot afford is to remain static. There is misconception between the notion of classic versus modern and static versus dynamic that any luxury manager should properly consider to avoid competitive mistakes.

Self-study questions

1. *Why a luxury manager should consider creativity as a key driver to achieve extraordinariness?*
2. *Creativity is commonly considered as a synonym of fashion. Is there any significant difference between creativity and fashion?*
3. *In a meeting, a manager points out that in luxury technology is less relevant, as it is ultimately concerned with handmade products. Do you agree with this statement?*
4. *Why the role of creativity goes beyond the definition of the product aesthetics?*
5. *Why there is a potential conflict between the creator and the luxury firm?*
6. *What is the difference between a static luxury firm and a luxury firm with a classic style?*

Notes

1 Grant, R., *Contemporary Strategy Analysis*. Wiley. Chapter 1. 9th edition, 2016.

2 Amabile, T. "Social Psychology of Creativity: A Consensual Assessment Technique", *Journal of Personality and Social Psychology*, Vol. 43 (1982), 997–1013. Page 1001.

3 Amabile, T. "The Social Psychology of Creativity: A Componential Conceptualization", *Journal of Personality and Social Psychology*, Vol. 45, No. 2 (1983), p. 360.

4 Hilgard, E. and Bower, G. *Theories of Learning* (4th ed.). Englewood Cliffs, N.J.: Prentice-Hall, 1975.

5 Amabile, T. "The Social Psychology of Creativity: A Componential Conceptualization", *Journal of Personality and Social Psychology*, Vol. 45, No. 2 (1983), p. 362.

6 Godart, F., Seong, S., and Phillips, D. "The Sociology of Creativity: Elements, Structures, and Audiences", *The Annual Review of Sociology*, April 3rd, 2020.

7 The theory behind the notion of creativity exceeds the boundaries of our study. Nevertheless, the reader can find an excellent and in-depth description of the different approaches to creativity in Godart et al., 2020.

8 The Oxford English Dictionary (OED).

9 The reader can find a very insightful description of the relationship between art and creativity for businesses on An, D. and Youn, N. "The Inspirational Power of Arts on Creativity", *Journal of Business Research*, November 2017.

10 Aspers, P. and Godart, F. "Sociology of Fashion: Order and Change", *Annual Review of Sociology*, Vol. 39 (2013), pp. 171–192.

11 Godart, F. Seong, S., and Phillips, D. "The Sociology of Creativity: Elements, Structures, and Audiences", *The Annual Review of Sociology*, April 3rd, 2020. Section.

12 Aspers, P. and Godart, F. "Sociology of Fashion: Order and Change", *Annual Review of Sociology*, Vol. 39 (2013), pp. 171–192.

13 Roberts J. and Armitage, J. "Luxury and Creativity: Exploration, Exploitation, or Preservation?" *California Management Review*, 1997.

14 For a more detailed biography of Velazquez, see, for instance, Calvo Serraller, F. "Velázquez", *Editorial Empunes*, 1991. Some of the comments made here are extracted from this book.

15 Amabile, T. "Motivating Creativity in Organizations: On Doing What You Love and Loving What You Do", *California Management Review*, 1997.

16 Millán Planelles, D. and Godart, F. "Creatividad: cadena o sistema de valor" *Harvard Deusto Business Review*, 2014.

17 You can see, for instance: Whelan, J. "The Revolution Will Not Be Serifised: Why Every Luxury Brand's Logo Looks the Same", *The Business of Fashion*, January 2019. Walker, R. "Why Fashion Brands All Seem to Be Using the Same Font". Bloomberg, November 2018.

18 Yoffie, D.B. and Kwak, M. "Gucci Group N.V." Harvard Business School Publishing, 2000.

19 Aspers, P. and Godart, F. "Sociology of Fashion: Order and Change", *Annual Review of Sociology*, Vol. 39 (2013), pp. 171–192.

20 See for instance: Solca, L. "The Path to a Better Prada", *The Business of Fashion*, June 2019.

Luxury as a creative industry. The creative value system

Introduction and objectives

Chapter 4 discussed the role of creativity within the boundaries of the firm. The chapter was dedicated to understand the concept of creativity and to unveil managerial lessons to guide the strategy formulation of the firm. This chapter is devoted to the role of creativity beyond firm boundaries. This complements and concludes a comprehensive analysis of creativity, which is an essential tool for the management of the luxury firm.

The first section introduces the need for an external analysis in creative firms. The relevancy of external factors is justified as essential for business success. This section builds on the lessons of the previous Chapter 4 to argue why creative firms cannot be understood in isolation. Likewise, as introduced in Chapter 2, this section justifies the need for specific analytical tools for the external analysis that responds to the challenges and characteristics of luxury firms.

The second section explores the different external entities that can influence a luxury firm's ability to succeed. The approach to value creation is characteristic in the case of luxury. The section argues how it is the collaborative ability of different entities that enhances value creation. The creative value system framework is discussed as a sound approach to analyzing this type of collaborative market. The framework suggests that four different entities are accountable for value creation in the luxury arena: the firm, the partners, the location and the appreciation. The section explores each factor in depth to perform the external analysis of the luxury firm.

To conclude, the last section explores the differences between creative markets and non-creative markets. In this way, the creative, the traditional, and the networked markets are described. This comparison is a meaningful way to explore and better appreciate each type of market's proper characteristics.

The comparison highlights the differences across the process of value creation and the external participants in this process. The variation across markets justifies that firms must adapt their strategy to the characteristics of its type of market. This external analysis is then a much needed analytical tool to support the strategy formulation of the luxury firm.

By the time you have completed this chapter, you will be able to:

- Understand the need for external analysis and its impact on the formulation of the luxury firms strategy.
- Understand the need for luxury specific external analysis as a consequence of the intrinsic characteristics of luxury firms and the role of creativity.
- Understand the collaborative role of value creation in the luxury market.
- Identify the different entities that contribute to value creation when creativity is relevant under the creative value system.
- Identify how the firm, the partners, the location, and the need for appreciation shape value in creative markets.
- Understand the limits and potential of the different entities of the creative value system.
- Identify the characteristics of the various business environments and identify their distinctive approach to value creation and external participants.
- Understand that the different business environments are not mutually exclusive and offer potential learning opportunities when a characteristic can be transferred.

Principles of creativity-driven industries

Why creativity is key (too) for the external analysis?

The firm analysis for luxury firms, provided in the previous Chapter 4, unveiled how creativity is hardly a matter of individual skills. This chapter complements the study of creativity with the external analysis. In this way, this chapter reveals that creativity is not based on the firm's sole effect, but external factors also influence it.

One way to approach the business environment is to consider the industry, which is the relationship between suppliers, competitors and buyers. As discussed in Chapter 2, Michael Porter's well known 5 Forces framework is based on this conception of the industry. Likewise, external forces can also include the so-called non-market forces. An initial framework to analyze these aspects is the PESTLE, which provides political, economic, social, technological, legal and environmental issues. A more refined approach is to consider the role of the non-market strategy as a set of different non-industrial activities that influence the firm's strategy. This entails the proper management of corporate business responsibility (CSR), the firm's corporate political activity, and the non-market risk that arises, among others, from cultural, economic and country-specific factors. Thus, the chapter considers the role of external aspects as both industry and non-market issues.

In the case of luxury firms, similarly to what we find in other non-luxury industries, the external factors play an essential role in the path to business success. Otherwise, the success of luxury firms would be explained only based on internal aspects. But the observation of successful luxury firms proves this is not the case.

For instance, some luxury firms do not entirely own their creative process (just like chapter's case study describes). This suggests that the analysis of creativity goes beyond the boundaries of the firm. Furthermore, on most occasions, luxury is heavily localized. This means that the geographic location plays a vital role beyond the firm's core organizational capabilities, or even location shapes creative potential and organizational capabilities. Other times, the appreciation of value is influenced by external factors, like experts or opinion leaders. A clear example is the wine industry, where the word of one individual, like Robert Parker, dramatically influences the assessment of value.

Therefore, the success of the luxury firm is the consequence of both internal and external factors. This chapter aims to clarify how to perform the external analysis to support the firm's strategy. Traditional frameworks might prove meaningful in this analysis to identify profit drivers (Michael Porter's 5 Forces) or valuable activities (value chain). Nevertheless, as introduced in Chapter 2, we might need to unveil new tools to adequately address the analysis of extraordinariness and the specific role of external aspects in such a path. This will be a pivotal point in the chapter.

The creative value system

There are two fundamental reasons why common industry analysis frameworks do not fully answer luxury firms' needs. The first reason is that these analytical tools are not designed to deal with the specific challenges of creative firms. Traditional external analysis is more in line with the normal type of competition's requirements, as we saw in Chapter 3.

The second reason is the specific characteristics of creativity. The observation of luxury suggests that creativity takes place more as a matter of collaboration than independency. In Chapter 4, we notice that creativity emerges as the combination of creative skills and the firm's environment, all aspects within the firm's boundaries. Here we go one step beyond arguing that creativity might be more valuable when it is the outcome of a collaboration with external participants. So the role of external entities is fundamental.

Therefore, we name as the creative value system the different participants that shape value creation in a creative environment (see Figure 5.1).

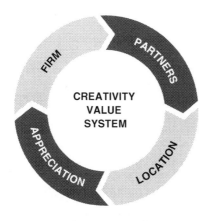

Figure 5.1 The creative value system.

The firm

For obvious reasons, a fundamental participant of creativity is the firm. This is what has been thoroughly discussed in Chapter 4. Therefore, here, only its role is summarized.

For a luxury firm to take full potential of their creativity, it is required not to stereotype the concept of creativity. As Chapter 4 explains, this might include a sound assessment of the value of creativity and its managerial implications. Fundamentally, the luxury firm should pay close attention to how the firm environment complements individual skills. This would include how the firm organizes its organizational capabilities toward a conception of extraordinariness and the management of creative skills, including the creator.

Examples like MB&F or Moncler, show the potential of a sound approach to creativity as a source of value creation in the luxury arena. They also show how vital creativity is as a broader notion beyond artistic design, another typical stereotype. As a result, successful luxury firms can choose their style meaningfully while protecting their source of extraordinariness.

Therefore, a sound definition of the firm's key organizational capabilities is a sound first approach to define competitive advantage. Then, to sustain it, it is useful to maintain a dynamic attitude toward business competition. This will prevent them from losing their source of extraordinariness and remain relevant.

The partners

The value from creative firms does not normally emerge from the firm alone. It is more frequently a combination of different actors. When Maximilian Büsser (see Chapter 4 case study) named his company Maximilian Büsser and Friends, he wanted to recognize the value that selective small companies, artist and independent watchmakers had in his company. This is a very good example of what the partners.

With the notion of partners it is aimed to identify all possible companies that contribute and shape in the final value of the firm. Partners are companies with the ability to shape the value. They are companies with expertise in terms of manufacturing, access to raw materials or the design abilities. Champagne houses have a special relation with their growers, luxury car

Luxury as a creative industry

makers with some exclusive part makers, watchmakers as illustrated above with part makers and designers, and fashion companies they equally have a close relationship with companies with certain know-how or access to scarce materials. They are all examples of partners, companies who influence the value produced by luxury firms in a way those firms could not do alone. Of course, the roles and relationships with partners do change depending on the industry or firm. Not all partners might have the same contribution to value either.

One would wonder at this point, that this is already captured with the notion of suppliers. However in luxury one might differentiate between partners and suppliers. The critical difference is that a supplier can be easily substituted without hurting the value of the outcome, while the partner is accountable for the value of the outcome. In other words, the outcome would never be equally valuable if the partners are abandoned or substituted. The key idea of a partner is its uniqueness.

Whenever we speak in terms of supplier, the idea of partners is not properly embodied. A supplier could be easily substituted as their function can be matched and it is normally a matter of reasonable cost. That is not the case for the partner who offer a valuable component hardly found otherwise.

The idea of partners could also in some occasions justify the vertical integration. Partners become so valuable that the firm might be interested in owning it. It is not uncommon to see that as luxury firms become bigger they acquire small suppliers that provide a scarce know-how. We have seen this in the 70s a luxury fashion was becoming global in Paris and in Switzerland in the 80s as the mechanical watch industry was beating the quartz threat.

The location

Luxury tends to be highly localized. The question is, what is the added value of location? The answer to this question is similar to what was discussed before in the partners section. Whenever partners concentrate on a given region, this allows the concentration of valuable and hard-to-find requirements. Fashion firms need to rely on specialists for several tasks, which are located on the outskirts of Paris, or Florence if we speak of leather goods. One would need to go to Switzerland to run a watchmaking firm appropriately. Otherwise, it would be too far away from many different and valuable partners. This is precisely the difference between Cristobal Balenciaga and Manuel Pertegaz, explained in Capsule 5.1.

137

Capsule 5.1. Balenciaga and Pertegaz

Cristobal Balenciaga was born in 1895 in the little town of Guetaria, near San Sebastian, Spain. By the moment the Spanish civil started in 1936, he had achieved some recognition in the Spanish market with stores in Madrid and Barcelona. But nothing compared to the fame he would end up obtaining in Paris.

The Spanish civil war forced him to leave Spain to Paris. He opened his atelier in the George V street and soon became the most expensive house couture house in Paris. It is commonly credited to Coco Chanel to have said that Balenciaga is the only among us who is a true couturier, not just a designer. Balenciaga dominated all the activities from the sketching to the sewing, and he was able to make the entire dress.

Balenciaga's global recognition relied on his own artistic and visionary skills. But also to the fact that he was based in Paris, the global capital of fashion for house couture. This is a clear example of how location adds value.

Manuel Pertegaz was born in 1918 in Olba, in the region of Teruel, Spain. He is considered one of the best Spanish fashion designers. Pertegaz was some years younger than Balenciaga. This might be one reason why Pertegaz did not have to leave Spain. The reason why Pertegaz remains in Spain goes beyond our story. The intriguing question is, why Pertegaz is not so well known outside Spain?. He did not lack the skills.

One plausible explanation is the role of location. While being at the cornerstone of fashion Balenciaga was able to explore and expand its ability to create value as an extraordinary couturier. Being based in Paris provided not only the clientele but also the skilled labor force, the partners in the form of the artisanship needed, the contacts with other designers like Coco Chanel or Christian Dior, and media attention on the Parisian fashion shows (see section Appreciation). All these aspects contributed significantly to the recognition of Balenciaga.

Luxury as a creative industry

> This is not, however, a discussion of who is a better designer Balenciaga or Pertegaz. Extraordinariness can be achieved in different ways equally valuable. The point is that location contributed to Balenciaga in a way it did not to Pertegaz. This is an example of how external components do shape value.

In luxury, as the concentration of scarce know-how is relevant, the idea of a cluster is sound. The different parties offering expertise might provide the best environment for firms to develop. Geographical concentration is then valuable as a way to put useful parts together. This also includes other participants beyond manufacturing. Educational institutions that foster scarce skills, logistics, or media can also be considered an essential part of a cluster. But geographic concentration offers the possibility for collaboration. And, this is a crucial difference in luxury.

In luxury, value creation is the result of the creative approach. This creativity can emerge more as a result of the collaborations that can arise from different companies and partners. The proximity of partners is then not only a matter of physical distance (which means lower cost) but a matter of relationship, enabling more creative collaborations.

Sometimes locations add also valuable as a way to access scarce raw materials. A clear example is the wine industry, which is typically concentrated on areas with excellent soil. However, that is not always the case. Marco Polo's silk way is the example of traditionally scarce and available materials transferred to the location where it can be transformed into more valuable goods. In Chapter 1, we observed how the textile industry was the source of moving precious materials into luxury goods. So the luxury industry was concentrated in the location where this transformation took place. Similar thought could be said about the jewelry industry, which is not located where the scarce raw materials are, but where those materials are transformed into pieces.

Appreciation and its 3T's

We have explained how creativity, and therefore extraordinariness, is complex to be assessed. In luxury, value creation is shaped by two fundamental factors. One is the difficulty in its conception (as explained in Chapter 3).

Principles of creativity-driven industries

And the second is the complexity of its appreciation (as described in Chapter 4). Therefore, the appreciation of creativity is a fundamental piece in the achievement of extraordinariness by any luxury firm.

There are three different stages in the appreciation of extraordinariness or creative value. The first is the transfer of valuable information, the second is the translation of the message, and the third is the teaching needed for its understanding. Hence, transfer, translate and teach are the three requirements for value appreciation. For this reason, they are named the 3T's of value appreciation framework.

As a result, there are three different ways to influence the appreciation of creativity. Any party, individual or organization that plays at least one of these roles affects value creation. Value appreciation is an essential role in value creation, and luxury managers should carefully explore how to collaborate with them to unleash their value potential. Let's examine each stage for appreciation in more detail.

Transfer

It is widely known that awareness is a fundamental driver of value creation. In simple terms, if the audience is not aware of the firm's existence, the audience can't buy from that firm. Making sure that the audience receives the message is the first step in the appreciation of value. Therefore, the crucial role of transfer is to send selected and relevant information.

At this stage, anyone can perform this task as long as they make sure that the audience receives the message. Traditional marketing and communication have covered this area extensively. Here we could speak in terms of intermediaries, distributors, points-of-sale, and of course, communications means. All entities can transfer the information.

Luxury firms need to be selective when transferring their information. The selection of intermediaries, points-of-sale, and communication channels must be considering that the message is sent correctly. As said in Chapter 3, given that value is mainly emotional or expressive, the channel selected needs to ensure that the firms' unique considerations are appropriately transferred. This is why luxury has also been very selective with the channel selection when transferring information.

A typical example is mass media. This has never been an ally of luxury firms as it sends a not complicated or sophisticated message to a broad audience. This channel works fantastically with functional benefits. Simplifying

140

Luxury as a creative industry

a bit, mass media is about simplicity and volume, exactly the opposite a luxury firm requires. In luxury, the transfer of information must be to a more limited audience and with a more complex message due to the emotional and expressive benefits of luxury (as explained in Chapter 3).

For this reason, luxury firms tend to rely on specialized intermediaries (like merchants, or selective distributors) or specialized media.

Traduce

One key aspect of appreciation is understanding. In luxury, it is not enough to receive a message. Most of the time, it is also required some additional clarification. This is what is referred to as traduce. Consumers might need to receive a message in words and concepts that they can understand. Too complicated, too ambiguous, or also abstracts messages can be hard to understand, and hence the appreciation of value will suffer as a consequence.

The translation enhances the appreciation of value as it provides the clarity needed to understand the message. Here complexity does not only mean a given technical expertise. It is the consequence of the complexity involved in explaining the path to extraordinariness, as seen in Chapter 3, which involves creative choices.

This stage is frequently performed by third persons or entities able to land a complex message. They are also accountable for organizing and filtering the relevant information for a better understanding. Firms are complex entities per se, and they have limited possibilities to send information, so they have to be selective on the information they submit. But the more and better we understand a firm, the better we can appreciate its value. So it is meaningful to filter and organize the information to be shared.

This role is often performed by recognized experts and specialized media, whom we commonly know as opinion leaders. The purpose of opinion leaders is to help understand a complex message. This has been one of the roles of fashion experts and magazines, being able to appreciate the sophisticated talent of designers and being able to show it to consumers. This industry is exciting as the role of the different opinion has evolved, as Capsule 5.2 shows with the arrival of social media. Opinion leaders can include a wide array of participants, but some other times are heavily concentrated in a few hands. We find an excellent example in the wine industry and Robert Parker, as Capsule 5.3 describes. Consumers might find easiness in the appreciation of complex emotional benefits when the information is filtered and clarified.

Principles of creativity-driven industries

Capsule 5.2. What makes an opinion leader? The fashion industry: from magazine editors to Instagrammers

In 2009, The New York Times made an intriguing article (*) stating how young bloggers occupied the first time the front row of fashion shows. On a fashion show, the front row is a privileged area reserved for the most influential opinion leaders. Until then, those seats were coped by senior editors from the most prestigious magazines. Among the most well-known fashion editors is Anna Wintour, editor-in-chief of the Vogue magazine. For many years, she has been a key opinion leader in taking a stand on trends and pointing out the role of young designers.

Perhaps more interestingly is the way the article noticed the subjacent tension between two worlds that a blogger on the front row showcased. Getting to a fashion show front row was the career peak. For a magazine executive, it meant achieving a senior editor position after a long professional career. Suddenly those executives saw how teenagers were occupying those seats. The difference in age, profession, and experience was evident. But this situation also showed to approaches to fashion communication. While editors wrote some professional reviews on paper, bloggers shared their opinions in almost real-time. In this way, the article showed pieces of evidence of how senior editors despised the young and inexperienced bloggers. This was the early seed of what we know today with the arrival of social media and digital communication. The word "influencers" is skipped purposely, as there is always influence in opinion leaders. This situation also unveils one of the most intriguing questions for those who aim to explain the value to others: what makes an opinion leader?

One way to approach this question is through the expert perspective. An expert's influence comes from the ability to understand a complex message on one side to simplify it, organize it and share it in a way that helps the appreciation of the other side. Therefore, training, expertise or experience might be expected from an opinion leader. So, how come a teenager with no expertise can be an opinion leader?

142

Luxury as a creative industry

The fundamental idea is that influence does not only come from expertise. Consider why celebrities, with recognized skills for one activity (like a movie star), can be a valid (influential) view to advertise a good beyond their area of expertise (like coffee). The advice is accepted as there is a shared emotion (like trust) or an aspiration (like recognition). Influence can occur without relevant experience in the good advertised (there is no proven expertise) as long as there is an emotional acceptance. Just like brand ambassadors have worked for many non-luxury and luxury firms alike.

So young, unexperienced teenagers do not need to be "experienced" in the good or industry to become an opinion leader, or at least to hold particular influence. They can instead be able to share a meaningful emotional relationship. This emotional acceptance from the audience might come from a similar perspective (we are of the same age or generation), a similar channel (you are like me) or aspirational acceptance (you have achieved what I dream). All these are examples of accepted influence without proven expertise in the good being communicated. Back in 2009, the mere use of a similar channel (digital vs. paper) was enough to establish this emotional acceptance from younger consumers. Today, with many more attempts to be influential on social networks, a more refined ability to build an emotional link would be required. But no wonder that the ones who are followed on social networks based their influence on their ability to establish an emotional relationship with or without "product" expertise. This is what we often refer to as engagement.

In a way, it is very similar to the three types of benefits, discussed in Chapter 3. A piece of advice from an expert is comparable to the discussion of functional benefits. In the same way, we said that value should not be assessed only from the lenses of functionality; influence does not only occur through expertise.

There is another aspect to be considered on what makes an opinion leader, the evolution of society. As seen in Chapter 1, luxury is a sociological entity that evolves as society does. Therefore, it is not for the firm to decide what is valuable for society. It is for the firm to create value within those circumstances. The digital change underneath the editor versus blogger situation is a clear example. New digital formats are not an end on itself. They represent a mirror of social change. It is an interesting exercise to observe how young generations behave to see, as they are, on many occasions, the peak of the iceberg of social change. (*)[1]

Capsule 5.3. Opinion leaders. Robert Parker and Wine

The wine industry is a clear example of the role of opinion leaders. Several entities and experts publish wine notes and elaborate wine rankings. But it is perhaps Robert Parker, the most influential opinion leader in the wine industry. He created the Wine Spectator, which includes an annual "ranking" on a 100 points scale.

The wine industry is an example of how complex it is for clients to appreciate value. Rankings and wine notes support the consumer path to wine selection and enjoyment. While no ranking is necessary for the consumer to enjoy good wine, additional support helps the consumer understand the differences in elaborations (like the type of grape, blends, time in barrel, type of soil, etc.) and appreciation of good wine.

This also helps consumers to appreciate value beyond the price tag. When there is little potential for appreciation, the price remains the only variable. How the consumers ascertain value beyond the price tag? Hear the role of opinion leaders is to supports the appreciation journey of the consumer. An extraordinary wine is not defined by a single metric or by a closed definition. A remarkable wine is open to different variables, and many are based on the winemaker's choices. This is an example of what was discussed in Chapter 3 as multiple ways to achieve extraordinariness. But this makes it harder for consumers to appreciate it.

An example of a Spanish winery is self-explanatory. The firm was awarded as the best wine in the world under 20$ by Robert Parker.

Right away, they sold the annual production even before putting the wine on the market.

But the role of opinion leaders generate in the wine industry has generated criticism as well. Wineries have adapted to flavors more likely to obtain higher punctuation in rankings. The term "parkerized" has become popular to describe wines that have been crafted to be liked by Robert Parker, and get a better ranking. Other areas of criticism point out that rankings, like the Wine Advocate, select wines based on personal likes and dislikes, leaving aside excellent wines only since the ranking editor does not like them, or does not share a similar approach. With no single path to extraordinariness, opinion leaders can be biased by their own extraordinariness approach.

What Robert Parker and other opinion leaders in the wine industry have done, is to transfer a complex language of winemaking into an easier-to-understand language to assess value. But also they aggregate, organize, and filter the immense information needed to understand and appreciate wine. Consequently, they show the most relevant aspects, making it easier to embark on a journey of appreciation by the consumer without the burden to be an expert or invest as much time as an expert to ascertain value.

As we have said profusely, art is always an excellent way to understand the value creation process of luxury. The appreciation of the value of a painting or an artist might arise from getting to know its work (the transfer stage), but this is hardly enough. The moment we understand the artist, which intentions own, which motivations pursue or how a given feeling or expression is aimed, eventually, we might appreciate his work better. But maybe getting to that point, consumers might understand selected information, a different language or tone from that from the artist. As said, the artist might find his inspiration, but he might not be as eloquent to express in simple or easy to understand terms of its work. To appreciate the value, the receiver might need a more natural message traduced from a complex artistic source. This is what we showed in Capsule 2.2, with the example of the movie "Untouchable."

Something similar happens in business schools when a firm's case study is discussed. Commonly, the moment students read a case study, they are more sensitive toward that firm. Getting to know better, the firm provides more room to appreciate it, as we have seen with the role of transferring information. But it is not a matter of awareness. The appreciation is more powerful when the company is better understood.

A case study is aimed to explain complexity, not only in terms of technical aspects but also in organizing and filtering the tons of information required to understand the firm (such as values or approach to the market). Typically, firms have limited space and time in their communication, so they send a competitive message (their competitive advantage or unique selling proposition). But they have limited time to speak about themselves. A case summarizes and organizes lots of information, so it is easier to get to know better their origins, their story, and the problematic moments lives by the founders. Typically this generates an emotional link with the firm. As a result, a case study is a way to help to appreciate the firm by organizing and filtering relevant information.

Appreciation of beauty is a personal feeling. It is not for firms to determine the tastes of consumers. The point of appreciation is not to tell another what to do, what is good from bad, or what someone should buy. The main point of translation is that with more precise information, the consumer can get to know it better. It can appreciate it, rather than be convinced. This is the role of traducing.

In this context, traduce does not mean translating words. Nor treating consumers as ignorants. It is the idea of explaining creativity with simplicity. But it is also the idea of selecting and filtering to help understand complexity in terms of massive information. As previously said, one does not need to be mechanical engineering to enjoy a sportscar but eventually understanding the firm and how they work help the appreciation of a particular sportscar.

However, opinion leaders also represent a potential conflict of interest. On the one hand, they might not be independent, which makes their comments biased. Likewise, the opinion leader view can represent or defend only one approach to extraordinariness. As a consequence, luxury firms need to carefully consider to what extent adaptations to opinion leader comments are sound and not deviate the firm from its approach to extraordinariness, just as Capsule 5.3 shows with the example of wine or Capsule 5.2 with social media. Luxury managers should consider the role of opinion leaders as support to create value from the lenses of appreciation, but not as a commercial tool (transfer information).

Luxury as a creative industry

Teach

The last component in the appreciation of value is the learning curve. In Chapter 3, the complexity involved in assessing emotional and aspirational benefits was provided. It was noticed as well in Chapter 3 that as a consequence of this complexity, and also ambiguity, the appreciation of value might require a learning curve.

The appreciation of value might increase once the consumer learns certain aspects that improve his ability to understand the value offered. Aspects like manufacturing techniques, processes used, materials selected, or fundamental artistic choices made can be a guiding path toward a better appreciation of value. It is the learning effect around the value being created that is essential in the teaching stage.

Once again, we might notice that the goal of a luxury firm is to show why the product is better. The critical aspect is to define and characterize the value offered. For this reason, the approach to teaching should be clarified. Here one might see the role of teaching is more in line with showing. The goal is never to tell apart right from wrong (this would be more useful when functional benefits are dominant). The goal is, on the contrary, a more subtle and sophisticated approach toward teaching. Luxury firms need to clarify and explain who they are and why they do what they do. This is why usually are the firms and not external entities who provide the teaching.

Another characteristic is the tone. It should be avoided as a hierarchical or snobby approach where people in the know (the firm) tell what to do and how to feel to their apprentices (consumers). Luxury firms must be more humble and use the teaching effect to explain themselves and not as a way to judge what value is in absolute terms.

Frequently we hear that luxury is a learning or appreciation journey. This is because appreciation needs times and experience. The satisfaction of fine wine, an elegant leather good, a beautiful piece of jewelry, or an excellent watch comes after a particular time and experience with it. And it can also continue growing over time.

This is not a matter of teaching particular expertise. It is a matter of showing the firm choices and personality to explain its path toward extraordinariness better. Just as mentioned in Chapter 3, one does not need to be a mechanical engineer to enjoy the pleasure of fine watchmaking or driving a sportscar. Nor does one need to be an enologist to appreciate a fine wine.

Principles of creativity-driven industries

It is after its exposure and experience that consumers can complement and enhance its enjoyment.

The role of teaching is hence fundamental. It is the consequence of the notion of extraordinariness, which is based on creative choices and allows multiples possibilities to achieve it meaningfully (see Chapter 3). We noted in Chapter 1, the role of fashion merchants in Paris was the key player in the appreciation of fashion as luxury items. Today luxury firms take the importance of the learning effect in the appreciation of value very seriously. Several formats are available—a real demonstration of the craftsmanship on the point of sale in one option—for instance, a live construction of a leather bag on a Hermès or Loewe store. Another option can be a visit to the manufacturing facilities like Patek Philippe does. Or it could also be a winery experience in the cellar with the chef de cave like Krug performs.

Complementary roles of value appreciation.

The 3T's of value appreciation framework provides a fundamental tool to enhance the competitiveness of luxury firms by lowering the difficulties associated with the achievement of extraordinariness. It is interesting to realize that the three stages are complementary and can be performed by different players. Some entities can take only one role, like an advertisement on a specialized magazine that transfers information, while some other entities, like an opinion leader, can, at the same time, transfer information and clarify the complexity of the message. This opens many possibilities for luxury firms to maximize the way consumers appreciate their extraordinariness by using the different roles in a complementary way. Table 5.1 summarizes the key aspects discussed with the 3T's of value appreciation framework.

To do so, luxury firms should not confuse the different roles and use them properly. For instance, let's consider an advertisement, a typical form of transferring information. In non-luxury industries, an ad could potentially be used as a commercial tool. As functional benefits dominate, the appreciation of value tends to be easier, so the transfer of information can serve as a basis to share the firm's competitive advantage. However, this is not the case in luxury, as emotional and expressive benefits dominate, and the appreciation of extraordinariness is significantly more sophisticated.

Luxury firms must pay close attention to the complexity involved in appreciating value. They must avoid the temptation to use all resources to raise awareness and provide a selling pitch. As said, the role of opinion leaders and the in-store learning effect is frequently more important.

148

Luxury as a creative industry

Table 5.1 The complementary roles of 3T's of value appreciation framework

Transfer	– Key role: send information to the audience – Who can be: anybody, particularly media and communication channels. Characteristics: – Importance to select the relevant information to be transferred. – Focus on creation of awareness.
Traduce	– Key role: make the message clear to understand – Who can be: opinion leaders (experts, specialized media). Characteristics: – Focus on making the message clear to the audience. – Role is to lower the potential complexity of the creative approach (including technicalities), and organizing and filtering the relevant information for clarity. – Potential conflict of interest in the approach toward extraordinariness between firm and opinion leader.
Teach	– Key role: link specificity of the firm with value, explain extraordinariness. – Who can be: mainly the firm, but also opinion leaders. Characteristics: – Focused on the needed clarification of extraordinariness. – Focus on explaining and clarifying the firm own approach. – Avoid the teaching by imposition or a hierarchical approach.

The difference between the translation and the teaching stages is perhaps more subtle. The idea is that in the translation stage, there is an intention to make the message clear, but this also includes, to a certain extent, a learning experience. The idea of teaching is more referred to the learning effect based on the specificity of the firm and its extraordinariness.

The analysis of value appreciation can help luxury managers to improve the firm competitiveness and improve at the same time the consumer appreciation journey. This analysis supports the selection of all possible collaborators, highlighting its different roles. Like we see in Capsule 5.4, with the case of shows in the fashion and watchmaking industries. The capsule explains the different functions that have made shows have so crucial in these industries, but also unveils how this relevancy can be threatened.

Principles of creativity-driven industries

Capsule 5.4. Are shows still relevant? Fashion shows versus Watch shows

A show can fulfill different roles. On the one hand, it is a commercial event where distributors or intermediaries can do business with companies. It is also an opportunity to stimulate demand, especially in industries with longer lead times, like fashion. And of course, it is an excellent opportunity to influence the appreciation of value. Shows are a useful tool as they combine under the same roof the three aspects of value appreciation.

Transfer role of a show

It is an ideal scenario to combine the different firms to showcase novelties. It is a platform that allows firms to send a message and be known. Companies can benefit their exposure by combining their activities at the same time and place. Shows have been traditionally known for being a promotional platform.

Traduce role of a show

Likewise, shows gather opinion leaders such as specialized media, magazine editors, collectors and aficionados. This gathering supports the transferring stated before and is an effective way to make the industry's complexity easier and more transparent for the consumers.

Teach role of a show

Last but not least, companies can take this unique gathering opportunity to display their collection and share their specificity know-how and personality. Firms have a great venue to comment with opinion leaders and media about their codes and philosophy, an excellent opportunity to stimulate the learning journey.

Are fashion shows still relevant?

For many, the idea of a fashion show is to promote. There are four fashion capitals based on the relevancy of their fashion-week shows; Paris, London, New York and Milan.

Out of these four, only Milan is not either a country's capital. The reasons why Milan and not other Italian cities became the fashion capital are examples of clarity in the role of shows and the strategic vision of a cluster. In the 1950s and 1960s, Italy had different fashion active regions. Florence was an important industrial region, Venice had a fashion show and Rome had an influential role in emphasizing haute couture. The city of Rome was pushed by its position as country capital and was also the epicenter of other relevant cultural organizations, like the Cinecittà Studios. There was where Federico Fellini filmed his famous film La Dolce Vita (1960), which supported the black dress's status and cemented a particularly voluptuous image of Italian style (*).

But it is the configuration of the Camera Nazionale Della Moda Italiana (CNMI) created in Milan in 1958 that brought organization, and more importantly, agglutinated all efforts to support Italian fashion. Indeed, there was tension between Rome and Milan. The Centro Romano Alta Moda (The Centre for Haute Couture in Rome), opened a Camera with a similar name.

But Italian fashion would not be the same today if different cities and different institutions would be working on their own, or even fighting against each other. The role of an industrial organization like the CNMI is to aggregate rather than desegregate efforts. Despite the difficulties and regional tensions, the fact that the Milan Fashion week became the single country fashion show, where the different stakeholders unite under one organization, is the result of a clear industry perspective.

The main function of the Camera Nazionale Della Moda Italiana was to be the self-regulatory body to which all the Fashion Houses adhered spontaneously. The fragmentary nature of the different organizations that existed in those days would find a measure of co-ordination in this way.

**

It is curious to observe how Spain still suffers the tensions between two fashion capitals (Madrid and Barcelona), with fashions, shows each, which suggests an inferior industrial perspective.

Principles of creativity-driven industries

This story of how Milan became a global fashion capital helps us face our question: are fashion-week shows still relevant? On the one hand, shows are costly, and there is an opportunity cost for the participant firms. Can firms achieve a similar goal with a different approach and a lower investment? Today digital technologies provide a real competitive alternative.

Shows must sustain their commercial potential, but also their crucial role in value appreciation. Even if the commercial function is limited, shows can still be valuable. But one should not evaluate the value appreciation role only in terms of promotion (transfer role). It also should be considered the traduce and teaching roles. The importance of gathering opinion leaders and having a venue to clarify the firm's approach to extraordinariness is equally essential.

Fashion shows still signal their potential, and while digital means can threaten the promotional role, the combination of the 3T's of value appreciation seems to suggest its relevancy. But if there is an effective alternative to meet those 3T's that alternative eventually will emerge. (*),[2] (**),[3] (***)[4]

This notion of value appreciation also clarifies a stereotype in the segmentation of luxury consumers. Traditionally, luxury clients have been divided between the knowledgeable (frequently used the French word "connoisseur") and the status. However, this segmentation does not tell apart two different types of consumers, but two different value appreciation levels. Therefore, it might be a simplification to differentiate between the connoisseur and the status consumer as two different types of consumers.

What is essential is to identify the level of appreciation of the consumer and improve it. In the early stages of value appreciation, consumers might find difficulties in ascertaining the value and hence might follow their best alternative, which is the price. After repeated consumption and more experiences related to its use and more interest in the good, the consumers will improve its value appreciation and become more knowledgeable. And more demanding too. This is what we have witnessed in the previous decades with the American, the Japanese, and, more recently, the Chinese consumer, for instance. But as said earlier, we should not confuse value appreciation with technical expertise. As mentioned before, one does not need to be a mechanical engineer to appreciate a sportscar.

Creative versus non-creative markets. The three types of business environments

The previous sections have explained the relevancy of understanding luxury as a creative industry. With the support of this chapter, the luxury manager is better prepared to define two critical components of value creation: how value is constructed and who takes part in this process, including the influence of external players—both fundamental aspects to guide the strategic formulation of a luxury firm.

This chapter also provides another lesson. We can now define the different types of business environments and see how the creative market differs from the remaining markets. This improves the understanding of the specific characteristics of a creative market.

In this section, three types of environments are identified, as shown in Table 5.2. First, we have the creative market, which has been previously

Table 5.2 The three types of business environments

	Traditional	Networked	Creative
Competitive mindset	Substitutive (zero-sum game) Winning over competitors Focus on efficiency Market need Economic logic	Focus on large user base Aggregation, volume	Focus on creativity Collaborative
Type of benefit	All but functional dominate	All but functional dominate	All but emotional & expressive dominate
How Value is created? (Source of CA)	Competitive advantage own key activities Own key R&C	Network externalities driven by: – User base – Complementary goods	Extraordinariness
Who takes part in value creation?	Mainly firm Efficiency—value chain	Firm and complementors	Creative value system

153

Principles of creativity-driven industries

discussed. Then we have the traditional market, which was introduced in Chapters 2 and 3, with the notions of the traditional paradigm and normality. Finally, we have a third type of environment, the networked market. This is a market that rules the so-called platform markets, with the likes of Amazon, Google or Facebook.

The key idea is that the different environments represent different forms of value creation and hence competitiveness. So companies by learning the characteristic of their market can compete more meaningfully. And not also firms, but executives can benefit from getting to know the different types of markets. The case study of Chapter 2 highlighted the difficulties executives face when entering the luxury market. Learning the features and differences between markets can be a practical guide to managers as well.

Furthermore, firms can learn from the characteristics of other markets. This learning is perhaps more limited, as the critical aspects of the value creation process differ in each type of market. But still, the understanding of all the different types of environments can unveil room for improvement.

Creative market

Chapter 4 and this chapter have discussed the role of creativity in the firm and the market. There is no clear definition of what a creative industry. We will rely on the lessons we have gained to identify its principal characteristics from how value is created. In Chapter 3, we unveiled how value is created in luxury. The notion of extraordinariness combined set luxury apart from the normal market. Value creation in luxury was intimately related to the type of benefit provided, and this offered a distinctive form of competition.

In Chapter 4, creativity was observed as a crucial ingredient of extraordinariness. It was highlighted how creativity is not the effort or talent of an individual creator, but on the contrary, it was the outcome of a collective effort within the firm. This chapter has complemented the study of creativity to observe how the firm is not the only entity accountable for value creation. This has led to the creative value system, which identifies the different entities taking part in the value creation process: partners, location and appreciation.

In a creative market, the competitive mindset is not directly driven toward rival companies, but toward the stimulation of extraordinariness, which requires a collaborative effort. Rival firms are not necessarily responsible for the decline in sales or lack of attractiveness of a luxury firm. The absence of

154

Luxury as a creative industry

a zero-sum game makes demand mainly stimulated by the firm's ability to achieve extraordinariness and hence obtain a share of the market.

In summary, a creative market is characterized by a value being created as a search for extraordinariness where emotional and expressive benefits dominate. And this is a collaborative process between the firm and external players.

Traditional markets

The traditional market as an alternative to a creative market was discussed in Chapter 3. And Chapter 2 highlighted how the classic paradigm characterized it. Here, there is a wide array of concepts and frameworks in the area of marketing and strategy to understand who takes part in the value creation process and how to face competition.

The idea of competitive advantage, the value chain, and identifying key organizational capabilities have worked very well to define the strategy in traditional markets. Likewise, core marketing themes like the understanding of the consumer (functional) needs and how to competitively develop the firm to achieve the sale have been a predominant theme in marketing.

The competitive mindset is here different. Companies compete basically for the same consumer and the corresponding need (a zero-sum game), forcing companies to hold a much more fierce or "winning over competition" type of mentality. This difference in the value creation process and competitive mindset generates difficulties in managers when moving to a luxury firm.

While distinctive principles rule each market, there is still room for learning. Let's take, for example, the Apple stores or the experiential environment at Starbucks. While not luxury firms, these are two examples of how the control of the experience can stimulate emotional benefits, which ultimately benefit the competitive advantage of the firm on a traditional market.

Networked market

There is a third type of market or business environment, the networked market (also called platform-mediated markets). The managerial tools we use in strategy should help us understand the competitive dynamics of a given market and explain why some firms are more successful than others. Suppose one tries to apply classical strategy or marketing principles, like the

Principles of creativity-driven industries

ones we discussed for the traditional market, to firms like Amazon, Google, Facebook, or Apple. In that case, it will be tough to explain their success. Of course, one would never understand the success of these sorts of companies applying the tools of creative markets.

The reason is that a different value creation process characterizes a networked market. So the way value is created, and its participants are merely different. On a networked market, the fundamental driver of value is network effects that generate positive externalities. This means, in simple terms, that the value for a user increases with the number of users. The classic example is the phone, whose value would be zero if there were one in the world.

The relationship between sellers and buyers through a platform is commonly known as a two-sided platform. Professors Jean-Charles Rochet and Jean Tirole elaborated on the idea that a two-sided market involved a platform-based competition, which was, in nature, a competitive landscape where success was determined differently from other markets.

The work of Professors Thomas Eisenmann, Geoffrey Parker, and Marshall Van Alstyne complemented this theory elaborating on how firms could be successful in a platform-mediated market. The idea that positive network externalities force firms to get and maintain their user base and identify the convenient business model, where even one-side of the market could be subsidized. This generates a new set of strategies in terms of pricing and profitability. It is not unusual to see platform valued based on their ability to gather a large user base, despite their short term profitability.

A great example can be seen in The Social Network (2010), the movie that describes the early days of Facebook. The dispute between the two founders is a critical strategic decision. One aims to get New York advertising agencies on board to make Facebook profitable. The other aims to extend its user base at the expense of short term profit (no more details provided to avoid spoilers).

The role of complementary good becomes also a competitive issue. Stimulating the availability of the complementary good can be a sound move, like in the case of consoles and games or the music industry with Spotify. Or even owning the complementary good can be a sound strategy. Today we witness how entertainment platforms like Netflix or HBO compete based on their own portfolio of shows (the likes of Breaking Bad or Game of Thrones).

Interestingly, the networked market generates new forms of competition. The idea of envelopment is a clear example. An envelopment is a form of competition where one platform can threaten a rival platform by offering a combination of services the rival can't match. In this way, a competitor (a platform in this case) no longer needs to be better or to defeat competitors. It can merely leverage common platform components and shared user based to increase the offering of a platform and hence steal competitors' user base. A classic example is when Microsoft included Internet Explorer in their Windows ecosystem and eliminated Netscape's threat as a raising web browser.

Of course, the description of this type of market is short, as it goes beyond our study area. But here it can be appreciated the distinctive value creation process and the different players involved. In this way, the luxury manager is ready to identify and ascertain the differences between the three types of business environments.

Case study. Maximilian Büsser and Friends (Part 2)

Maximilian Büsser (Max) vision went beyond the product aesthetics. Max also wanted to collaborate with people who shared his vision and values. People who could also contribute with the skills and expertise he needed. That was the reason to call the company Maximilian Büsser and Friends (MB&F).

In this way, MB&F conceived and crafted their products in collaboration with different experts in the fields of watchmaking, engineering, design and art. Max was not interested in working to create shareholder value but rather to create his own products with his own rules. A clear illustration of this philosophy was the way he named his products. Max believed that the term Horological Machine (HM) better described MB&F's emphasis on art and creativity.

> It was very important to me to signal that this is not a watch anymore. It is true that it will tell you the time, but that is not even its core value. I define a Horological Machine as a piece of kinetic art, which also tells time.

With the passion of a young entrepreneur, Max started a very challenging journey: to create a brand in the high-end sector from the ground up. He definitely had some valuable assets to get started: a successful career, a sound knowledge of the industry and a unique vision about watchmaking. He also had a clear idea of what his main goals had to be: to build a company with only 15 employees, to manufacture a limited number of 300 pieces per year and to reach an annual turnaround of 15 million Swiss Francs (CHF).

On July 25, 2005 MB&F was born in Geneva. The first years proved that creating a new company was more challenging than expected. Max invested his personal savings in the venture, which consisted of almost one million dollars. The initial investment was 700,000 CHF. This capital was meant to cover the first two years' expenses (design, manufacturing, salaries and other fixed costs). Max himself relied on his personal savings and did not have a salary during that period.

It was obviously a limited investment considering the requirements to enter this exclusive industry. Maximilian started working in his own apartment on the engineering and design of his first piece, the Horological Machine 1 (HM 1).

One of his first steps was to attract the attention of selective watch dealers. To do so, he took advantage of the knowledge and contacts he had developed in his years at Jaeger-LeCoultre and Harry Winston Timepieces. He felt that there was no better way to capture their attention than by meeting them directly. So during the first months, he traveled around the world to meet with selective watch dealers to let them know about their new personal venture.

He needed to be smart and take advantage of his limited resources. To save time and money, he decided to build a 3D printing model of the HM 1, which he painted by hand. This allowed him to show a replica, but without the investment needed for a real piece and much sooner than the first piece would have been ready. "That was my primary support for showing my product. It worked quite well as in 2005 a 3D printing model was uncommon, and it helped me to increase the attention."

Retailers had to make a tough choice. They had to take a chance on a new brand with only the promise of the founder's passion and a beautiful, plastic-based reproduction of the final product. On top of that, retailers would need to pay at least one-third of the final price in advance. MB&F had no other way to secure the manufacturing of

Luxury as a creative industry

the first pieces other than early payment by retailers. MB&F was short on cash, and they were unable to finance the horological machines in advance. Finally, the retailer would receive the final piece 18–24 months after the deposit, given the long product cycle involved. Therefore, convincing exclusive retailers, who were used to working with long-established brands, seemed like a titanic task for such a young company.

After many miles and meetings, six brave retailers, as Max used to call them, decided to order the HM 1. With a total presale of 28 pieces, MB&F secured an additional income stream of 700,000 CHF to start the manufacturing of the first pieces. Financing the venture and convincing selective retailers was not the only problem—perhaps not even the main one. The delivery of HM 1 was scheduled for January 2007. However, an unexpected problem came up in 2006. One supplier forced MB&F to push back their HM 1 deliveries. The first pieces were still not ready for delivery in May 2007, and MB&F was running out of cash: "By then I had money for one more month, and I was close to bankruptcy ... for the first time."

In June 2007, the first two HM 1 were delivered, which was a twofold relief. On the one hand, the company had made their first delivery. On the other hand, the income stream would help the firm to secure the fixed cost for the rest of the year. MB&F continued to deliver the remaining HM 1 orders until the end of 2007 (Exhibit 2). The stability provided by the HM 1 deliveries helped MB&F to embark on the development of their second piece, the Horological Machine 2 (HM 2). HM 1 was received positively in the market. Based on the early commercial acceptance and the close contact with retailers, the expectations for 2008 and HM 2 were excellent. Total deliveries in 2008 grew to 125 pieces, accounting for a total revenue of 6.1 million CHF.

Things started to look promising, but MB&F still had to face another major drawback in its beginnings. In August 2008, the Lehman Brothers scandal and the financial crash hit the global market. While most industries plunged, the luxury market seemed to be more resilient. MB&F continued shipping pieces at a constant pace until December 2008. "It was with the Madoff scandal in December 2008 when I

Principles of creativity-driven industries

sensed that the market was changing. Retailers started to panic and to reconsider orders."

In January 2009, during the "Salon International de la Haute Horlogerie" (SIHH), MB&F rented a hotel suite. This was aimed at leveraging the fact that Geneva becomes the epicenter of high-end watchmaking—gathering companies, retailers, press and a selected clientele—during the SIHH celebration. This approach helped Max get the intimacy he needed to continue building the relationships with retailers and specialized press. In this more private environment, MB&F had the time and the perfect audience to introduce their new pieces.

However, 2009 did not seem like an excellent year. MB&F could only secure 17 orders during the celebration of SIHH. That was roughly 10% of the previous year's production.

I was, for the second time in two years, close to bankruptcy. I needed to secure more orders. I focused again on personal meetings with retailers around the world. In that year I traveled for 230 days doing product presentations and talking to the specialized press.

After months of hard work, MB&F took 143 orders in 2009. That was a milestone for MB&F, and from that moment sales were no longer based only on direct contacts and personal visits to retailers worldwide.

By the end of 2009, Maximilian had already realized that he was facing bigger challenges than expected. "I thought it would take five years to reach my goals. Then I realized I would need at least ten years."

Adapted from Millán, D., "MB&F. The management of creativity". IE Publishing, DE1–219.

Summary

This chapter provides the fundamental tools to ascertain the external analysis of the luxury firm.

The need for an external analysis in luxury twofold. First, since external entities do influence significantly the ability of the firm to compete, so the analysis beyond firm boundaries is essential. Second, because creative firms have specific characteristics shaped by external factors.

The creative value system is a framework that aims to solve these two requirements. It is a framework that helps the luxury manager perform an external analysis highlighting the specific factors that influence value on creative markets. It is a framework that places value creation as the consequence of a collaborative effort between the firm, its partners, the location where it is placed, and the role of value appreciation entities. As described, all the components of the value system shape the outcome, so the firm would not be able to create as much value without them.

Unlike widely perceived value creation in luxury takes places as a collaboration between the firm and external players. This can bring specific skills, know-how or materials that set them apart from suppliers. In essence, a supplier is easily replaceable, while partners are fundamental for the value created.

The role of location as a geographic cluster is an essential part as well. The location gathers together different external aspects required for extraordinariness. Scarce know-how or expertise is better protected when concentrated. But also, knowledge is enhanced when supported by educational institutions and specialized media nearby. Aggregating entities with similar interests are indispensable ingredients for extraordinariness. It is not a coincidence that most of the luxury industries we know are based on selected locations.

The last component is the appreciation of value. Creativity as a source of extraordinariness poses several problems for value creation. It is hard to conceive, it is hard to achieve and it is hard to explain. For that reason, several are the external entities that play a role in making value be appreciated. The 3T's of value appreciation framework is a way to identify and support all possible enablers of value clarification. This is an essential tool for luxury managers as it is the bridge between the firm and its audience.

Finally, this chapter concludes with a comparison between the creative and non-creative markets. Collaborative efforts characterize creative markets. However, this is different in the traditional market, more oriented toward traditional zero-sum game competition. The third business environment, the networked market, suggests the notion of user size as a driver of success. The differences in approach to value creation, collaboration in the creative market, zero-sum game competition in the traditional market and user base seeker in the networked market generate entirely different business dynamics and ways to achieve success. Hence, the role of external analysis under the creative market condition for the luxury firm is of utmost importance.

Principles of creativity-driven industries

Self-study questions

1. *Why do firms need to perform an external analysis?*
2. *The creative value system does not refer to suppliers, but partners. What is the difference between a supplier and a partner in the luxury arena?*
3. *Select a luxury firm and identify different entities that can help the firm achieve the 3T's of value appreciation.*
4. *How do you see fashion shows in the next ten years? And watch shows?*
5. *Why is a creative market so different from a traditional market? What are the key differences?*
6. *Why is a creative market so different from a networked market? What are the key differences?*
7. *Can you think of potential lessons that a luxury firm can learn from how firms compete in networked markets?*

Notes

1 Source: Wilson, E. "Bloggers Crash Fashion's Front Row", *The New York Times*, December 24, 2009.

2 Jana, R. "A Brief History of Milan Fashion Week", *Vogue.com.au* (edition Australia), September 2019.

3 Camera Nazionale della Moda Italiana. www.cameramoda.it

4 Thompson, J., "Breitling Pulls Out of Baselworld 2020", *Hodinkee.com*, April 2019.

PART

Principles of luxury competition. The *means* of luxury

Principles of business level rivalry. The *means* of the luxury firm

Introduction and objectives

Parts 1–3 have defined the basis of strategy formulation applied to luxury firms, from the concept of luxury to the role of creativity.

This last part of the book integrates all these lessons to facilitate the competitive challenges of luxury firms, what is defined as the *means* of luxury. This chapter will start this approach with the business strategy level, which is concerned with the quest for a competitive advantage in a single market. The chapter's main objective is to explore the challenges that firms face when implementing their strategy and how they can effectively deal with market rivalry.

The first section serves as a link between the strategy formulation learned in the previous chapters and the need for implementation. The second section stresses the differences across luxury categories that influence strategy implementation. The scale potential and the category's business model are emphasized as essential aspects that firms must consider when landing their intended strategies. The third section describes the most common rivalry issues that can undermine the firm's ability to compete meaningfully.

The fourth section discusses a pivotal topic of the chapter. It provides fundamental lessons to enhance the ability of the firm to compete. The section identifies the core principles that rule luxury rivalry into the 3C's of the luxury competition framework.

The last section covers the example of turnarounds and successful transformations as a summary of all the components discussed in the

Principles of luxury competition

chapter. These situations gather all the ingredients to observe how a well-crafted strategy is executed successfully.

By the time you have completed this chapter, you will be able to:

- Identify the difference between strategy formulation and strategy implementation issues.
- Identify the main characteristics of luxury categories to be considered in the strategy implementation process.
- Understand the main competitive problems that affect the ability of the luxury firm to succeed.
- Assess the likelihood of a threat to the firm's strategy and differentiate between complementary and substitution types of risks.
- Identify the principles of luxury rivalry and the rationale behind its importance.
- Understand the importance of turnarounds and successful transformations as examples to showcase the relationship between strategy formulation and effective implementation.

Business strategy into practice. From formulation to implementation

Up to this point, the book has provided all the needed information to formulate the firm's business strategy. Chapter 2 introduced the general theory of strategy. The notion of strategy formulation was then defined as the main aspects determining its ability to compete meaningfully. This included the firm's positioning and direction.

Following Professor Robert Grant's approach,[1] the positioning is concerned with two questions. The first one is, "How the company competes?" This question ultimately seeks to determine the firm's source of competitive advantage. The second question is, "Where the company is competing?" which aims to determine the firm's markets and activities. The direction is concerned with setting the long-term goals and values of the firm. Therefore, the firm has formulated its strategy, the moment it has determined the way it aims to be competitive in the market, which are the markets and activities it seeks, and which are their long-term goals and values.

This chapter covers the business strategy, or as often called competitive strategy. The main goal is to determine the firm's ability to compete in the

166

Principles of business level rivalry

market (the "How" question stated above). The next Chapter 7 will deal with corporate strategy to define the firms' scope of activities (the "Where" question as mentioned before).

Chapters 3–5 adapted these principles to the particular luxury environment. Chapter 3 showed how extraordinariness could serve as a guideline to the concept of competitive advantage in the luxury industry. This part was named the *essence* of luxury as it deals with the fundamental tools to analyze the firm's ability to create value. Chapters 4 and 5 covered the analysis of creativity as a system of value creation. This part was named the Nature of luxury, as it deals with the intrinsic characteristic of the luxury business environment.

Combining the generic principles showed in Chapter 2 with the needed adaptation guidelines to the luxury arena provided with Chapters 3–5 have provided the fundamental tools to formulate the luxury strategy, as Figure 6.1 shows.

The previous chapters have provided the rationale behind a fundamental strategic question: Why some firms are more successful than others?

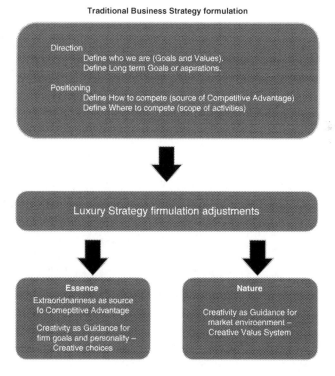

Figure 6.1 Essence and nature of luxury. Adjusting traditional business strategy to luxury specific challenges.

Principles of luxury competition

Nevertheless, one crucial piece is still missing. The strategy is not just about thinking beforehand, it is also about transferring those intentions into the reality of the marketplace.

Therefore, this chapter is mainly concerned with the difficulties involved in implementing the strategy. Transforming intentions into market realities can be more challenging than expected. It requires practice and adaptation. Strategy has a fundamental role in guiding support to meet complex, competitive choices. And these choices can arise unexpectedly based on the intensity of the market rivalry or the needed adaptation of the intended goals.

Differences across luxury categories

Luxury associations and research companies write luxury reports on the industry's state and insights about the evolution and trends of the market. Commonly these entities organize luxury into different categories. A frequent term used is the personal luxury category, which aggregates fashion, accessories (mainly referred to leather goods), watches, jewelry, perfumes and cosmetics. Fashion and accessories are commonly named soft luxury, while mechanical watches and jewelry are often called hard-luxury. Additional luxury categories considered might vary, but the most frequently considered are automobiles, hospitality, wines and spirits, gourmet food (also known by the French expression *art de table*), yacht, aviation, and arts.

Altagamma Foundation, the Italian association that gathers High-End Italian Cultural and Creative Companies, with the consultancy company Bain & Co., elaborates an annual study of the market. The Altagamma Bain Worldwide Monitor report is one of the first and still one of the most significant data sources in the luxury market. This report considered initially personal luxury categories, and more recently included additional categories, as shown in Figures 6.2 and 6.3.

So far, the frameworks and tools provided in the previous chapters have not explicitly addressed the differences across industries. In the chapter's examples, capsules and case studies, different sectors have been selected indistinctly to illustrate the various tools. Purposely, no specific mention was given to the differences between categories. Therefore, a tough question would be, do the managerial tools discussed require further adaptation to each luxury category? Or in other words, are the tools provided only valuable to some industries while not to others?

168

Principles of business level rivalry

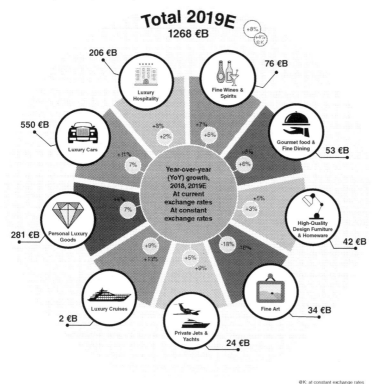

Figure 6.2 Global luxury market.

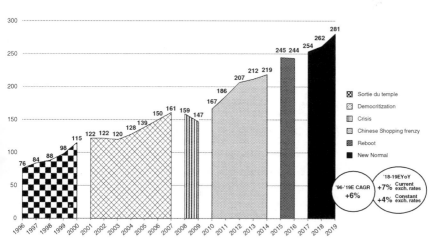

Figure 6.3 Personal luxury market.

Principles of luxury competition

The answer is no. In the non-luxury arena, the general principles of strategy and marketing are commonly applied to different industries. Concepts like competitive advantage or value proposition do not need to be fundamentally modified to various sectors. Similarly, the luxury-specific concepts and frameworks detailed in the previous chapters are meant to describe the luxury phenomenon in different industries.

We observe the same in the luxury market. Investment and research firms provide luxury indexes combining different industries. For instance, Standard & Poor's provides the S&P Global Luxury Index, which, in their words, is "comprised of 80 of the largest publicly-traded companies engaged in the production or distribution of luxury goods or the provision of luxury services that meet specific invisibility requirements".[2] While it is typical for investment firms to different aggregate industries to mitigate risk, the critical aspect is the notion of luxury goods and services as a shared characteristic.

Another example of the similarities among luxury firms can be seen when Ferrari landed on Wall Street. The firm valuation made by analysts followed the financial ratios and multiples of the automobile industry. However, at that time, Ferrari's CEO, Sergio Marchionne, claimed that Ferrari was not an automobile firm, but a luxury firm. Hence the financial ratios and multiples that properly valuated the company were those of the luxury industry.[3] The latter examples show that while intrinsic differences exist, luxury firms share certain principles (see Chapter 1), which allow us to identify and apply standard managerial tools.

Of course, differences across industries shape the strategy. Each luxury category might require some specific adaptation of the tools provided, but not new tools. The previous chapters offered useful guidance of the core and shared principles, which are of utmost importance to define the luxury strategy's main aspects. This is the reason why the book does provide an in-depth overview of each luxury industry. It is not the ambition of this study; it is not needed to apply the main luxury strategy principles.

However, some category aspects should be considered. These differences, as said, are not the intrinsic differences in terms of product or service features. Of course, selling a yacht is not the same as selling a watch. But as discussed above, the strategic principles apply homogeneously with little adaptation. Nevertheless, two category-specific factors are important to be considered in the strategic process:

- How powerful the category is, and
- The business model of the category.

170

Principles of business level rivalry

Powerful categories in personal luxury

Most of the luxury industries tend to be independent of each other. The industries shown in Figure 6.2 are usually are led by different companies. Players in luxury car, hospitality or winery are generally not involved in other sectors. In other words, Porsche is fundamentally a carmaker, Azimut is a yacht builder, Four Seasons is a hospitality firm and Krug is a champagne house. The ownership can form conglomerates (this will be reviewed in Chapter 7), but the individual firms are mainly concentrated at the business level.

However, personal luxury is not the same. Under the personal luxury umbrella, there is a broad set of categories. From the business lenses, some of those personal luxury categories can be more important than others. The relevancy can emerge from the profitability potential, the potential for growth, or even better perception in the marketplace that can ease competition (for instance, with a higher willingness to pay). In short, the firm's development will vary if the firm achieves success in a category with more considerable scale potential.

In a way, the firm can become more powerful if it achieves success in these kinds of categories. Hence the concept of a powerful category is meant to describe this reality. The notion of powerful categories refers to the differences across categories based on the potential of the category to leverage the business. As a result, deploying the strategy and becoming successful on a powerful category can be more competitive, which adds complexity to the business formulation and implementation process.

Capsule 6.1 shows Montblanc's example of how a firm can leverage its scale by achieving a powerful category's success. More recently, Burberry, under the leadership of Marco Gobbetti, as CEO, and Riccardo Tisci, as creative director, has made a similar move. To enter into a powerful category to develop the firm's scale. In this particular case, Burberry has decided to move upscale in the leather goods accessories category. The company had previously leather goods accessories, which accounted for about 40% of its revenues. The new focus was to increase the percentage of revenues from this category to more than 50%, alongside increased prices.[4] This is a significant strategic change that sets a new way of competing with a new or at least adjusted, source competitive advantage, which means an evolved source of extraordinariness to compete in a new market space. The company's goal is not to diversify their portfolio of products, but to conquer success in the lucrative leather bags category. For that, they have created a new line of products, with an emphasis in the core category of bags, and strengthen their in-house manufacturing of fine leather goods in Italy.

Principles of luxury competition

Capsule 6.1. Montblanc. Building success

Today, Montblanc is a successful and diversified firm—a vital firm alongside Cartier, within the Richemont group. Visiting a Montblanc store offers a wide array of possibilities, from their writing instruments to a broad portfolio of products like leather goods or accessories. Montblanc has become, with its own merits, a remarkable example of diversification.

A key event in their diversification story is their entry in the watchmaking industry. The firm built its facilities to produce in-house movement and watches, Montblanc Montre SA. The facilities, located in Le Locle (Switzerland), were inaugurated in 1997. Their first modern watch collection, the Meisterstück, was unveiled the same year. The firm leveraged its acquisition of Minerva, with heritage in the watchmaking industry since 1858.

Entering the fine watchmaking industry was a bold move for a pen maker. The next Chapter 7 discusses in depth the rationale behind diversification moves. Here the attention is driven toward how relevant is success in powerful categories.

Montblanc would not be the company we know today in terms of scale if it not have achieved success in a critical category like watchmaking. The size it has reached (growth), their profitability level, and the company landmark would not be the same. To a certain extent, their diversification move on leather goods also plays a role in achieving such a scale. But getting to the scale and success is not only a matter of successful diversification. It is a matter of success in powerful categories. Consider for a moment that Montblanc would have successfully diversified into shoes and belts instead of watches. Indeed, the firm's dimension would be much more limited as success on a powerful category, like watchmaking, allows the firm to develop at a different scale.[5]

Principles of business level rivalry

As said, the nature of diversification moves, and the likelihood of success is addressed in the next Chapter 7. Here, what is interesting is the rationale behind their move, as Burberry aims for a larger scale in sales and profits. This also improves how the firm can compete in the market by leveraging a stronger luxury player's perception.

The underlying reason is that leather goods are the most attractive category in terms of profitability. It is not the same to be a successful company in the leather goods industry, particularly in the lucrative bags category, than to be successful in the shoe or even the ready-to-wear sector. See Chanel, Hermès, Louis Vuitton, Gucci, Prada or, more recently, Bottega Veneta. Their relevant role in terms of scale is related to being key players in this category.

Conglomerates are also built around success in specific categories. Size and relevancy are fueled by success in powerful categories like leather goods, watches or jewelry. The remaining categories are extensions of this (non-leather accessories, perfumes), or only not enough to create a firm with such scale. Consider, for instance, a shoemaker alone. It will never reach the scale that a leather goods bag firm can get.

The largest companies in the personal luxury space in terms of profits, size or market reputation have something in common. They all have a solid position on a powerful category. For instance, if we look at Interbrand's valuation of luxury firms, we will find something similar. The most valued firms are the key players of the powerful categories. One can now understand why Burberry ambitions to be successful in the leather goods space to reach a larger scale.

Fashion can be considered as a powerful category. But it is a bit trickier. The reason is that it is challenging to reach a large scale only with fashion. Haute couture is for an elite, and today, most firms do not achieve profits with it, as it is mainly a vehicle to sell other extensions, like perfumes and accessories. Ready-to-wear is also a tough category. It changes very quickly (it is very dynamic), and the supply chain complexity possesses a high barrier to consistent profits. While there might be some exceptions, we don't often find firms doing only fashion. The power of fashion relies on its ability to be the basis for additional (often more lucrative) activities.

The underlying question is what set apart powerful categories. Why do bags in the soft luxury or watches and jewelry in the hard-luxury fuel firms to a larger scale in the personal luxury arena? One part of the answer lies in what has already been covered in previous chapters. These categories can be a better platform for extraordinariness. The creative process and

Principles of luxury competition

manufacturing complexity (craftsmanship) provide more room to express extraordinariness.

However, there is a second reason. As seen in Chapter 1, luxury is a social phenomenon, and powerful categories are its consequence. A bag or fine jewelry are categories widely seen as feminine. They are the products to enjoy a particular lifestyle (emotional benefit) or display it (expressive benefit). Watches, until very recently, widely seen as a male luxury category is the same. Unlike cufflinks, belts or shoes, a watch is placed on the wrist, a symbol of power and strength. So it is not the extraordinariness involved in the category. It is also what the category psychologically means for individuals. There is no empirical evidence of the previous statement. Still, it is not coincident that the largest and more recognized luxury firms are built upon categories with such powerful psychological meaning.

Consider the scale of Rolex. A clear example of a large firm based on success in a powerful category. Its success in terms of profits, size and recognition is unparalleled in other categories. It is unthinkable to find in the cufflink, shoe or writing instruments category a firm with a similar scale.

Firms can reach extraordinariness and success in different categories. But what triggers a large scale is success in powerful categories. As a result, one can anticipate more rivalry and more barriers to success in powerful categories, as many will be the firms attracted by this potential. Just like the examples of Montblanc and Burberry have shown.

Differences across business models

The second category-specific factor to be considered is the influence of the business model. Until this point, no fundamental difference was mentioned between products and services. As argued before, luxury concepts and frameworks can be applied indistinctly. However, the business model of products and services does not often be the same, which is worth considering.

Fundamentally there are three distinctive types of business models. Their differences rely on the intermediaries' role, as they can influence both margins and prices (see Table 6.1 for a summary).

Service-based, or direct-to-consumer

This is the business model most common on services, and therefore the model we see in the hospitality, restaurant or cruise industries. In this model, there is a direct relationship with the consumer and no physical exchange.

174

Principles of business level rivalry

Table 6.1 Characteristics of the different types of business models

	Service-based	Single investment	Point-of-sale
Example of industries	Hospitality, restaurants, cruises.	Art, jet, yacht, car	Personal luxury
Key characteristics	Common on services Intermediaries as commercial tool with influence over price and visibility, but little control over client.	Common on single acquisitions. Intermediaries do frequently own the relationship with consumer. Intermediaries do not only serve as commercial tools.	Common on recurrent consumption. Role of point-of-sale as fundamental tool for sale. Proprietary versus non-proprietary Offline versus online. Digitalization is a complementary threat, not a distinctive model.
How prices and profits are influenced	Direct relationship with consumer involves cost and expertise	Intermediaries influence price and margins	Point-of-sale influence price and cost. Point-of-sale provided the needed control over experience.

Here intermediaries work as a commercial channel. They can shape visibility (accessibility), and price. But the intermediary does not significantly shape the service provided. Just like a booking portal can influence visibility and price, but the quality of the service depends entirely on the firm. Consequently, companies have to control the relationship with the consumer, which is both complex and costly.

Single investment

The purchase process shapes some strategies. Some products can be seen as more of an investment given the expense and lasting possession. The decision is hence more thoughtful and entails different stages. Often they are named operation rather than a sale, given the complexities of legal requirements or eventual financing. Examples of this are art, boats, jets and cars.

Unlike in the previous service-based model, here, it is expected that the firm does not own the relationship with the final client. And price negotiation

Principles of luxury competition

and conditions are heavily influenced by intermediaries. Hence it becomes a paramount aspect to control and select intermediaries properly. Sometimes, the firm has the power to control intermediaries tightly, and even claim exclusivity, like in the car industry. But some other times, volumes and barriers to access exclusive intermediary make it more complicated, like in the yacht industry.

Point-of-sale. The evolution of the retail-driven model

This is the most common business model in the personal luxury categories. The point-of-sale is needed when consumption is more recurrent. As a result, the point-of-sale influences prices and consumption.

The point-of-sale can be proprietary and non-proprietary. On the one hand, owning the point-of-sale adds complexity and cost. This limits profit potential. But it is needed as it allows a better execution when emotional or expressive benefits are dominant (more details are given in the next section, "The need for control").

However, sometimes volumes, consumption frequency or tight margins do not justify point-of-sale ownership, just like we see in cosmetics, perfumes, gourmet or furniture. These industries heavily rely on third parties to control the point-of-sale.

Commonly a proprietary point-of-sale is known as a direct operated store (DOS). Powerful categories command larger profits and the odds of pursing a DOS approach increases. Hence this is the frequent model in fashion and accessories. And it is open to debate in watches and jewelry, where different players choose between proprietary (DOS) and non-proprietary (exclusive retailers).

The business model is named point-of-sale, but not the retail model. There is no need for the point-of-sale to be physical, although it is the most frequent form. This is made purposely to note that the role of digitalization is not opposed to this model. A digital store, proprietary or not, is also a point-of-sale. While there are noticeable differences in physical and online store management, they both serve the same purpose (Chapter 8 deals with such distinctions). But there is no need to claim for a new digital business model, as the fundamental aspect is that the model is based on the role of the point-of-sale.

What is interesting to note is the complementary role of the two point-of-sale formats. The reason for buying on the physical store is complementary to the reasons to buy online.[6] This makes the two forms complementary rather than substitute. The consumer in personal luxury categories buys online fundamentally for convenience (moment of purchase, or assortment). The choice

176

Principles of business level rivalry

to go to the store relies mainly on the experiential value of the physical contact (value touch and feel, or pleasure of shopping), see Figure 6.4. This is why there is no need to speak about a digital business model and physical business model. Both are formats of the same point-of-sale business model.

Fundamental problems of luxury rivalry. What can go wrong in the market?

The market reality put assumptions into question, shows new or unforeseen events to think about, and forces firms to adapt. This section aims to provide some overview of the most common problems firms and strategists face when implementing their strategy and facing market rivalry.

Poor strategy formulation

A strategy that is not well conceived is likely to set apart the firm from business success. Here, we explore the main reasons why the conception of luxury strategies tends to fail.

No clear goals

Lack of clarity can be the starting point of a value destruction journey. Most of the concepts and tools provided in the last chapters are fundamentally aimed to help managers have clarity about their strategic choices. These choices are fundamental as they define what the firm seeks to achieve and how to do it. In Chapter 2, it was unveiled the luxury paradigm as a way to help managers realize that the competitive environment is different in the luxury arena. The source of extraordinariness (Chapter 3) and the treatment of creativity (Chapters 4 and 5) are fundamental tools for confidence in the firm's primary goals.

So luxury managers should feel comfortable with these principles to have certainty and clarity in their decision-making. Whenever this clarity is missing, firms are exposed to the ambiguity of the market without guiding tools. It is not uncommon to see firms that change from one day to another based on short term trends or market expectations, making the firm a follower rather than a creator. A great example can be seen with the arrival of the Millennial generation. With the arrival of a new generation, luxury firms started to question their strategies. However, luxury is not about following what consumers demand, as Capsule 6.2 shows. It is based on a tricky balance between adaptation to social change while keeping creative leadership.

Principles of luxury competition

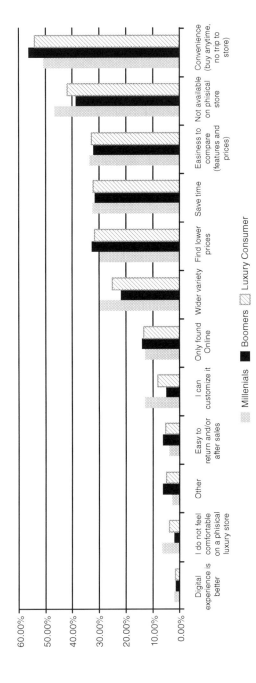

Figure 6.4 Luxury consumption: Online vs. physical store. What are the main reasons for buying luxury online? (3 choices per respondent); What are the main reasons for buying luxury at a physical store? (3 choices per respondent).

Source: IE Premium & Prestige Observatory. Millán Planelles, D. "Luxury Surrenders to the Internet. The Role of Millennials", March 2017.

Principles of business level rivalry

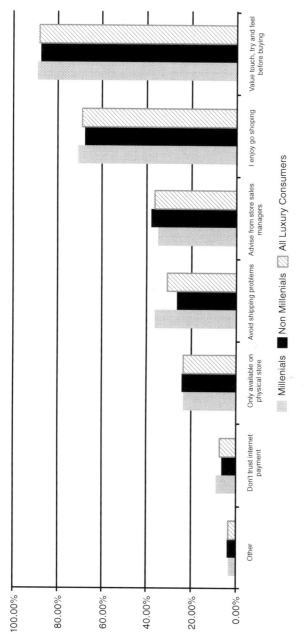

Figure 6.4 (Continued).

Principles of luxury competition

Capsule 6.2. Gucci and the arrival of the Millennial generation. Creative leadership under social change

A new generation of consumers always brings changes and new perspectives to the idea of luxury (see Chapter 1). The logical approach is to understand this new generation and respond to their needs. However, this is much in the line of the classic paradigm seen in Chapter 2. The luxury firm should not rely mainly on the demand aspects and provide creative leadership (luxury paradigm). Again, this is not to say that demand is not essential, and luxury is always based on what society defines is luxury (see Chapter 1). So if the Millennial generation has a different attitude toward luxury, it is vital to consider it. But one thing is to consider it, and another thing is to act based on what the demand suggests. This is a tricky dilemma, but luxury firms should take the lead on this change, not react to offer what is expected. So there is a balance between adaptation to how society is changing while keeping creative leadership that sustains extraordinariness.

Gucci has provided a great example. Under the creative leadership of Alessandro Michele since 2015, the firm has reinvigorated sales and profits significantly. But the success at Gucci seems a contradiction with the Millennial generation. Most of the research done on Millennials highlights that this generation is characterized by a focus on experiences, rather than products, and a certain detachment toward logos. Then how come Gucci has been selling so successfully t-shirts heavily "logotized" to Millennials?

The answer lies in the difference between social change and creative leadership. If a luxury firm takes a generic report on Millennials and follow it, it will most likely fail. Specific luxury research suggests that the attitudes toward luxury consumption do not differ much across generations. What is different is the way that consumption takes place (see Figure 6.5). Something at which Gucci has also excelled. Therefore, this goes beyond logo yes or no. The firm must provide proper creative leadership while considering social change. Something Alessandro Michele has made beautifully.

180

Principles of business level rivalry

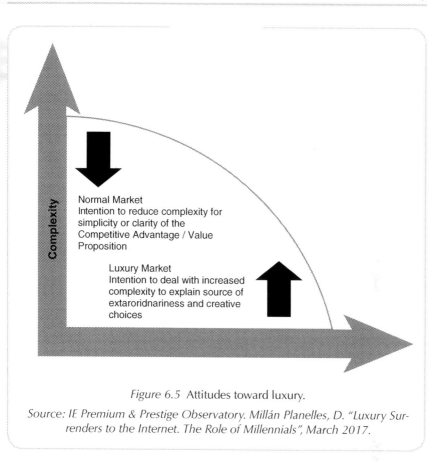

Figure 6.5 Attitudes toward luxury.
Source: *IE Premium & Prestige Observatory. Millán Planelles, D. "Luxury Surrenders to the Internet. The Role of Millennials", March 2017.*

Avoiding complexity

The way the firm treats complexity is another way to ascertain poor strategies. The strategy formulation process is often perceived as a way to find clarity through simplification. The competitive advantage needs to be widely communicated and has to be easily understood. Hence simplicity is pursued, and it creates the temptation to reduce complexity. However, this does not fit well with luxury principles, especially with the notion of extraordinariness. As argued in Chapter 3, the source of extraordinariness involves dealing with complexity.

Luxury firms can be tempted to simplify, rather than going deep into their complexity. Figure 6.6 shows the role of complexity in the *normal* and *luxury* markets. In the *normal* market, the intention is to reduce complexity,

Principles of luxury competition

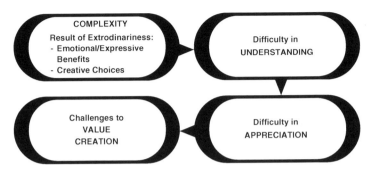

Figure 6.6 The role of complexity in the *normal* and *luxury* markets.

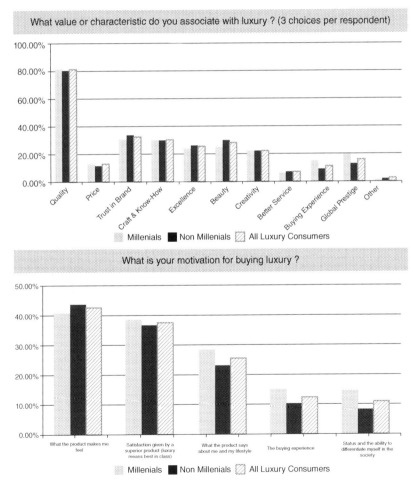

Figure 6.7 Complexity as the start of a path toward value creation.

Principles of business level rivalry

whereas, in luxury, the idea of increasing complexity means that luxury firms should not avoid complexity but explain it.

In luxury, as a consequence of extraordinariness and creative choices, complexity is the start of a path toward value creation, see Figure 6.7. Complexity must be considered, rather than avoided. This is why simplification works well with volumes but does not go hand in hand with luxury. Take the example of fine watchmaking; if one does not appreciate the value of mechanical watchmaking, it is, indeed, complex to sustain a long-term strategy. It might work in the short term, however. Early on, in the consumer appreciation journey (see Chapter 5), the consumer might ascertain value by price. And at this stage, it is no need to deal with complexity. But later on, as that same consumer advanced in their value appreciation journey, the selling process becomes more demanding, and the complexity to deal with extraordinariness has to be managed, just like seen in Chapter 5 with the 3T's of value appreciation framework, for instance.

Misuse of storytelling

There is another way to identify a poor strategy formulation, the inadequate use of storytelling. This is mainly a consequence of the previous points. Whenever a firm does not have clarity to define its goals or follow a simplistic approach avoiding complexity, the chances are that it fails in telling its story.

In luxury, storytelling can be a fantastic tool to build value, as it helps to communicate complexity, build trust and empathy. Good storytelling goes beyond a simple story and shows the firm philosophy, attitude, and personality. It helps to get to know the company beyond its products and commercial messages. As complexity raises and creative choices are involved, value creation is not a quest for being the best or solving a problem. It is more a particular approach toward extraordinariness. As seen in Chapter 5, value must be appreciated. In this line, a story explaining the origins, founders' personalities, challenges and choices is a fantastic way to clarify how extraordinariness has been conceived.

But storytelling does not equal telling tales. A story must be realistic and have the purpose to explain extraordinariness. Here, it is denoted as a tale a fictionized story, often exaggerated or even based on lies, to convince the consumer about something the firm is not. Luxury firms must take to their advantage the positive aspects of storytelling. But they should avoid at all cost telling tales.

Successful luxury firms are the ones who know themselves very well, not necessarily companies that know themselves better than others in the

Principles of luxury competition

market. This is a result of the role of creativity. This is not to say that market analysis is irrelevant, but market analysis can never undermine its creative leadership.

Successful luxury firms are commonly making appropriate use of storytelling. Good storytelling involves excellent self-understanding. It requires self-discovery and research in companies with a long heritage. Whenever a company is making fair use of storytelling, there is an intention to take care of their own story. Self-knowledge is a perfect way to have clarity in the strategy and guide companies to make complex choices. Good storytelling is frequently a sign of the patience and effort needed to have clarity in the path toward extraordinariness.

Poor strategy implementation

Not only a well-conceived strategy is enough to achieve business success. Even great strategies can fail if execution fails. Ultimately, execution or implementation is about transferring into reality an intention defined previously. A fundamental reason companies fail in their execution is the lack of coherence between the path toward extraordinariness and all the firms' facets.

In Chapter 3, it already introduced how consistency is a requirement for extraordinariness. The reason being is that consistency supports the complicated development of emotional and expressive benefits. This is why, in this section, we provide an overview of the most common sources of inconsistency.

Looking at the development of the firm, one can find sources of inconsistency. Distribution is an important area. In the personal luxury arena, a poor selection of the distribution system (for instance, favoring third parties, when DOS can better deliver the strategy) is a typical example. Third parties, like exclusive retailers, can be the right approach as long as the partner is aligned with the firm's intentions, and it is protective of the source of extraordinariness. If the relationship is based only on sales targets, the chances are that a retailer can fail to develop the strategy consistently. Prada suffered, both in profits and in perception, in the second decade of the century after an excessive focus on an expansionary distribution strategy.

A key measure to ensure consistency is price discipline. Dealing with third entities or having global distribution calls for sound price management. Otherwise, the firm can send a confusing message or even contradictory

Principles of business level rivalry

messages. Any change in price like increase/decrease, discounts, outlets, or bad adaptation to local currencies influence the strategy.

Price is the most important communication tool of the firm, and it is accountable for most of the perception generated in the consumer's mind. This is why changing the price is a tricky move, and there has to be a reliable strategic reason for doing so. There can be minor price changes to adapt to economic issues, like currencies or tariffs. But firms are often tempted to increase prices based on popularity or increased demand. But one should be careful that this is not just a short-term move to capture sales, as in the long run, it damages the perception of extraordinariness. The moment the price is significantly changed, there should be a reason consistent with the source of extraordinariness behind it. Otherwise, there is not value-added, only opportunism.

In the same way, a price decrease destroys the perception of extraordinariness. Discounts and outlets are often considered a not desired but needed way to eliminate stocks; however, they are at the expense of ruining the strategy. There might be subtle ways to do discounts, like through employees or special events. In any case, the most successful luxury firms in the personal luxury arena are consistent in two things, excellent price discipline and no store discounts.

Some other sources of inconsistency have been covered already—a misleading communication in one example. As seen in Chapter 5, with the 3T's of value appreciation framework, a mistaken communication can deviate the consumer's attention to less competitive aspects. But more importantly, it can also fail on the critical role of communication; to build the value appreciation needed in extraordinariness. Krug communication in the early 2000s supported a status-driven position that was disconnected from the real source of extraordinariness in blending. This generated surprise among loyal customers and did not help new clients appreciate Krug's value. Only when communication came back to support Krug's strategy is when the company regained its position.

Likewise, another source of inconsistency is poor product portfolio management. The risk and perils of moving to another category are mainly a diversification move, covered in Chapter 7.

But poor execution does not only come in the form of a marketing mix. Poor financial discipline and internal family conflicts are common problems behind business failure in the luxury market. For instance, this is what put Gucci at the edge of bankruptcy before the arrival of Domenico de Sole and

Principles of luxury competition

Tom Ford. The lack of management skills to put into practice the strategy can be the reason for the failure of a luxury firm.

Poor assessment of threats. Dealing with change

Luxury is a social phenomenon that is subject to change (see Chapter 1). But at the same time, companies tend to rely on constant and stable factors to enhance their competitiveness and ensure better market results. This creates a tension between change and stability that luxury firms need to address.

One way to deal with change is the analysis of threats. As soon as the strategy works well, there might be little incentive to change. But companies sooner or later need to be responsive to social evolution and its consequent market change. Therefore, identifying threats to the strategy is required to adapt to it accordingly.

Complementary versus Substitution threats

There are two types of threats to the strategy. The first type is a complementary threat. On a complementary threat, the market grows with more alternatives. This is a threat as it influences the market and the ability of the firms to succeed. Still, at the same time, it does not fundamentally change the relevancy of the firm's source of extraordinariness.

This type of threat can come through new product segments. A very well-known example is the sneakers (see Chapter 1). This results from social evolution toward a less formal lifestyle at all ages, not only at young ages. As a new product segment, the sneakers are a complementary threat as it expands the options of the firms. Some were more rapid to see this threat and adapt to it. Therefore, a complementary threat can be positive if the firms react soon enough, as Chanel did, for instance, in 2014. It was the first time a luxury house included sneakers in its haute couture show, capturing much of the attention.[7]

But complementary threats can affect the luxury firm. Salvatore Ferragamo, in 2018, dropped its profit by 42%. Analysts suggested a twofold reason:[8] lack of online sales and a too static collection not gathering new consumers' attention. This can serve as an example of what was described as a static company in Chapter 4. Not only is not adapting to the latest styles and demands of society a lost opportunity, but it can also affect the relevancy of the firm. This can be recuperated when the firm comes again to a dynamic path to reinvigorate its extraordinariness source, with creative talent and luxury management discipline. That was the path Salvatore Ferragamo took in 2019.[9]

186

Principles of business level rivalry

Another source of complementary threat is new technologies that can alter the current state of the industry. We see this with the new category of headphones. As society and technology allowed better products and services to listen to music, this category flourished. But the leader and the perhaps the spark that ignites this change was surprising, Dr. Dre's Beats. This was great news for successful incumbents like Sennheiser, Bose, Bang & Olufsen, or Bowers & Wilkins.

It is interesting to observe how this was, for some time, a missed opportunity for luxury audio players to capitalize, or even lead this new trend and obtain sooner a better market share. But this success is not far from the understanding of social change. The arrival of hip hop has been a cultural and sociological change that, of course, has brought new leaderships. Zack O'Malley Greenburg explains beautifully in his book *3 Kings* the intertwinement between society, success and Hip-Hop.[10] Therefore, the understanding of social change is at the heart of luxury business potential. The Hip Hop culture has been a key influence behind the raise of headphones. This category grew from 70 million units in 2008 to 650 million units only in 2009. The stunning leadership role of Beats in this growth signals how complementary threats can affect incumbents.

Another example of a complementary threat can be observed in the luxury hospitality industry. The arrival of Airbnb signaled both a social change and technological advancement. However, Airbnb's success is based on a more straightforward service offering, just the opposite of what luxury hospitality's extraordinariness is all about. The study of Professors Blal, Singal and Templin[11] evidence that Airbnb's arrival is a complementary threat and does not affect the Hotel revenue per available room in general terms. In the particular case of luxury, the study suggests how, on a given destination, the higher the prices on Airbnb equals the higher demand for luxury rooms. This confirms that the threat is complementary, and hence the market expands with it.

Therefore, complementary threats can alter the strategy of a firm and calls for action. But this does not mean that luxury firms must react directly. Luxury firms can try to leverage the opportunity if possible (sneakers or headphones) or focus on its core strategy to reinvigorate it (luxury hospitality).

The second type of threat is the substitution threat. This is a threat that not only influences the market but also alters the ability of the firms to succeed in it. Unlike in the previous type, the market does not grow to allocate more options and new firms. When a substitution threat appears, a part of the market, or in the extreme case, the whole market, is taken by new players.

Principles of luxury competition

So incumbents are partially or entirely substituted. Therefore, this is a more severe problem that does not offer potential but introduces a critical menace to its existence. As a result, when a substitution threat appears, a strategic decision is required.

The nature of luxury, the fact that luxury is a creative industry (see Chapters 4 and 5), suggests that substitution is less likely to occur. Industries are more likely to be substituted when the demand for the industry's output decreases, given that a better one exists (like superior technology) or social change making the industry obsolete (new lifestyles or trends). Therefore, substitution is more likely to take place when functional benefits dominate.

It should be noted that substitution is referred to the industry scope. Any other industry cannot substitute art as an industry. But this does not mean that individual artists can increase or decrease their popularity for several reasons. The latter is more of an internal competitive issue, not a substitution. The same occurs for companies. For instance, as discussed earlier, some categories within the personal luxury arena can decrease their popularity based on social change (sneakers increase and ties decrease, for example). This is not a minor theme, and it can modify some firm's success within the industry. But this is a competitive issue, not an industry substitution. A similar situation can be observed in the gourmet, hospitality, yacht or automobile. It is unlikely that these industries can be substituted, in the short term, although not impossible as society or technology can supply new forms of extraordinariness.

Indeed, technology can change the industry demand. Cars substituted horses as a transportation means, and luxury companies adapted to a new reality (see the example of Hermès). But this type of substitution usually takes more time, and it happens less frequently—society changes at a different tempo than technology and functional driven industries.

Still, substitution is a threat to be considered, especially when the technology that sustains extraordinariness is threatened. A clear example was the quartz revolution in the mechanical watch industry in the 1980s. Only by capturing the leadership as emotional and aspirational products is how the Swiss watchmaking industry survived the superior technology of quartz watches. That vision was primarily put in place by Mr. Nicolas Hayek, and it was the origin of the Swatch Group. After a period of severe substitution, the mechanical watch industry emerged as a complementary industry to the quartz segment as they appeal to entirely different audiences.

Today, electric vehicles and smartwatches can be two of these examples of likely substitution threats. New competences and skills to develop a car

188

Principles of business level rivalry

can pose a threat to incumbents. Here the latest technology, electric, shows specific improvements compared to combustion (like emissions and consumption), which offers a similar driven experience. So a clear threat of substitution exists. No wonder why luxury players, like Porsche, have reacted quickly, expressing their commitment to build (extraordinary) sportscar, regardless of the engine technology.

However, sometimes new technology does not improve the previous one, so it is unclear to what extent this is a complementary or substitution threat. This is what reveals the analysis of the smartwatch threat shown in Capsule 6.3.

Capsule 6.3. Complementary versus substitution threat: smartwatches versus mechanical watches

The Apple watch in Gold. A luxury menace?

In March 2015, Apple released a gold version of its smartwatch. An average smartwatch had a price in the realm of $500. The precious metal version could reach $17.000. Given the material and price tag, this product became a clear threat to mechanical incumbents. To what extent this a threat to luxury timepieces?

The reason why this product did not succeed can be found in the lack of substitution threat. The product fundamentally offered functional benefits, where the ability to raise extraordinariness remained solely on its gold cage. Hence, beyond the cage the product was the same as their steel version, with a price 30 times lower. On top of that, there was obsolescence. Every year key technical features would be enhanced (better battery, better screen…). What left not much as remaining value. It was not a good investment, and it did not look like a substitute for a mechanical watch.

Smartwatches as a lifestyle choice. Industry substitution?

The role of smartwatches is more in the realm of a complementary threat. Indeed, a smartwatch can perform a better task and more efficiently than a mechanical watch, so there is no question about the technological improvement.

Principles of luxury competition

There are differences in the type of benefits provided (consumer need). Smartwatches are mainly a functional driven product, whereas mechanical watches are emotional or expressive. Form these lenses, the threat looks complementary. The organizational capabilities to compete successfully are also worlds apart. Smartwatches rely on operating systems (software) and technical components (hardware) like screens or batteries. Mechanical watches, on the other side, rely heavily on mechanical engineering and mechanic craftsmanship. It would be hard for a mechanical watchmaker to excel at some of the smartwatch organization capabilities on their own.

Therefore, smartwatches are mainly a complementary threat. This new category introduces more choices to more consumers. A significant increase in volume in this case, given that smartwatches have a lower price tag and signal a new demand from a large part of society, clearly exceeds the excess competition realm. This can raise concerns for luxury firms. Fundamentally, we have two concerns: internal cannibalization and category attractiveness.

The reason why some luxury watchmakers are more concerned than others is the likelihood of cannibalization. With new categories, there might be a transit of consumers from one to another in some spaces. This is relevant when a zero-sum game exists; this is consumer buying one product equals not buying another. This is what we can see in the entry-level categories. Consumers here can choose between a smartwatch or a mechanical watch, and therefore this is a substantial threat. This is very unlike to see for companies competing in the higher spectrum. Such companies like Tag Heuer are certainly more exposed to smartwatch cannibalization than Patek Philippe. Not because smartwatches directly compete against mechanical watches, but because some consumers might trade-off one need for another, as they can choose only one.

Smartwatches are not a luxury item. Competition in this market would most likely fit with the parameter of *normal* competition (see Chapter 3). Nevertheless, this is a signal of social change, which influences luxury categories. The popularization of smartwatches would make most consumers enter their mechanical watchmaking journey and have already experienced smartwatches. This can lower its expo-

Principles of business level rivalry

> sition to the category, the moment to get engaged, or their appreciation of value to a certain extent. The new category can, indeed, shape perceptions. So eventually, new forms to communicate and help consumers appreciate the value might be needed, but never at the expense of believing that this is a substitution threat, but as a way to enhance value under a complementary threat.

The analysis of threats is an essential factor in ascertaining the need for change in luxury firms. The two types, complementary and substitution, shows a distinctive approach to industry evolution. While a complementary threat can offer potential, a substitution threat does affect the firm's ability to sustain its relevancy.

Likewise, both types of threats summarized the effect of change in society and technology. The close observation of social factors, combined with a fair appraisal of the firm's source of extraordinariness, can help luxury firms ascertain the impact their strategy, hence the need for change, as summarized in Table 6.2.

The *means* of luxury. Principles of luxury rivalry and the 3C's of luxury competition framework

The way luxury firms decide their strategy is based on the principles explained in the previous parts: Part 1, the concept of luxury, Part 2, the way value is created (*essence*), and Part 3, the principles of creative industries (*nature*). With the *essence* and the *nature*, the luxury firm is ready to formulate its strategy. The lessons of this chapter complement this process with the way luxury firms can face market rivalry to implement its intended strategy. This third component of the strategy is denoted as the *means* of luxury.

Therefore, this section provides some guidelines to put the strategy into action and hence face, in better terms, market rivalry. Luxury firms must carefully consider three components to ensure their approach to business rivalry is sound. These components are the 3C's of luxury competition: control, consistency and confidence.

Principles of luxury competition

Table 6.2 The analysis of complementary versus substitution threats

	Complementary	Substitution
Market impact	– Market growth – New options comple- ment existing ones	– Market replacement. – New options steal share from incumbents.
Source of extraordinari- ness impact	– Similarity in the type of benefit – Similarities in the orga- nizational capabilities – Low influence of zero- sum game (consumers do not trade-off)	– New or modified type of benefits – Different organiza- tional capabilities – Influence of zero-sum game (consumers do trade-off)
Internal competition impact	– Internal competition exist, with likely cannibalization.	– External competition exist, from one indus- try to another. – Internal competi- tion exist with likely cannibalization.
Industry relevancy impact	– Source of extraordi- nariness still relevant. – Social change points toward new ele- ments which build on existent elements (Sneakers vs. Ties)	– Source of extraordi- nariness questioned. – Social change points toward new elements which does not build on existent elements (Car vs. Horses)

The need for control

The need for control is a consequence of the way value is created in luxury. Chapter 3 provides a rationale for it. Extraordinariness is based on benefits (emotional and expressive) that difficult to quantify and explain. Likewise, Chapter 5 explained how value is complex to be assessed with the 3T of value appreciation framework.

The result is that creating and sustaining an advantage in the market is always open to fine lines of interpretation. And the link between creative choices and value creation can often be hard to maintain. This is the reason why control is so relevant. The lack of control puts the risk of passing this fine line and ruining value creation's demanding job.

This is what is meant with the idea of controlling the experiences. If one thinks about it, controlling the experience is always valuable, and it is not

Principles of business level rivalry

only an issue for luxury firms. McDonald's controls their experience excellently. In the personal luxury arena, owning the store (DOS) seems like a good idea, but it was not always like that.

Louis Vuitton was among the first to explore DOS as the best system to control their international development in Japan in the 1990s. It was not standard back then for a luxury firm to own the point-of-sale, and the perception was that the benefits of controlling the experience would never compensate for the cost involved in DOS. The reality proved that to ensure the meaningful development of a tricky value proposition, there is no better way than doing it oneself. Third parties might not be the best choice to explain the firm's creative decisions, its personality, and its source of extraordinariness. These aspects are complex to master for a third party that might also have their problems, like attention to other companies, or the temptation to discount. The experience at McDonald's can be easily understood and replicated. This is why a franchise model works. This is very unlike to work on luxury firms, given the complexities involved.

So there is a delicate balance to evaluate between costs and benefits. In the accessories and fashion categories, DOS might compensate, given its volumes and recurrent sales, while in the perfume or gourmet categories might more likely not. In other types, the answer is not so clear. Hard luxury, as it is a less recurrent purchase, can put this at the edge. For instance, some players have opted for DOS in the watchmaking industry, like the Swatch Group, and others rely almost entirely on selective retailers, like Rolex or Patek Philippe.

The previous examples suggest that the firm's business model and objectives determine the specific areas to be controlled. Therefore, it is critical for a luxury firm to identify what needs to be controlled. Table 6.3 shows a summary that put into perspective the lessons gained in the strategy formulation and what should therefore be controlled.

A sound approach to identify likely activities to be controlled, like the store discussed above, is the touchpoint notion, or as Jan Carlzon described in his excellent book *Moments of Truth*.[12] Identifying how the firms interact with their consumer is a fundamental way to remember how value is constructed. What ultimately determines what activities need to be controlled to ensure that motional/expressive benefits transform into market value. It should be considered that consumer interaction is not only about selling; other very relevant activities like after-sales activities are often forgotten. Another analysis that can be performed is the creative value system, as it

Principles of luxury competition

Table 6.3 The need for control

	Service Business model	Intermediary Business model	Point-of-sale Business model
Why control is relevant?	Control reduces the challenges involved with Emotional/Expressive benefits Control allow a superior development, and a better communication of source of extraordinariness		
What needs to be controlled	Firm—Sources of Extraordinariness (Creative drivers, organizational capabilities) Creative Value System components (Partners, Location, Appreciation). Development—Touchpoints (moments of truth—distribution, interactions, after sales)		
How to effectively control	Corporate culture and practices	Dealership network Selective distribution	Own—DOS Selective distribution

will also identify potential areas of control, like partners or value appreciation activities.

As a result of the activities' analysis to be controlled, the firms must determine the best alternative to ensure control. As seen above, with the example of DOS, for instance.

The need for consistency

Consistency supports credibility

The second component to ensure meaningful development of the strategy toward business success is consistency. The rationale is similar to the arguments provided for the need for control. Consistency is needed due to the characteristics of luxury and the challenges introduced by emotional and expressive benefits.

The need for control is based on the importance of ensuring the proper development of the firm's intentions. The need for consistency is based on the necessity to align all facets under the same objective. Ultimately it is about sustaining the firm's credibility to be considered a luxury player.

The achievement of extraordinariness is a complex equilibrium that is hard to get but easy to lose. A minimum inconsistency can ruin it. A luxury

194

Principles of business level rivalry

firm can quickly lose its credibility once its source of extraordinariness is questioned. Examples seen in previous chapters, like discounting or exaggerating the source of extraordinariness (see Chapter 3), show clearly the risk involved in sustaining the firm's ability to compete as a luxury player.

In short, if the firm does not deliver on what they claim is its luxury essence, its credibility will suffer. This is not only an issue of reputation only. It is about a weak source of extraordinariness, which limits its ability to create value. So it is at the very heart of the firm's ability to compete. Therefore, the idea of ruining the firm's reputation or diluting the brand should be considered through the lenses of valuable consistency.

Consistency is not only about consistent communication messages (as seen in Chapter 5 and the 3T of value appreciation framework). It is about any aspect that can ruin the complex task of raising the notion of extraordinariness. Therefore, luxury firms must review their whole source of extraordinariness to ensure consistency between its source and how it is developed in the market.

Another aspect to be clarified is that consistency does not equal homogeneity. A common misunderstanding relies on the conception of consistency as a synonym of similarity or homogeneity. A homogeneous product line, store design and communication theme are useful ways to be clear in the marketplace. Indeed, in the *normal* market, this is helpful support. But similarity does not go hand by hand with creativity. Consistency must lie in the value creation drivers, but not just on its visual display.

Maximilian Büsser was surprised when he designed purposely radically different horological machines; yet consumers kept saying those pieces were consistent. With no visual or design similarities between the products, how come consumers recognized consistency? The answer lies in where clients saw consistency. In MB&F, clients saw a consistent creative philosophy, not product similarities. That is what Max found out that consistency lied in his unique approach to watchmaking. At Hermès, no store equals another. Some aspects are undoubtedly similar, like excellent client service and experience. But an internal bidding process makes that the product assortment is unique in each store. Annually different events are held internally where country and key stores managers choose from the products offered in a sort of internal contest. As a result, no store equals the offering of any other, and the store is somehow adapted to its environment. This also creates an invitation to visit different stores and discover something new.

Luxury firms must carefully differentiate between consistency and homogeneity. Consistency is concerned with supporting the source of extraordinariness, and sometimes certain aspects, like a homogeneous product portfolio, cannot be in line with it.

Consistency builds and explains meanings—the role of codes

The second component of consistency is the role of meaning. As explained in Chapters 3 and 4, value creation in luxury is related to extraordinariness and creativity. And this is turn, is difficult to be conceived and explained. Therefore, in luxury, the meaning is paramount. The moment consumers can appreciate value, it is more likely that value creation (and consumption) takes place.

This is why consistency is paramount to help luxury firms conceive and explain their source to extraordinariness. A key concept that can guide firms to ensure it is the idea of codes. By codes, we understand the set of self-defined facets that the companies believe in and respect in their development. This, of course, entails all visual elements (like its logo, fonts selected, packaging or commercial messages). But it goes beyond. Codes set the tone, personality, beliefs and commitments of the company. Codes are the consequence of the creative approach and singularity of the firm. Hence, it is the way to explain the firm's meaning, what they do and why they do it. It is not only about visual recognition. Companies face a lot of choices in their development, visual choices, packaging choices and location choices. Codes support consistency for the firm while respecting what the company is really about.

What to be consistent with

The dilemma that consistency brings is to decide on change. Initially, one can perceive that consistency in luxury might contradict change. However, as discussed in Chapter 1, luxury is intimately associated with change. The idea is not to consider change and consistency in absolute terms but to question which aspects are subject to change and which, on the other hand, are needed to strengthen the consistency. This can be clarified by facing these two critical questions: What should we change? And with which aspects do we aim to be consistent?

Dealing with this question requires a previous analysis of the source of extraordinariness, as explained in Chapter 3. This focuses the discussion on the ability to create value rather than a debate about superficial product features.

Principles of business level rivalry

A clear example is the arrival of streetwear in the luxury fashion industry. On the one hand, streetwear is a desirable trend that can increase sales and capture younger consumers' attention. However, this can contradict the original categories offered, the expertise involved, or the clientele served, in short its value proposition. This is why change (like here offering new products or serving new clients) offered) might seem "inconsistent" with the core strategy.

However, change per se is not a synonym of inconstancy. And here is where we tackle the second question: what to be consistent with? If one believes that consistency lies in keeping the same product category, clearly entering a new category is inconsistent. But is that what the firm aims to be consistent with? Consistency must resonate with the source of extraordinariness, not with secondary aspects (like product features, distribution methods, or communication channels).

When Maximilian Büsser launched very distinctive horological machines to the market, he was surprised to see how clients saw consistency in timepieces conceived and designed purposefully, not to have any visual similarity. He then realized that consistency was found in his approach to the market, the idea that a watch could be a piece of kinetic art, as Chapter's 4 and 5 case study explored with more detail.

On the contrary, streetwear can be understood as a new possibility to explore and even develop its capabilities. And as seen in Chapter 3, there is an intimate relationship between extraordinariness and organizational capabilities. In this case, streetwear can be a means to convey the creative ability of the firm to offer new materials, new forms, and new meanings in fashion. In short, to evolve firms as society does (this was also seen in Chapter 1 with the sneakers introduction by Chanel).

An essential aspect that distinguishes successful luxury firms is hence the ability to analyze change and consistency. Success is often found when luxury firms identify what can be changed and need to be protected to ensure consistency. This is, indeed, a very tricky dilemma but a powerful tool to sustain its relevancy in the market.

The need for confidence

The last component to help companies to compete better is their mindset. Parts 2 and 3 have introduced the need for a luxury managerial approach. This is not only a matter of concepts and tools. The appreciation of the

Principles of luxury competition

concept and management tools of luxury does also influence the mindset of luxury managers. This is why while successful manager could navigate between different non-luxury industries with a short period of adaptation. In luxury, the transformation needed for managers entering the industry is more profound as luxury is based on other principles (as seen in Chapter 2). Successful executives in non-luxury industries often recognize that moving to a luxury industry is much harder than expected. It is common to hear how it takes more than six months to know what the luxury firm is all about and how it works.

The luxury principles must be interiorized in the manager's mindset to enhance their decision-making and, hence, the firm's ability to compete meaningfully. This will become clear with the typical example of setting the price. Suppose a manager is not familiarized with the concept of value creation through emotional benefits and the functionality trap. In that case, the chances are that their pricing decision would be biased toward a cost justification price, leaving aside the fundamental aspects of extraordinariness.

This is why a sensitivity toward luxury principles is needed. This is referred to as confidence. Luxury managers need to be the first to be confident in their luxury approach. Only confidence in what the firms do and its principles allows more sound decision-making and avoids critical mistakes, like the temptation to discount prices, following the previous price example. And discussed in earlier chapters, the appreciation of extraordinariness as a value creation process is time-consuming not only for the consumer but also for the manager. So confidence comes with time, understanding of the luxury principles, and an honest belief in its source of extraordinariness.

Lessons from luxury turnarounds and transformations

There is no better way to identify how strategy can be transferred to the reality that the observation of turnarounds. This situation entails a problematic approach that is solved by a combination of clear strategic guidelines and an exemplary implementation. Likewise, successful transformation in scale and recognition is also an excellent platform for observing the best strategic practices.

The reasons why luxury firms can enter into difficulties vary, but they are frequently related to key strategic issues in any of the two key components

Principles of business level rivalry

formulation and implementation. A poorly formulated strategy would face problems to ensure business success, as noted in the chapter's introduction. Likewise, Chapter 4 showed how the firms' creative component needs to be complemented with managerial discipline, especially financial rigor, to avoid turbulent situations. It is frequent to observe luxury firms entering into trouble with good creative skills, but lacking the managerial discipline to transfer that creativity into a sustainable business.

Fashion turnarounds are among the most recognized and studied. On the one hand, fashion is a very dynamic industry that can raise risks in shorter times. Furthermore, fashion is an industry with high social exposition and impact, making successful stories within very popular. Very well-known are the transformations of Gucci by Domenico de Sole (as CEO) and Tom Ford (as creative director) in the 1990s, Burberry by Angela Ahrendts (as CEO), and Christopher Bailey (as creative director) in the early years of this century. Here, we could add the very successful transformations of Louis Vuitton in the 1990s under the leadership of Yves Carcelle (as CEO) and Marc Jacobs (as creative director), and more recently in Gucci with Marco Bizzarri (as CEO) and Alessandro Michele (as creative director).

These two companies offer a great example of the dilemma between change and consistency, described in the previous section. These companies embraced change but ensure at the same time consistency with their source of extraordinariness.

In Gucci's case, the 1990s represented a modernization of their imaginary, the quest for new consumers, and a more fashion-oriented company. But this also shows that consistency is needed. In the end, Gucci modernized something they had already excel in the past and represented the history of Guccio Gucci. Gucci won back its position as an avant-garde reference of fashion. It is remarkable how all these changes and the consolidation of its consistency were made simultaneously and without any logo changes.

However, there are also great stories of transformation. Watchmaker Breitling has regained a stable competitive position under the leadership of George Kern (as CEO). Another example is Porsche, which was at the edge of bankruptcy in the 1990s. In 1993, the sales of the German sportscar maker dropped to 3.000 units from 50.000 units in 1986. The introduction of a new model offered the possibility to increase sales and provide a much-needed manufacturing scale. This was the rationale behind the Porsche Boxster launch,[13] which ended as one of the most successful transformations

Principles of luxury competition

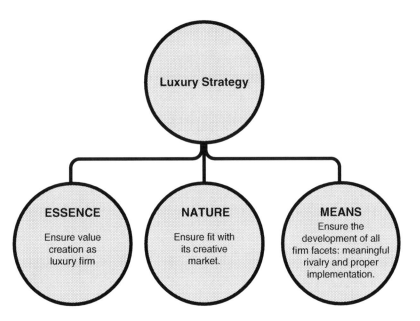

Figure 6.8 The three components of luxury strategy.

in the luxury automobile industry. Porsche, by 2010 was among the most profitable car companies in the world with a broader portfolio.

What all these stories have in common is a sound balance between formulation and implementation. These are great examples to put into perspective the three components of a sound luxury strategy: *essence*, *nature* and *means*, (see Figure 6.8).

The first component is the *essence*, the way the luxury firms create value. There is no luxury strategy without a sound approach to its source of extraordinariness. Successful transformations and turnarounds are examples of that. Frequently, companies need to take a look backward to study when and why they became extraordinary in the first place. This is why coming back to origins is so important. It is not needed to claim heritage per se. It is required to discover or recuperate at what point the firm became extraordinary and why. Maggie Hernandez transformed Krug by placing back the art of blend at the firm's heart.[14]

The second component is Nature. Luxury firms need to consider their creative choices and how they interact with the environment as a creative value system. This is what Tom Ford meant for Gucci or Marc Jacobs for Louis Vuitton. They not only sparked a new creative light into their firms but

Principles of business level rivalry

also supported the CEO to enhance its creative system, making the role of partners and value appreciation equally crucial for the firm. Louis Vuitton was able to double capacity while keeping quality, and Gucci was able to regain a stable relationship with key suppliers (partners) while refocusing on core products. What successful transformation has in common is time. Enhancing the *essence* and *nature* of luxury requires times, so shareholders need to be aligned with managers to allocate enough resources and time for the transformation.

The third component is the *means*. While the *essence* and *nature* provide the rationale for the decision being made, the *means* are accountable for transforming those choices into realities. As described in the chapter, this would require consistency, careful control and confidence. Consistency is necessary to achieve credibility. Gucci decided in the 1990s to reposition to a more fashion and young-minded customer. This required many changes in the same line, from the collections (product) to the store's design and shared message. Everything needs to be consistent with the same intention, with the exact source of extraordinariness. Control ensures that complex value propositions are adequately delivered, as we have seen previously with the leading role of Louis Vuitton, introducing the DOS.

And last but not least, confidence. This is needed to gain a luxury mindset and take risks. This is what Breitling has done when reducing some of their core models cage sizes, introducing collectors' perspective, and developing new stores and designs with such successful results.[15] In summary, successful transformation and turnaround allow the identification of the three components of the luxury strategy.

Summary

This chapter provides the fundamental tools to deal with the complex task of strategy implementation. A well-defined strategy is, indeed, an ideal starting point. Luxury executives face several sources of complexity when transferring their planned strategy into the real settings of market rivalry.

The chapter has depicted the typical face difficulties that luxury firms face, both at the formulation and implementation level. Therefore, implementation is also a key requirement for business success.

Principles of luxury competition

The differences between luxury categories are the first aspects considered in the analysis of the factors that shape the firm's development. These differences are not mainly related to the product or services' features, as luxury principles are on a general basis relevant to all industries.

The category's characteristics that impact the firm's development are more in line with its scale potential and business model. The identification of a powerful category aims to shape the strategy and the development of the firm according to the scale potential of the category. Similarly, the business model does influence firm development. The three business models proposed, service, intermediary and point-of-sale, also introduce characteristics to be considered when implementing the firm's strategy.

Another area of study to better put strategies into practice is the assessment of change. The analysis of complementary and substitution threats can help companies to identify the likelihood of strategy adaptation better. This analysis is also an excellent way to observe society and its constant evolution. Therefore, the assessment of change and the study of threats can be a good motivation to stimulate the firm's continuous need for the development of the firm's source of extraordinariness, as a society, and hence luxury evolves.

But ultimately, the way the firm faces market competition determines its ability to transfer intentions (formulation of the strategy) into reality. The 3C's of luxury competition framework shows the requirements to ensure value creation. These requirements are consistency, control, and confidence. The need for consistency is based on the challenges to bring extraordinariness to reality, as any minor inconsistency can ruin the whole value proposition. Consistency is not aimed at delivering homogeneity in the message or displaying a similar (often called recognizable) perspective, but to ensure the credibility behind the drivers of value creation. The need for control is needed as luxury firms have a significant likelihood of failure when third parties are responsible for value creation's key drivers. Finally, the need for confidence is based on the risks associated with creative choices, and the necessity for luxury managers to embody the principles of luxury as a distinctive market phenomenon. This complements the previous chapters, offering a new argument to support to need to adapt generic managerial tools to the luxury arena.

Finally, the chapter concludes with the lessons of successful transformations and turn arounds teach. These situations serve as an example of the relevancy of both strategy formulation and execution. Pieces of evidence drawn from the recuperation from problematic situations, or significant expansions, signal the crucial role of the three different variables shown in the 3C luxury competition framework.

Self-study questions

1. What is the difference between strategy formulation and strategy implementation?
2. Why is a luxury strategy not complete if we only consider its formulation?
3. What evidences support the fact that luxury frameworks can be applied to different luxury industries?
4. Which are the two category-specific aspects that influence the luxury strategy?
5. What is the difference between a complementary and a substitution type of threat?
6. Can you find a current example of a firm which might be experiencing a low performance due to the lack of control? And one firm due to the lack of consistency?

Notes

1 Grant, R. *Contemporary Strategy Analysis*. Wiley. Chapter 1 provides an overview of the concept of strategy. 9th edition, 2016.

2 See S&P Global Luxury Index. https://www.spglobal.com/spdji/en/indices/equity/sp-global-luxury-index/#overview

3 See for instance, Sharman, A. "Ferrari Files for IPO", *The Financial Times*, July 23rd, 2015.

4 Shannon, S. "Burberry's New Strategy Takes Shape", *The Business of Fashion*, May 16th, 2018.

5 Source: Section company on Montblac.com

6 Millán Planelles, D. "Luxury Surrenders to the Internet. The Role of Millennials", *IE Premium and Prestige Observatory*, March 2017. Report accessible on https://observatoriodelmercadopremium.ie.edu/en/category/reports

7 See for instance, Cartner-Morley, J., "Chanel Couture: The Trainers Say It All", *The Guardian*, January 21st, 2014.

8 Sylvers, E. "Ferragamo, Once Cobbler to the Stars, Stumbles", *The Wall Street Journal*, April 11th, 2018.

Principles of luxury competition

9 Sanderson, R. "Shoemaker Salvatore Ferragamo Turnround Begins to Reap Benefits", *The Financial Times*, May 15th, 2019.

10 O'Malley Greenburg, Z., "3 Kings. Diddy, Dr. Dre, Jay Z and the Multibillion-Dollar Rise." Ed. Little, Brown, and Company, 2018.

11 Blal, I., Singal, M., and Templin, J. "Airbnb's Effect on Hotel Sales Growth", *International Journal of Hospitality Management*, Vol. 73 (July 2018), pp. 85–92.

12 Carlzon, J. Ed. "The Moments of Truth", *HarperBusiness*, June 1987.

13 See for instance: Conrad Bell, L. "A Look Back at the Car that Saved Porsche: 20 Years of the Boxster", *Roadandtrack.com*, March 16th, 2016.

14 For a detailed description of the transformation strategy in KRUG, see Millán, D. "KRUG Champagne: "The Savoir Faire of a Luxury Turnaround", DE1–230-I, 2020.

15 See, for instance, Bandl, N. "Georges Kern and The Future of Breitling – The Cool Alternative to Traditional Luxury", *Swisswatches Magazine*, April 14th 2020.

Principles of corporate level rivalry. Diversification and the conglomerate power

Introduction and objectives

The previous chapter discussed the challenges that firms face when implementing their strategy and how they can effectively deal with market rivalry. This chapter complements this analysis by exploring competition with a diverse set of business activities, commonly known as diversification.

Exploring the potential of diversification is an area of great interest. Increasing their activities and competing beyond their core market offers great potential to luxury firms. However, competing in more markets brings complexity and risks. Identifying the rationale for selecting the markets where the firm can meaningfully compete is a priority in any corporate strategy.

The chapter explores the complexity of diversification in four sections. The first section provides an overview of the fundamental principles that sustain the analysis of diversification. The second section stresses one typology of diversification, the diversified firm. This section shows the study of the potential and the perils of diversification moves under the firm's umbrella. The third section covers the second typology of diversification, the diversified conglomerate. In this case, diversification is analyzed through a conglomerate's lenses where a diverse set of companies cover different markets under the same ownership. Finally, the last section provides an overview of the potential of diversification.

DOI: 10.4324/9781003015321-12

Principles of luxury competition

By the time you have completed this chapter, you will be able to:

- Identify the difference between business strategy and corporate strategy.
- Identify the two major diversification moves that a luxury firm can perform, diversification within the firm boundaries and diversification as a conglomerate of firms.
- Understand the main theoretical background to analyze strategic diversification, especially the analysis of synergies.
- Differentiate the challenges of diversification for a firm from those for a conglomerate of firms.
- Assess the potential to create synergies both on the cost side and on the value side.
- Understand the analysis of synergies required to assess diversification moves and identify the balance between potential and complexity that this analysis entails.
- Identify the qualitative aspects that the study of synergies involves.

The business level and the corporate level of strategy

In Chapter 6, we reviewed the business strategy (also referred to as a luxury firm's competitive strategy). Here the key is how to achieve business success in a given market, and it is usually encapsulated as the "How to compete?" question. This chapter wants to explore the potential for competition beyond a single business strategy, known as corporate strategy. This was introduced in the previous Chapter 6 as the "Where to compete?" question.

Corporate strategy is fundamentally concerned with choosing the scope of activities of the firm. This scope of activities can entail the product scope (diversification), geographic scope, or a vertical scope (vertical integration). In this chapter, however, the attention will be mainly focused on diversification. Luxury is more of a global industry, where the geographic barriers to the business strategy are less relevant. While there is some need for adaptation and exploration of geographic differences can be considered, they are more related to the implementation covered in Chapter 6 than with the firm's primary source of extraordinariness. Hence, the geographic scope is

Principles of corporate level rivalry

more in line with an international expansion challenge than a core strategic issue. Furthermore, vertical integration was covered with Creative Value System, as in luxury rather than looking at vertical integration as chained activities, the approach is collaborative.

However, entering a broader set of markets offers, in turn, managerial challenges and strategic risk. Identifying a sound rationale for each of the activities under a common strategy is indeed a complicated task. Success in a new market is often more complicated than anticipated. The firm might need to build new organizational capabilities, understand new competitive dynamics and prioritize its limited resources. Therefore, deciding which markets the firm can compete in while owning a competitive advantage requires a sound strategic rationale. Otherwise, firms can never overcome the challenges involved in diversifying the business.

Fundamentally there are two approaches to explore diversification. The first approach is the analysis of diversification within the firm's boundaries or firm diversification. In this case, it is a single firm that enters different markets. This analysis should provide light on the rationale behind the aggregation of activities within the firm. A diversified firm makes sense when the accumulation of all the activities that the firm performs adds value. So the question here is why it makes sense for the firm to compete in all these markets?

The second approach is the analysis of diversification with several firms or the study of the diversified conglomerate. In this case, different firms are entering into one or different markets. Here the analysis is aimed to find the rationale for the aggregation of other firms under the same strategic leadership. A conglomerate makes sense when the aggregation of the different firms is more valuable than those firms' value independently. So the question here is a bit trickier. It is something like, why it makes sense for the conglomerate to compete in these markets and what strategic rationale links the different companies of the portfolio?

These approaches are not mutually exclusive, of course. For example, LVMH is a diversified conglomerate. It is composed of a diverse set of firms competing in different markets like wine, fashion or jewelry (to name a few). One of those firms under the LVMH umbrella is Louis Vuitton, an example of a diversified firm. We see a firm competing in its core market (leather goods and accessories) and other markets like fashion, watches or jewelry.

Similarly, Richemont is a diversified conglomerate, even if most of its companies focus on two markets, jewelry and mechanical watchmaking. As

Principles of luxury competition

introduced before, the analysis should provide a rationale for adding different firms under the same leadership, despite the fact they compete or not on
the same market. Montblanc, a company within the Richemont portfolio, is
another example of a diversified firm, as seen on *Capsule 6.1*.

A short review of corporate strategy fundamentals

The notion of synergies to approach corporate strategy diversification

The way to address diversification has been traditionally through the analysis of synergies. One of the most well-known approaches for doing so is
Professor Robert Porter's essential tests.[1] These essential tests are three main
aspects to analyze whether a diversification creates values. The first two tests
are concerned with the attractiveness of the industry and the cost of entry.
The third one is the fundamental one, as it is concerned with ensuring that
the diversification is valuable. This is the better-off test.

The principle is simple. In business strategy, firms compete on the market
and are ultimately driven by their ability to compete successfully in that
market. So basically, they do one thing, compete. However, aggregating
more competitive activities add complexity, so firms need to ensure that
their benefits compensate for the complexity acquired with all those activities. In other words, firms need to find a strategic rationale to argue why they
are better off doing more activities than doing only one.

Following Professor Porter's approach, the way to ensure a firm passes
the better-off test is through transferring skills or sharing activities. A complementary view is provided by Professors David Collis and Cynthia Montgomery, where they associated corporate value with the ability to share key
resources.[2] Both approaches are similar as they describe how diversification
is intimately related to sharing organizational capabilities. This builds on
what was discussed in Chapter 3 and the importance of crucial organizational capabilities to achieve a competitive advantage. In the case of diversification, the competitive advantage will be based on sharing (transfer or
enhance) those key organizational capabilities.

In summary, this approach helps us realize that the natural answer to
aggregating activities' dilemma lies in the firm's ability to build synergies. Synergies are nothing else than the rationale for value creation when

Principles of corporate level rivalry

different (and complex on their own) activities are aggregated. It is the rationale to ensure that total benefits overcome the increase in complexity. The fundamental aspect to understanding synergies is that it balances potential and complexity, not pursue benefits in absolute terms. Even if diversification could add tremendous potential, we don't have synergies until it is understood why that potential overcomes the complexity of pursuing all those activities.

Considering these lessons, the strategy of any diversification move must provide a twofold approach. On the one hand, it has to make sense, but it has to make sense considering it as a part of a more comprehensive set of activities.

Why the analysis of synergies is so complex

Getting synergies right is perhaps one of the most challenging tasks in strategy making. Professor Porter's essential test was based on his empirical research showing that diversification tends to fail in most cases. The difficulty to get diversification right lies in the complexity that firms face understanding the balance between potential and complexity. There are some fundamental aspects to consider for a proper analysis of synergies to deal with such complexity.

Synergies are hard to understand and measure. The assessment of synergies often deals with lots of ambiguity, uncertainty, and many variables that are difficult to measure. Some organizational skills can be intangible and also challenging to measure. For these reasons, it should be provided an extra effort into the comprehension and measurement of the value that synergies can provide. Otherwise, firms risk performing a too simplistic or unrealistic evaluation of the synergies.

Synergies exist on both the value side and the cost side. A typical mistake is to consider only one side of the potential benefits of synergies. Firms tend to simplify and assume that synergies are a form of cost reduction processes, where similar processes, structures, and employees can be shared while keeping a similar outcome. This is a risky simplification, as synergies do not equal a simple cost improvement. But more importantly, synergies are not only cost-driven. Synergies can be leveraged to raise the firm's ability to be more valuable, not only more cost-efficient.

Synergies do not equal the aggregation of benefits. This is another significant simplification that surrounds the analysis of synergies. As a senior

Principles of luxury competition

executive once suggested to me, "if you put together a great guitarist, bass, drummer, and singer, you don't have U2. Synergies are one step beyond the mere aggregation of positive things". Many diversification failures are related to an over-optimistic reading of the benefits expected, combined with an inadequate assessment of the complexity acquired. Managers should be extra careful in balancing expected benefits with risks and organizational complexity. If not, diversification can be argued with very simplistic approaches, such as the client base is shared.

Synergies are harder to understand when emotional or expressive benefits are present. There is a final remark, more specific to the luxury arena. Synergies, by their nature, are difficult to assess, as described above. One could imagine that this process can become even trickier if we add complications. In luxury, value creation is linked to emotional and expressive benefits, challenging to ascertain, as discussed in the previous chapter. Luxury firms must ensure a proper understanding of their source of extraordinariness and creative value system before venturing into diversification moves.

As a result, firms have difficulty getting a realistic overview of the real synergies that can be created. This is why Professor Porter emphasized the notion of avoiding "imagined synergies", as "real synergies" can't be analyzed following a simplistic or optimistic approach.[3]

The analysis of the diversified firm

Many luxury firms have the potential to go beyond their core market successfully. They can leverage their skills and reputation to travel to another market. Personal luxury, and particularly fashion and accessories, is a great example. Like Louis Vuitton, Hermès, Chanel, Gucci, Cartier, or Montblanc, the most well-known luxury houses are just a mirror of the great potential of diversification. But getting it right is not a comfortable journey.

However, this is less likely to be seen in other industries like watchmaking and jewelry. It is even more challenging in non-personal luxury categories like hospitality, wine, cars, or yachts. Hence, the potential to travel beyond the core activity is an opportunity but not suited for every company. This section explores how to identify this potential and also limit the risks involved in diversification.

The fundamental idea behind the extension of a firm beyond its core market is the ownership of certain aspects that makes the firm competitive in a new market. Traditional marketing has been looking at this as brand

210

Principles of corporate level rivalry

values that can be used to the firm's advantage in a new market. And in strategy, the focus is placed on key organizational capabilities. In reality, both approaches are consistent, as brand values are nothing else than the consequence of excellent organizational capabilities.

In the end, these two approaches are not that different as they both rely upon the principles discussed in the previous section. A firm aiming to diversify into a new market should identify which aspects will make it competitive in a new market. And this has to be related to the elements that make it competitive in the first place. There must be some link, some common aspects that can be used to the firm's advantage in its core and new market. This is what real synergies are all about.

Operational-driven approach. Cost side synergies

The most common approach to evaluate synergies is to identify how companies can share operational activities. Firms can share similar distribution networks, similar manufacturing facilities, or a similar cost structure for different activities. This is commonly known as economies of scope. As a result, the firm will become more cost-effective in both markets. This is why they are referred to as cost side synergies, as these synergies improve the firm's operational efficiency, ultimately influencing its market performance and profitability.

When markets are initially perceived as similar, one can imagine certain easiness to share operational activities. This is commonly known as related diversification. However, there is no empirical evidence to date that related diversification provides better results than unrelated diversification. The main driver of success is the firm's ability to share organizational capabilities, not that market or products are similar.

In luxury, we can better observe why related or unrelated diversification can't be a guiding light. In reality, defining relatedness is very ambiguous. Through management and strategic complexity lenses, a luxury bag can be more similar to champagne than a mass-market market bag. So what does it mean related? This question is tough to answer, and it is unlikely to offer any managerial support to guide a diversification move.

Consequently, it seems more interesting to explore the likelihood to share operational activities beyond the similarities of markets. The boundaries between industries like fashion and accessories are indeed not very clear. This offers great potential to share similar activities for the benefit of the firm

Principles of luxury competition

in different markets. For instance, similar manufacturing facilities to perform best in class leather products are quite frequent to observe in the most powerful luxury houses.

However, luxury relies frequently on proprietary expertise, creative independence and genuine know-how. And this is a limitation to share operational capabilities. In some other industries, these limitations are even harder to achieve as most organizational capabilities are relevant to a single market. Carmakers, yacht builders, or watch manufacturers have very specialized capabilities that can hardly be the basis of an advantage in any other market.

Operational synergies can be very relevant to gain a competitive advantage in markets where a minimum efficiency scale might be required. This is what happened to Porsche when they launched the Porsche Boxster in the 1990s. Despite some critics losing the purity of the 911, the Boxster gave Porsche the scale needed to run its business profitably. Between 1996 (the year the Boxster was launched) and 1999, the company was able to double sales and gain enough economic and operational scale to develop the business.

Value-driven approach. Value side synergies

Frequently, synergies are considered a cost-cutting approach, which is a misperception to avoid. Synergies can also arise on the value side, making the firm more valuable and competitive. This would mean that the diversified firm can become a better firm than what it would be without being diversified. The synergies that help the company become a better firm are here named value side synergies (notice the difference with the previous section when it was discussed how the firm could become more effective). That is at the very heart of what Professor Porter meant with its Better-off test.

In luxury, the value side synergies are fundamental. As said earlier, synergies on the cost side or operational synergies can be present, and they must not be dismissed. But they are not the only way to achieve synergies, and even some times are not the most critical source of synergies. Furthermore, in luxury, improving the firm efficiency does not always transfer into a better competitive position, and this is why value side synergies become paramount to analyze a diversification move.

The lessons gained in the way luxury creates value (Chapter 3) and the creative value system (Chapter 5) can be used to analyze the value side

212

Principles of corporate level rivalry

synergies. These will be the analytical guidelines to assess why luxury firms can, at the same time, increase the scope of their activities and enhance their position.

Value creation synergies. As discussed in Chapter 3, the *essence* of luxury firms is tightly linked to the conception and execution of extraordinariness. This notion was better explained as creative choices, to highlight the difference with goals in absolute terms. It was discussed how key organizational skills are the key driver of the firm's ability to compete (or competitive advantage). Once a company owns organizational skills, it can achieve extraordinariness in a given market. Those skills can become the bridge to value creation in other markets. This is the fundamental idea behind transferring creative skills from one market to another.

Through these lenses, we can observe how companies can easily travel personal luxury categories. They rely on similar creative skills, which are both valuable and proprietary. For instance, Hermès is a clear example of how their creative skills can be transferred to a better position in different personal luxury categories. The firm can compete meaningfully with its core expertise in leather goods and share its approach to craftsmanship to other categories in personal luxury like fashion. Once this approach to care and artisanship is created, it can also be the basis for their approach in other not related businesses like fragrances. In these categories, there are few operational activities to be shared. The Hermès approach to fragrances shares is the same approach to excellence through expertise and a shared creative approach. In the case of fragrances, Jean-Claude Ellena was the creator of the Hermès fragrances, or "nouse", between 2003 and 2019. He improved the fragrance business for Hermès significantly. Based in Cabris, in the French Provence, he could enjoy the creative freedom to express his talent, understand better Hermès, and creates perfumes that respected and develop the French house. This notion of excellent artisanship in the task and respect to the house principles is what Hermès can share across initially unrelated categories.

It is not a coincidence that Christine Nagel, who took over when Jean-Claude Ellena retired in 2019, comments that creative freedom and coordination with Hermès creative leadership is paramount for her to create.

Each perfume I create, I have always responded or adapted to a particular brand or client. But today, at Hermès, I have such freedom that I create perfumes that match my philosophy. I am completely

213

Principles of luxury competition

free, and I don't have to follow any fashions. At Hermès, they do not believe in market testing. At Hermès, (the artistic director) Pierre-Alexis Dumas chooses the perfume with three other people – we are a tiny group that makes these decisions. And this is unique, and we are able to take risks.[4]

This example suggests how sharing common organizational skills can explain business success. But this should not only be observed through the lenses of sales or value propositions when companies share organizational skills. As a result, the company nourishes and develops their creativity further. Hence the company is better than it would be without entering into new categories. This is the right notion of synergies. While undertaking more activities, the firm competes in more markets, and its organizational skills develop and enhanced. So the firm is better doing more activities than doing only one, and hence the firm is better off.

Consider here that the approach is not consumer-driven, but a skills-driven approach. Diversification is not considered thinking about what consumers might expect, but where the company has the potential to share meaningfully its core organizational skills (that would be in the end what consumers will respect).

This approach also explains the limitations that firms face to diversify when their core organizational skills are only valuable to a given activity—for instance, watchmaking, automobiles or boatbuilding. Luxury houses can enter watchmaking from the fashion world. However, we barely see the contrary, a watchmaker entering any different activities as key organizational capabilities in watchmaking are very specialized and relevant only to that product category.

Creative value system synergies. As said before, synergies can arise by sharing key organization skills. But the firm's ability to compete is not only determined by its organizational skills. This was the lesson gained in Chapter 5 and the notion of the creative value system. Creativity might require the firm's creative skills, but it is also based on the partners' role, the influence of the location, and shaped by how value is appreciated.

So a firm can also be better-off by leveraging the components of its creative value system. Let's explore how synergies can arise at each of the creative value system stages.

Partners. Increasing the set of activities in different markets can improve the relationship with key partners or provide a more diverse or rich group

Principles of corporate level rivalry

of partners. This can be, in turn, enhance the ability of the firm to create and be competitive. Traditionally luxury fashion houses have relied on key partners to ensure excellence in the making. This can be the basis for a move to another category and further develop its capabilities for its core market at the same time. For instance, a company with close links with a best in class leather good provider can leverage that partnership to explore a move toward a category where this expertise is valuable. But on top of that, this will help the firm gain better control and develop its own core capabilities.

Location. Expertise supports excellent capabilities, and this tends to be geographically concentrated. By gaining access (through partners or own facilities) to the location with great expertise can create synergies. On the one hand, this allows the firm to complement the expertise needed to diversify. Still, it also serves as a learning platform for the firm to gain or develop further its skills, just like we saw with Hermès and perfumes being based in the French Provence. Another example would be securing partners or developing their own facilities in Tuscany in Italy or Ubrique in Spain, which are very well known for their best in class lather expertise. It provides the firm with an edge to enter new categories.

Value appreciation. Last and not least, synergies can be raised in the way companies explain their value. By competing in a broad set of activities and linking those to a shared organizational skill set, the firm can raise better perceptions around those skills. The example provided with Hermès and perfumes is also relevant here. By sharing their creative skills in care and artisanship in different categories, the firm can raise a more credible communication on their core values and beliefs on craftsmanship. The way they protect and develop the firm in various categories under common skills helps explain what creativity and craftsmanship mean for the company. So the more activities they do, the better they can provide a credible message around it. Experts and opinion leaders can comment on this view in different areas, and ultimately the core message prevails. Then clients find examples and reasons to appreciate the house of Hermès. It seems like a potential contradiction. Common sense would say that the more activities a firm does, the more complicated it becomes to gain credibility. But in reality, sharing creative skills can benefit the firm's position in all its activities.

In summary, diversification is not only a means to sell more products. It is also a way to develop and gain credibility around essential organizational

Principles of luxury competition

skills. It is clearer why a company like Hermès can compete in fashion, accessories, and fragrances meaningfully. But more importantly, from the lenses of synergies, this explains why Hermès is a better company as a result of doing all these activities.

The analysis of the diversified conglomerate

Most luxury markets include great independent companies and also great conglomerates. A conglomerate is hard to achieve for some of the reasons outline in the previous section. This section adds a connotation. The difference here is that a conglomerate combines companies under the same ownership, but they are competitively independent.

The synergies' analysis at the conglomerate level is similar to what was discussed in the previous section. However, in the conglomerate case, it should be considered the role of the independent companies. The distinction is then to observe a common rationale for the conglomerate while integrating the independence of companies. The main point is how the strategy can become more meaningful by the aggregation of all these different companies.

Operational driven approach. Cost side synergies

Conglomerates can benefit by sharing different activities back office or similar distribution systems. Scale can also be valuable to gain bargain power on the supply side and the demand side. Conglomerates can better negotiate deals for their companies from suppliers (including here access to capital). They can also use their scale to negotiate lower advertising costs or rentals at better conditions.

As discussed in the previous section, operational synergies have certain limitations. Luxury houses need to claim independent expertise and creative leadership. And this limits the ability to share organizational resources. Therefore, operational resources can be shared across companies while always respecting the room for individuality and independence. This is something LVMH frequently communicate when explaining their corporate strategy. LVMH provides an ecosystem where every company can benefit but always respecting the autonomy of each house. This explains the potential operational benefits that conglomerates can share among the different companies of their portfolio.

216

Principles of corporate level rivalry

Value-driven approach. Value side synergies

The previous section unveiled how luxury firms require a strategic rationale to reveal the power that diversification can bring. Similarly, conglomerates need to find their strategic cause to achieve how the aggregation of different companies under the same roof results in a better-off conglomerate. Value side synergies are a fundamental tool to find the strategic rationale for conglomerates. While operational synergies can increase efficiency and reduce costs significantly, most of the time, a lower cost is not enough to claim a competitive position in the luxury arena.

As introduced in the previous section, this could be perceived as a contradiction since luxury firms rely on their individuality. The approach is then the same it was discussed earlier. Synergies can arise in the way value is created and in the way creativity, it is managed.

Value creation synergies. A firm under the umbrella of a conglomerate can benefit from better access to a broad set of capabilities to better develop their organizational skills. This is the core idea behind value side synergies in luxury. By sharing best practices, allocating talent, and sharing luxury expertise, all the conglomerate members can take advantage of these insights to better develop their own organizational skills. In other words, the firm alone can never reach the level of expertise that it can acquire without being part of the conglomerate. This idea relies on what was studied in Chapter 2 when it was pointed out that despite luxury industries are different, managerial approaches can be shared.

Creative value system synergies. Synergies can not only be achieved by sharing among firms their organizational skills. Synergies can also arise by sharing the whole creative value system.

Partners. Conglomerates can have better access, sometimes exclusive access, to key partners. In this case, scale benefits conglomerates not only by gaining economies (organizational synergies as discussed above) but also by securing access to a key partner. Notice here the difference that the operational synergies would highlight cost reduction and efficiency. Here, the point is different as value side synergies arise when best practices acquired through key partners benefit the firm's competitive position, just like it was discussed for the case of MB&F in Chapter 5.

Location. Synergies might arise by aggregating activities or firms in the same region. This might be the basis to access key organizational skills to

Principles of luxury competition

develop the firm's source of extraordinariness. Those skills are frequently localized geographically, like watchmaking in Switzerland, or leather and fashion expertise in France and Italy.

Value Appreciation. Aggregating different firms also improves the conglomerate's ability to explain their value through the three components of value appreciation: transfer, traduce and teach. While respecting the individuality of each company, conglomerates can improve their engagement with media and opinion leaders.

As the creative value system shows, synergies can arise despite the required firm's independence. Some of the value drivers are found beyond the firm's boundaries, and they also provide an opportunity to gain competitiveness by sharing them with other firms.

From complexity to potential. Creating synergies to achieve corporate success

The limits of potential. Possible does not mean it makes sense

The recognition of luxury firms and their brand's equity suggests that they can travel to many different markets, raising their brand name. However, a proper analysis of synergies unveils that this initial potential is more complex to achieve in real life. Only when key organizational skills can be used meaningfully to claim extraordinariness on a new market and secure a competitive position we can conclude that synergies are present.

When Professor Porter developed the essential tests for corporate advantage, he stated how diversification should not be considered based on similarities or industry fit. A vague notion of synergies based on similarities rather than a sound strategic rationale is what he described as imagined synergies. However, a more realistic analysis of synergies relies on the link between organizational skills and the firm's competitiveness, unveiling what Professor Porter described as real synergies.

Here the question remains to what extent improving the operational efficiency of the firm justifies a diversification move. A better cost structure that arises from product similarities can be, without a doubt, an improvement, but this alone might not improve the firm's competitiveness. Particularly

218

Principles of corporate level rivalry

in luxury, where a better cost can improve profitability, but it might not increase the product's desirability, as they do not compete on prices in the first place.

Consequently, managers should be careful in analyzing synergies and avoiding simplistic or over optimistic approaches to (imagined) synergies. They must search and find the strategic rationale behind value creation in their (real) synergies analysis.

This is the reason why some diversification moves tend to fail. They might be based on a flawed analysis of the organizational skills shared or the likelihood of using those to succeed in the destination market. Suppose the study only considers the potential of future sales or positive consumer perceptions. In that case, the chances are that the firm will not consider that getting to those sales requires competitive excellence in some key organizational skills. This is why sales potential does not equal diversification success.

A typical example is the cosmetic industry. Diverse fashion houses have tried to enter the cosmetic industry with poor results. This industry heavily relies on science, focused research and development, and less on creative skills. This is not the same in the fragrance market, where creativity can be shared between fashion and perfumes as they both rely on those skills for their success.

Creating business success from synergies

Despite the strategic challenges of diversification, sharing organizational capabilities in creative industries can provide positive results. Unlike commonly perceive, synergies do not arise to increase the firm's efficiency and scale alone. Cost synergies are valuable, but they are not the only ones present.

Luxury firms can benefit by creating value side synergies to the best benefit of the firm. And this is valid for the diversified firms and the diversified conglomerates. The analysis of value creation through diversification in luxury requires two primary sources of study. First, a sound comprehension of the notion of synergies (both in the cost and in the value side), and second is the notion of luxury value creation and creative value system. Once the luxury manager has a profound understanding of both, a meaningful strategic diversification move can be made.

219

Principles of luxury competition

Case study. LVMH and watchmaking

LVMH's watchmaking division generates less income than most of the conglomerate's other businesses. Thus far, the group's leadership of the "soft luxury" industry (fashion, accessories, leather goods and accessories) has not been replicated by its watches and jewelry division. Strengthening the performance of this particular business line is a strategic challenge for the group.

LVMH joined the watch industry in 1999 when it acquired TAG-Heuer, Ebel and Zenith in quick succession (September, October and November, respectively). The move was carried out in conjunction with several jewelry acquisitions such as Chaumet. In 2012, the group acquired Bulgari, watchmakers Hublot and Montres Dior and jewelers De Beers and Fred. LVMH's director of acquisitions from 1998 to 2004 Pierre Mallevays supervised the French group's entry into the watch and jewelry industry. As he recalls, the conglomerate found it difficult to develop a luxury brand at the top end of the market as this is where both the Swatch Group and Richemont were well established.

Over the years, these brands have helped LVMH strengthen its position within the watch industry. TAG-Heuer enabled the group to offer products at accessible prices, while Zenith's reputation as a more prestigious watchmaker allowed the conglomerate to compete with brands toward the upper end of the market.

LVMH acquired Hublot from founder Carlo Crocco in May 2008. The firm had been set up in 1980 and, despite its youth, had acquired a certain level of renown and prestige within the industry. However, at the beginning of 2000, Hublot's initial success began to wane and by 2004 the company registered a loss of SFr 2.6 million on sales of SFr 26 million.

That same year, one of the sector's well-known and experienced executives, Jean-Claude Biver, acquired 20% of Hublot from Mr. Crocco. Biver had a history of success within the watch industry; at the beginning of the 1980s he acquired Blancpain with a partner for just SFr 22,000. In 1992 he sold the firm to the Swatch Group for SFr 60 million.

220

Principles of corporate level rivalry

Under Biver leadership, Hublot experienced unparalleled success, increasing its income five-fold in the period 2004–2007. Hublot's exceptional performance was, in part, based on the resounding success of the firm's new Big Bang model. Biver also focuses on a brand's identity. At Blancpain, he managed to turn the fact the company had been overwhelmed by competition from the quartz watch industry into an asset by launching the slogan, "There has never been a quartz Blancpain watch. And there never will be." This policy is still in place today and has helped define Blancpain as a traditional watchmaker. At Hublot, Biver chose to promote the brand by highlighting the fact the company had always remained true to its identity of mixing materials. Hublot had been the first company to design watches incorporating both a gold case and a rubber strap. Thus, it seemed logical that the Big Bang collection would follow the same principles. In Hublot, Biver saw an opportunity to develop this particular identity within the sphere of traditional watchmaking.

Hublot's first achievement as part of LVMH was to strengthen its manufacturing process. In 2009, the firm's tourbillon supplier, BNB Concept, went bankrupt. The first movement manufactured by Hublot, "Unico", was unveiled at Baselworld in 2010. Hublot no longer needed to acquire movements from Swatch Group subsidiary ETA now that it was manufacturing them in-house.

In March 2011, LVMH acquired Bulgari for 3.7 billion Euros (4.3 billion Euros including debt). The cost of the deal represented a 60% premium on the firm's trading price a few days before. The amount LVMH was prepared to offer for Bulgari showed it saw great potential in the firm. Furthermore, the acquisition enabled the French group to literally double the capacity of its watch and jewelry division. At the time, the deal was praised by many analysts who realized that LVMH and Bulgari made a good match. Bulgari's former CEO, Francesco Trapani, took over the reins of LVMH's watch and jewelry division.

Bulgari had launched several watch collections throughout its history, but only ever as a minor business line. The first of these collections was introduced in the 1940s, but it was not until the 1970s that the firm launched its first, highly acclaimed, complete collection of timepieces featuring the BVLGARI BVLGARI logo.

Principles of luxury competition

It was not until the beginning of the twenty first century that Bulgari decided to develop timepieces as a major business line. Subsequently, the firm entered an era of strong vertical integration through acquisitions, purchasing Daniel Roth and Gérald Genta in 2000, two prestigious businesses involved in complication watch design and manufacture. Further acquisitions included key watch component manufacturers such as Prestige D'or, which makes gold watch straps, and Finger which specializes in luxury cases. In 2005, Bulgari increased its industrial capacity by merging the activities of Daniel Roth and Gérald Genta at its Le Sentier installations. The firm had also set up a new manufacturing plant at La Chaux-de-Fonts in the heart of Switzerland's watchmaking region where it performed all its timepiece manufacturing activities.

In 2010, Bulgari's efforts in the watchmaking industry began to bear fruit. This was the year the firm launched the "Calibro 168", which was followed by a number of other movements developed in-house including the BVL 261 (retrograde hours), the BVL 347 (moonphases, retrograde day and date), the BVL 416 (tourbillon, perpetual calendar and dual time zone) and the BVL 465 (tourbillon and perpetual calendar with double coaxial retrograde display). The number given to each movement indicates the number of parts it contains (in brackets are the complications housed in each movement).

Louis Vuitton has become the latest LVMH brand to enter the watch industry, with Hamdo Chatti employed to lead the firm's watch development project. The number of personnel employed by the company's watchmaking division has doubled since Mr. Chatti took over the business in 2009, with around 60 individuals now engaged in the process. Louis Vuitton then performed a rapid vertical integration process acquiring, among others, the high-end movement manufacturer La Fabrique du Temps in 2011 for an unspecified price, widely believed to have been high. The firm's intention was to become a serious player within the timepiece sector, which is why it has LVMH continues to show strong growth, with organic growth (excluding acquisitions and interest rates) 6% in the third quarter of 2012.

The LVMH Group had committed itself to both the timepiece industry and, moreover, Bulgari. Mr. Burke was now responsible for dictating the direction of this symbolic firm, which would play an important role in LVMH's bid to secure a position of leadership within the luxury

Principles of corporate level rivalry

watch industry. Bulgari was therefore of substantial strategic importance for LVMH.

What strategy should LVMH now adopt with regards to the watchmaking industry? Did LVMH have everything it needed to succeed in the timepiece industry in conjunction with Bulgari?

Adapted from "LVMH & BULGARI, Luxury time", David Millán Planelles, IE Publishing DE1–189-A, and DE1–189-B, 2013.

Summary

This chapter provides the fundamental tools to analyze the diversification challenge. Managers face a different type of problems when assessing luxury companies' innate potential to travel beyond their core markets.

To start, luxury executives should differentiate single market competition (business strategy) from the complexity of the diversified competition (corporate strategy). To do so, the chapter has depicted the main theoretical background to identify and analyze diversification strategies. The better-off test and a sound assessment of synergies provide luxury executives with essential tools to navigate this type of complexity.

Unlike commonly perceived, the assessment of synergies should not prioritize operational elements or sales targets. The critical aspect behind the notion of synergies is the ability to find the rationale for value creation due to an aggregation of business activities. The best way to support this analysis is by sharing critical organizational capabilities to their advantage in their different business activities. However, as explained in the chapter, engaging in a more diverse set of activities is not only tricky, but it also hinders unexpected managerial problems.

Four main reasons are accountable for the difficulties in assessing synergies properly. The first is the qualitative nature of synergies. Synergies are frequently hard to quantify, and they are also open to ambiguity. Sharing a manufacturing facility is easy to picture; however, sharing manufacturing expertise and finding how this will provide an edge in diverse markets is complex to ascertain. The second factor is the misperception that synergies are a synonym of cost reduction. Indeed, synergies can improve the business's efficiency, but they can also represent a way to increase the firm's output. Not seizing the opportunity to leverage its ability to improve as a firm is an explicit limitation. The third aspect is the simplification of synergies

223

Principles of luxury competition

as an aggregation of synergies. This is a risky assumption as a key (often qualitative) aspect of synergies is identifying the problems and complexities that competing in several markets entails. As a result of the former, there is a fourth limitation related to identifying emotional and expressive benefits. Many synergies cannot be observed in the analysis of the benefits obtained are limited to functional benefits. This is a significant limitation for luxury firms specifically.

The chapter has shown how this analysis applies to the specific settings of the diversified firm. The distinction between the cost and value side synergies helps the luxury firm gain effectiveness and competitiveness as the scope of activities increases. This, however, should not be confused with reducing cost or increasing sales. Sharing organizational capabilities in either the cost or the value side must provide above all a strategic rationale to help the company own competitive advantage in all its activities. In the case of luxury, this must be intimately related to the source of its extraordinariness.

This is why value side synergies must be a vital part of the analysis, as cost side synergies might be more a complement than a core strategic rationale. It is unlike that luxury firms can meaningfully compete based (only) on cost gainings. Therefore, understanding how the luxury firm can be Better-off by increasing their activities should focus on the analysis of value creation and the creative value system. Unveiling the sources of value creation and the value system's collaborative forces might be a sound approach to reveal all the potential organizational capabilities that can be shared or transferred to the firm's competitive benefit.

Finally, the chapter concludes with an analysis of the diversified conglomerate. This is very similar to the study of the diversified firm. The situation here is different as the increase in business activities is performed under different firms with common ownership. This serves as a limiting factor for exploiting synergies on the cost side, as firms might be expected to keep independence. Nevertheless, a similar type of analysis is performed based on value creation and the creative value system.

Self-study questions

1. *Which is the difference between business strategy and corporate strategy?*
2. *What strategic principles would you use to analyze a diversification move?*

Principles of corporate level rivalry

3. *Which are the differences between a diversified firm and a diversified conglomerate?*
4. *What is the difference between the cost side and value side synergies?*
5. *Consider a diversified luxury firm and identify three cost side synergies and three value side synergies.*
6. *Consider a diversified conglomerate firm and identify three cost side synergies and three value side synergies.*

Notes

1 Porter, M. E. "From Competitive Advantage to Corporate Strategy", *Harvard Business Review*, May-June, 1987.

2 Collis, D.J. and Montgomery, C. "Creating Corporate Advantage", *Harvard Business Review*, May 1998.

3 Porter, M.E. "From Competitive Advantage to Corporate Strategy", *Harvard Business Review*, May-June, 1987.

4 Quote from an interview as appeared on: Benjamin. "How Christine Nagel Found Complete Freedom at Hermès", *The Sydney Morning Herald*, May 15, 2020.

The future of luxury

Introduction and objectives

The previous chapters have defined the foundations of a luxury strategy. Part 1 provided a comprehensive review of the concept of luxury. Part 2 discussed the principles of value creation in the luxury market, and Part 3 introduced the role of creativity. Finally, Part 4 complemented those lessons with the competitive principles of the luxury market.

This final chapter concludes this journey with an observation of change and an approximation to luxury evolution. As discussed in Chapter 1, luxury evolves with social change, and in this chapter, we want to pay attention to some of the drivers of that change. Of course, this is not a comprehensive overview but a summary of the main themes that luxury managers should consider when evaluating how updated their strategy is.

The first section approximates the relevant topics and key themes that luxury executives consider in the construction and development of their strategies. This serves as an introduction to the topics that are covered in the following sections of the chapter.

The chapter covers with more detail three main themes that are expected to shape the evolution of luxury. The first one is digitalization. The advancement of new digital technologies is a significant driver of social change. This section shows how to focus on the strategic side of digital transformation for luxury firms.

The second driver of change analyzed in the chapter is corporate social responsibility (CSR). While this entails a wide array of topics, the

The future of luxury

section describes how to face CSR strategically and link it to the luxury firm's strategy. Finally, the third driver change analyzed is the generational change. The section discusses how generational analysis can be a valuable source of knowledge and avoid frequent simplifications.

This chapter also aims to stimulate a sense of constant analysis and an observation attitude to social change. This attitude is about the trends and events that might shape the strategy in the short term and, more importantly, to build a long-term mindset to support the firm's development.

The section also provides an approach to understand how luxury will evolve after the 2020 pandemic. Rather than looking at the pandemic as an independent topic, the chapter discusses its effect by considering the influence on each of the drivers shown in the chapter.

By the time you have completed this chapter, you will be able to:

- Understand the long-term evolution of strategy and its relationship with social change
- Identify different social change drivers and become more sensitive toward how social change shapes the concept of luxury.
- Identify the strategic role of digitalization as a change agent in organizations that imply the development of core and new organizational skills.
- Understand the (subject to conflict of interests) complementary roles of the retail store and online channels.
- Appreciate corporate social responsibility a significant firm commitment that requires a clear link with the firm strategy.
- Identify the strategic role of corporate social responsibility as a change agent in organizations that imply the development of core and new organizational skills.
- Identify the potential and the simplification of the generational analysis.

An observation of change. The luxury that is coming

One of the lessons gained in the previous chapters is that the luxury firms' strategy is an ongoing process of creation, which is also influenced by social

Principles of luxury competition

forces. Chapter 1 provided an extensive overview of the luxury concept to argue the link business's importance with society. This chapter explores this ongoing relationship and provides some additional observation of the main aspects that can shape the constant evolution of luxury.

In a way, luxury is an ever-evolving quest for extraordinariness, and hence observing the forces that shape this change is an essential consideration for any luxury strategy. To build on this observation, this chapter covers some of the themes that might help the luxury manager be more sensitive toward the evolution of luxury and question the impact of this change on its major managerial decisions.

However, this chapter does not provide a comprehensive overview of all the themes considered. Therefore this is not meant to be a broad market or social analysis. The chapter's primary objective is to highlight social change as a factor in strategic decision making. It has to be noticed that this emphasis on external factors, like social change and consumer demands, should never jeopardize the primary strategic considerations raised in the previous chapters.

The IE Luxury Barometer, a study carried over five years to research the luxury executives' priorities, suggests that luxury managers are sensitive to the luxury market's constant evolution (see Figure 8.1). Priorities change over time, and they are influenced by core competitive issues like creating memorable experiences, the role of China, and tourism. Key priorities include the growing importance of corporate social responsibility, digital issues (like reinventing the role of retail or reaching new audiences) and social change (like new values of luxury).

The three themes discussed in this chapter are considered the most relevant and influential, as, for instance, the IE Luxury Barometer suggests. The first topic will be the digitalization of society and hence of business models. Digital technologies enable faster communications, better control, and more extensive access to data. This, of course, influences the ability of luxury firms to develop their business. We only need to consider how the traditional retail model requires an update or how companies can directly interact with consumers.

The second issue is the influence of corporate social responsibility. This is shaping more and more the evolution and practices of luxury firms. And this is also another example of how social change impacts the business of luxury. Today, society, not only luxury consumers, is more sensitive toward social and environmental issues. And they expect their favorite luxury companies to be sensitive as well. What started as a minor issue (and sometimes

228

The future of luxury

Figure 8.1 IE Mastercard luxury barometer.

perceived as a pure advertising aspect) has become a key strategic issue shaping the business and evolution of luxury firms.

Last but not least, social change is shaped by values and how they change. This, of course, is open to cultural and geographic differences. But in general terms, the evolution of social values directly affects the luxury market and the way luxury firms can (and will) compete. Indeed, younger generations are a mirror of social change. But this analysis should not be focused only on how younger generations differ from the previous ones. This analysis must aim to unveil how social values evolve our time.

A note on the post-pandemic luxury

There will be a major social influence in all these aspects, with the effect of the Covid-19 pandemic. This will not be considered as an individual factor but as an impact on all the topics introduced above. The pandemic will shape social values, push even harder the digital transformation, and most likely emphasize corporate social responsibility.

This book has been finished under the COVID-19 pandemic. It might be tempting to unveil ideas and projections to how luxury will evolve after the

Principles of luxury competition

pandemic and define the so-called post-pandemic luxury. However, a close read of Chapter 1 reveals that luxury is under constant change, so there is no need to add adjectives to the notion of luxury continually. This is why this book avoids terms like post-pandemic. Similarly, it has also been avoided terms like after-crisis luxury, to refer to the effect of the 2008 subprime crisis, or new luxury refer to the arrival of younger generations. It is always luxury, and it is ever-changing.

The author's view that this tendency to redefine luxury based on novel trends can be misleading to the core and strategic conception of luxury. As the chapter will explain, certainly observation of social change is indeed needed. But instead of redefining luxury as a post-pandemic luxury, it might be more accurate to observe how the pandemic impacts as a driver of change. The main idea here is to consider luxury as a single concept, which is subject to change and evolve (as introduced in Chapter 1). The addition of such adjectives (post-luxury, after-crisis luxury, new luxury, old luxury) can be misleading. It might convey the idea that luxury before and after the addition of the adjective are different concepts.

The luxury manager must sensitively observe future potential and have solid knowledge to avoid stereotypes. And this is a mindset to be always kept, not under specific changes. Balancing an own creative view while ensuring adaptation to the ongoing change remains a solid principle to navigate the luxury waters.

The role of digitalization

We consider digitalization as the impact of digital technologies in the evolution of business. This, of course, influences the ability to sell (digital channels) and communicate (digital means). But it goes beyond that. Digitalization affects the production means, it impacts the organizational capabilities of firms, and in the end, it changes the way firms can compete in the market.

Therefore, digitalization provides a new landscape of where to do business, and as such, it shapes the whole company. Hence, luxury firms should not consider only the direct effect on sales. The following topics provide an overview of the main strategic challenges that digitalization offers to luxury firms.

Store and online sales are complementary

In Chapter 6, it was mentioned how the retail and the online spaces are complementary. Both are different channels to benefit the firm to convey its messages and sell its products. From this perspective, digitalization offers more possibilities.

The future of luxury

These possibilities must be evaluated for each case, and luxury firms must ensure which their commercial partners are. For instance, in the watch industry, where firms tend to rely on retailers, the choice to open online channels might offer a potential conflict of interest that must be explored before taking solo online activities. If, on the contrary, the firm already owns its distribution network, like often in fashion and accessories, then the move to online is entirely complementary.

But this, of course, comes with complexity. To a certain extent, luxury firms were reluctant to embrace digital channels as their retail operation worked perfectly. And Chapter 6 also provided evidence on the similar attitudes toward luxury between Millennials and non-Millennials generations. However, with the arrival of younger generations, this started to shift to more digitally friendly windows (see Figure 8.2).

A digital business requires new organizational capabilities

The arrival of digital means has heavily impacted luxury consumption. Not only the consumption channels have been expanded, but also the consumption attitudes. Today, we have new ways to gather and share information and more consumption channels available. And here is where we find generational differences (see Figure 8.3). Younger generations show the path toward a luxury where digital consumption and interaction is more relevant.

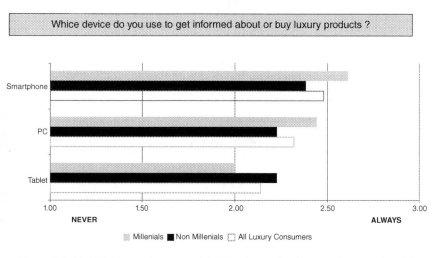

Figure 8.2 Multidevice web access. Mobile phone dominates all categories. PC still relevant for Millennials, tablets for non-Millennials.

Principles of luxury competition

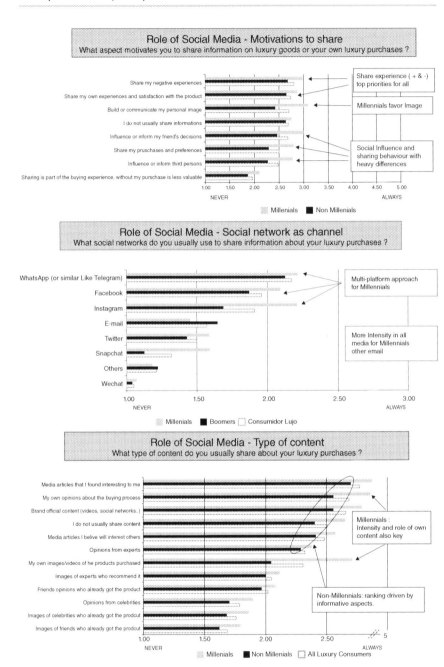

Figure 8.3 (a) Significant disparity. Millennials driven by personal image and social influence (b) Significant disparity. Multiplatform and intensity characterizes Millennials (c) Significant disparity. Millennials follow a generator role, while non-Millennials follow a distributor role.

The future of luxury

However, luxury firms should not consider only the commercial effect of digitalization. Firms must evolve in their whole set of organizational capabilities. Developing a digital business includes new challenges, like logistics. The so-called omnicanality, which means integrating all firm channels, is easier said than done. Companies face several difficulties in implementing it in real life. This view represents companies like platforms able to sell and communicate under an integrated system, but making it a reality might apply to only a limited (yet powerful) set of firms. Following the creative value system, partners might also include the vendors' function and future specialized online vendors. So choosing when to integrate an activity or when to collaborate is today a complex and strategic choice to take.

Likewise, there are new valuable areas that luxury firms can integrate into the lines of data mining or use their digital platforms to establish more trustworthy relationships. And all this, in turn, requires new skills to master a distribution that embodies digital channels or improves communication on new digital channels.

Digital is a change agent to the whole organization, not just an improvement on commercial channels. This is the main strategic point to consider. Some companies have been able to use them to their advantage, leveraging new channels to gain awareness and inform the consumer about their expertise. Today there are lower entry barriers in terms of capital, but only as long as those new skills are mastered. New fashion brands have been able to enter the market with a digital sound approach following the same rationale unveiled in the case of MB&F. Maximilian Büsser himself managed their digital platforms accounts for several years and responded directly to their customers and followers.

While services could be perceived as less affected, the platform approach is also valuable to the hospitality and restoration industries. As argued in the introduction, the core product is not altered, but digitalization represents a new landscape not only new commercial channels.

The role of corporate social responsibility

Another area to observe social change is through their values and beliefs. Perhaps an aspect that deserves an individual perspective is how our society is becoming more concerned with firms' impact. This includes a wide array of topics, where environmental and social effects tend to be the leading ones. This is commonly known as corporate social responsibility (CSR).

Principles of luxury competition

In reality, CSR is not a new theme. Initially, CSR was a minor topic concerned with raising the firm's awareness by being sensitive to social aspects. However, on many occasions, this was more of a commercial tagline than real interest. A second common concern, which is still an object of research, is how consumers are willing to pay a price premium for CSR activities. This trend is evolving, and managers need to be open-minded to observe the evolution.

However, over time CSR has become more of a strategic issue. This might be a consequence of multiple factors. Let's consider, for instance, environmental impact as an example. Today, one can witness with more clarity the effects of climate change, creating a more concerned mindset. As a result, companies have become more environmentally worried in the fashion industry. This has generated new processes and textiles, like Ecoalf's expertise in obtaining recycled fibers.

The consequence of social change is not whether consumers are willing to pay a price premium for more environmentally friendly products. The result can be that consumers might be more sensitive and more demanding from more environmentally concerned firms. Based in Spain, our research suggests the latter approach, as the luxury consumer expects luxury firms to be strategically involved (see Figure 8.4). Therefore, CSR is less of a way to differentiate the firm (hence claiming a price premium, for instance) and more of a future business requirement.

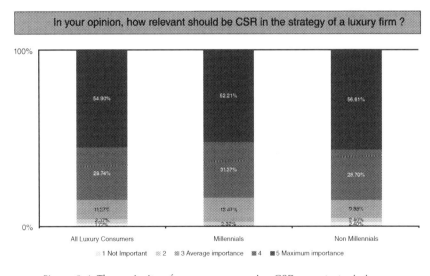

Figure 8.4 The majority of consumer perceive CSR as a strategic issue.

The future of luxury

In the specific case of luxury, CSR can become a real strategic aspect. For that luxury, firms must consider two fundamental factors: the level of strategic commitment and business impact.

CSR is a commitment shaped by positioning and direction

We unveiled in Chapter 2 how a well-crafted strategy might consider the way the firms aim to compete (Positioning) and the specific rationale behind the business (Direction). These are the first steps to evaluate the role of CSR in the firm. Responding to consumer trends, mimic what other companies do, or claiming generic taglines on social involvement with a little real link with the firm is the path to take miss-leading choices. Likewise, this will only bring confusion to clients and the firm's employees.

It is perfectly fine that a firm chooses to follow a philanthropic approach and support any cause. It is strategic the moment that support is linked to its strategy.

As explained in Chapter 3, the *essence* of a luxury firm is its source of extraordinariness. Therefore, any CSR must have a clear link with it. There are several ways to link CSR with strategy, such as protect their scarce resources.

It is not about being perceived as environmentally or socially concerned. It is about being concerned in a way to supports your business. CSR is not a contradiction with strategy. It can be a great ally. When the champagne house Krug builds strong ties with their growers, it is both a way to support the local community and protect access to the best grapes they need for their blends.

A second concern is the long-term perspective. When CSR is approached as a trend, companies over time decline in their efforts, and hence their focus on CSR can be short-lived. Luxury firms must consider that CSR is a commitment. And commitments are to be proved not to be told. Saying that we care about the environment or that the firm is socially involved can be easily conveyed. But demonstrating it requires the commitment of the whole organization, the allocation of specific resources, and, above all, a long-term involvement.

In the end, CSR can include a wide array of topics. Luxury firms should carefully consider their choices along with CSR topics. To do so, they must evaluate the strategic alignment and their willingness to commit. If correctly done, CSR is not a way to claim a "cool image" but to enhance and develop an organization's reason of being.

CSR as a change agent to develop core and new organizational capabilities

A strategic approach to CSR should also consider the impact on the firm's organizational capabilities. This might even imply the development of new ones.

Principles of luxury competition

This will become easier with a generic example. Let's consider a leather goods firm that wants to be protective (not only to be perceived as protective) with the environment. The firm might need to secure tannery partners (not suppliers, as seen in Chapter 5) with the ability to reduce their polluting processes, which is more costly, putting pressure on the firm to consider a price raise. This is the logic, and usually, firms would be considering how consumers will accept a price increase. That would be the logic behind a tactical approach to CSR. However, new processes, like less polluting tanneries, require a long-term strategy to consider that new organizational capabilities are needed. Partners might need to adapt processes or adapt their manufacturing expertise.

This might also imply a different set or a modification in the sourcing of raw materials. Like for instance, Chopard's commitment to ethical gold in all of their products. Chopard defines ethical gold as gold acquired from responsible sources, verified as having met international best practice environmental and social standards. This is a change in the sourcing, as Chopard has moved a significant part of their sourcing to small artisanal freshly mined gold from small-scale mines.

On some occasions, it is the firm that must evolve its core expertise. A great example is the car industry and the electrification change. CSR is not only about consumer trends. It is also about adapting to technological evolution. For instance, Porsche invested more than 600 million Euros in developing their first electric vehicle, the Taycan. This shows how even great companies need to acquire the necessary expertise to design and manufacture electric cars. Always in mind to deliver an ultimate sportscar experience.

In short, CSR is not only a matter of time and investment. It is also a matter of adapting the firm diverse set of expertise. So CSR is both a substantial commitment and a change agent across the whole creative value system. An excellent example to identify these two aspects of CSR, dedication, and development of organizational capabilities, can be seen in Loewe, as seen in Capsule 8.1.

Social change. The analysis beyond generational change

The previous section, combined with the lessons gained in Chapter 1, has provided examples of social change on luxury as a concept and the luxury market. The reason to name this section social change is to add some clarity

The future of luxury

> ## Capsule 8.1. Loewe's annual report on sustainability. A strategic approach to CSR
>
> Professor Joaquín Garralda, from IE Business School, describes in his excellent case study "Loewe: Sustainability and durable luxury"[1] how Loewe approached CSR.
>
> Loewe, in 2013, was among the first companies to publish an annual sustainability report. Their approach to CSR was not pursuing a philanthropic or an awareness goal; their commitment was acquired throughout all firm layers, especially in the top management, and with a clear strategic link.
>
> A key aspect in Loewe's approach was a classification of all CSR activities according to how important they are for Loewe and society. This helps to identify how strategic each activity is. Furthermore, Loewe ensured across the firm accountability for each project to ensure that CSR activities were realities with clear responsibilities and not mere advertisement themes.
>
> Among the different projects, one that deserves attention is the creation of a leather crafts academy. This aimed to protect and ensure the sustainability of their core expertise. The academy was also coordinate with local authorities to improve unemployment in their local community. This is an example of how a CSR project can benefit society, build the firm's strategy and protect core organizational skills.

to the stereotypes that frequently are considered when discussing the new generations' role.

The observation of new generations is an insightful source of knowledge to gather a better social change perspective. In this way, one can better understand the adoption of new technologies or social values' evolution. However, the luxury manager should be careful when extrapolating generic studies' based on non-luxury markets to gather luxury insights.

Specific versus generic themes

A generational analysis might unveil generic themes that require further refinement to get specific lessons. People at a given age are exposed similarly

Principles of luxury competition

to certain factors, like new technologies, but, of course, they do not all behave in the same way. This tends to create myths or stereotypes about generations rather than analytical perspectives to help dig into more details. Many have been the topics raised about the Millennial generation, but a generation is a comprehensive concept that entails differences across many variables, even age differences. In short, the idea of Millennials is not a homogenous or cohesive reality. Therefore, companies can rely on generational analysis to gain more details and not an end on itself. This is why a broad, often stereotyped approach to a generational analysis can be misleading.

The need for luxury-specific lessons

One should be careful when extrapolating lessons. Generational analysis can be misleading as the general studies might not be directly applicable to specific contexts, like the luxury market. For instance, research performed based on luxury consumers suggest, as seen with Figure 8.2, that the concept of luxury is not that different across different generations, while specific consumption patterns are. What highlight the need to luxury specific research to unveil lessons applicable to the luxury market.

Therefore, a generational analysis must also be focused on the population it aims to study. For instance, it was frequent for years to hear that the Millennial generation did not want logos or that experiences were preferred over products. Still, to a certain extent, Gucci's success in the second decade of the century is explained through younger generations' desire for their products, which frequently included prominent logo references. This might seem a contradiction with the generic lessons on the Millennial generation. The reality was that Alessandro Michelle's work and the transformation of Gucci were not based on those stereotypes. We might want to avoid this stereotype with the following generation Z. As said earlier, generational analysis can be a great source to understand social change. Still, it should be fine-tuned to transfer those lessons into specific audiences, like in the luxury market.

It might be too soon to tell

Another limitation of a generational analysis can be the time frame. In the previous section, we said that asking individuals who are not luxury consumers might be misleading to understand the luxury market. In the same way, asking individuals that can be luxury consumers in the future, but they are not present, can also be misleading. This is another area of stereotypes.

The future of luxury

An individual can convey their current attitudes, which is an interesting area to observe but not as a reality as those same individuals can change their attitudes when they become real consumers. Therefore, one should be careful when extrapolating generational analysis based on individuals who are not still the study's audience.

New categories, new values

In the end, the luxury manager should be curious about social change and its impact on the luxury market. The previous topics help to consider generational analysis as a valid source of knowledge and avoid stereotypes.

Social change can be observed through new generations, but it is not only about how the new generation differs from the others. One should never lose sight that the ultimate goal is to observe how society evolves. In Chapter 1, a clarifying example with sneakers as a luxury product was presented. It is not that younger generations prefer sneakers. It is that sneakers signal that our society as a whole feels younger. This helps us understand how the emphasis is not on how younger generations are different but on how society moves. And as said in Chapter 2, the evolution of technology now, among many other things, makes you, the dear reader, whatever your age is, feel younger than somebody your age some 15 or 20 years ago.

The sneakers example also clarifies how social change can be observed through changes in technology, of course, but also through changes in values. And as a result, new opportunities and new product categories arise. Chapter 6 unveiled Smartwatches as a new category, but not necessarily a direct threat to mechanical watches. Similarly, headphones, or the impact of urban mobility on the automobile market, are just a few examples of how social change can be observed through new categories.

Summary

As society changes, so will luxury. If our society enjoys the benefits of digital means, so it will evolve luxury. If we become more socially concerned, so it will be luxury. In the end, luxury is a mirror of the society it coexists with.

As a consequence, luxury managers should be attentive to observe social change and adapt when needed. One key lesson of this chapter is that luxury strategies evolve and are subject to change. Luxury should not be considered with an everlasting approach in terms of products or values.

Principles of luxury competition

The chapter provided three critical areas of observation. The first one is the digital evolution. Digitalization is a change agent for the whole organization. This implies developing organizational skills to embrace new distribution systems' challenges or new ways of communication. Likewise, digitalization provides new dilemmas. The balance between the retail store and online sales or the potential conflict of interests with key partners is a clear example. As such, firms' digital evolution should not be considered through the lenses of commercial development, but as the firm's strategic enhancement.

Another area where social change can be observed is the evolution of values and beliefs, especially those concerned with social and environmental issues (CSR). Approaching CSR is not an easy task. The luxury firm must be clear about the commitments it aims to make and be clear about the link with its strategy (in terms of positing and direction). This prevents luxury firms from engaging in CSR as a mere advertisement, an approach that backfires. Like the digital challenge, CSR is also a change agent, so the luxury firm must carefully consider the impact of their core organization skills to have a more realistic and strategic assessment of their move.

Luxury categories can also evolve. Generational analysis has been a common approach to observe social change, and, indeed, it can offer great insights. However, the luxury manager should be careful not to fall into stereotypes and be critical of how the lessons of this sort of analysis apply to luxury realty. Only then are we ready to observe social change and how new values and new categories shape the luxury market?

A special final request needs to highlight how the pandemic situation that the world lived in 2020 impacts luxury. A dramatic situation like this certainly has changed society. The analysis of the post-pandemic luxury is similar to the lessons gained in this chapter. Luxury will evolve as a consequence of social change. This can be observed with careful analysis of digitalization and how social values will shape luxury now and in the future.

Note

1   Garralda, J. "Loewe: Sustainability and Durable Luxury", IE Publishing, DE1-209-I, July 2015.

Index

Note: **Bold** page numbers refer to tables and *italic* page numbers refer to figures.

3C's (control, consistency, confidence), of luxury competition framework 191–198, **194**
3T's (transfer, traduce, teach) framework 140–153, **149**; fashion shows *versus* watch shows 150–152

Aaker, D. A. 62
Aduriz, A. 114
Ahrendts, A. 43, 199
Airbnb 187
Altagamma Foundation 168
Amabile, T. 102–104
Amazon 154, 156
anthropological perspective on luxury **27**
Apple 55, 65, 155, 156; iPhone 80; watch 189
appreciation 12–13, 17–21, 25–26, 82; value 139–153, 215, 218
Aristotle 11; *Rhetoric* 64
art: and creativity 105–107; definition of 105–106; and luxury 17–21, 45, 48, 53
artisans 13, 26
artists 13, 26
Arts et Métiers 109
Aspers, P. 106

Aston Martin 92–93; Cygnet 92
Audemars Piguet 29, 117
Audi 92
avant-garde 64
Azimut 171

baby-boomers 46
Bailey, C. 43, 117, 199
Bain & Co. 168
Balenciaga, C. 116, 138–139
Balmain 116
Bang & Olufsen 187
Barbon, N. 12
Barneys, J. 51, 55
Berg, M. 17; "Consumers and Luxury: Consumer Culture in Europe 1650–1850" 19; "In Pursuit of Luxury: Global History and British Consumer Goods in the Eighteenth Century. Past & Present" 16; *Luxury in the Eighteenth Century* 14
Berkeley, G. 15
Berluti 116
Berry, C. J. 8, 10–12; *Idea of Luxury, The* 10
Biver, J.-C. 220, 221
Bizzarri, M. 199
Blancpain 220, 221

241

Index

Blümlein, G. 126
BMW 92
Bose 187
Bottega Veneta 173
Bowers & Wilkins 187
Breaking Bad 156
Breguet, Abraham-Louis 107–108, 124
Breitling 199, 201
Bulgari 220–222
Burberry 43, 116, 117, 173, 199
business environments, types of **153**
business level of luxury strategy 206–208
business models; characteristics of **175**; differences across 174–177, *178–179*
Büsser, M. 55, 82, 87, 112, 124–128, 136, 195, 197

Cahn, L. 90, 91
Cahn, M. 90, 91
The Cambridge history of the eighteenth century on political thought 14–15
Carcelle, Y. 38, 57, 118, 199
Carlzon, J.: *Moments of Truth* 193
Cartier 172, 210
Cashin, B. 90
Celine 116
Chanel (brand) 23, 55, 173, 186, 210
Chanel, C. 108, 138
change challenge to luxury 40–41, **44**
Chatti, H. 222
choice: extraordinariness as 83; luxury as 79–82
Chopard 236
classic paradigm 46–47, *46*, 65, 67, 155
classic *versus* modern style 119–120
client satisfaction 47
Clifford, H.: "Consumers and Luxury: Consumer Culture in Europe 1650–1850" 19
Coach Inc. 90–91

codes, role of 196
Collis, D. 208
competition: excess 73–88, **74**, *77*; normal 65–73, *69*, **70**, 73, 82–85, 87
competitive mindset 50–52, **153**, 154, 155
complexity, avoidance of 181–184
consistency, role of 88–89
conspicuous consumption 20
consumer surplus 62
contemporary luxury 19–21
control challenge to luxury 42–43, **44**
corporate level of luxury strategy 206–208; diversified conglomerate, analysis of 216–218; synergies to approach diversification 208–216
corporate social responsibility (CSR) 134, 226, 227, 229, 240; role of 233–236, *234*; strategic approach to 237
corruption *versus* luxury 16
cosmetic industry 219
cost advantage 50, 51
cost side synergies: corporate strategy diversification 211–212; diversified conglomerate, analysis of 216
craftsmanship, luxury as 30
creative market 154–155
creative value system 132–161, *135*; appreciation 139–153; firm 136; location 137–139; partners 136–137; 3T's (transfer, traduce, teach) 140–153, **149**; *see also* value creation process
creative value system synergies 214; diversified conglomerate, analysis of 217–218
creativity challenge to luxury 38–39, **44**
creativity for firm analysis 99–129, **111**; adaptation 110, 112; assessment of 110–129; classic *versus* modern style 119–120; conceptualization of 102–110; definition of 102–103;

242

Index

external analysis 134–135; forms of 112–115; individual talent 115–117; innovation 107–108; management and 117–119; need of 100–102; roles of **118**; shapes of 105–107; static *versus* dynamic companies 120–123; technology 107–108, 124; will 110, 112

creativity-relevant skills 104

creators: *versus* firm 115–117, 122–123; role of 108–110, **111**

credibility 194–196

Crocco, C. 220

CSR *see* corporate social responsibility (CSR)

culture, and luxury 12

Daniel Roth 222

Da Vinci, L. 30

De Beers 220

designers, role of 108–110, 199

desire 10, 11; *versus* needs 21, 24

Diane von Furstenberg 116

differentiation advantage 50, 51

digitalization, role of 230–233, *231, 232*

Dior, C. 138

direct operated store (DOS) 42, 176, 184, 193, 201

diversification 207–211, 214

diversified conglomerate, analysis of: cost side synergies 216; value side synergies 217–218

domain-relevant skills 104

DOS *see* direct operated store (DOS)

Dr. Dre: Beats 187

Ebel 220

Ecoalf 234

economic factor, luxury as 14, 16

economic logic 52–54, 72

economies of scope 211

Eger, E.: *Luxury in the Eighteenth Century* 14

Eisenmann, T. 156

Ellena, J.-C. 213

Enlightenment debate on luxury 17–19, 28

"entry-level" category, management of 92–93

Erlin, M. 17

essence of luxury 3, 22, 60–95, 167, *167*, 213

ethos 64

European Enlightenment 14

excess competition 73–78, *77*; characteristics of 74–76, **74**

extraordinariness 76, 78–88, 100–102, 148, 155, 174; achieving 83–88; being *versus* looking 87; conceiving 79–82, *80*

Facebook 55, 154, 156

fashion 105–107, 142–144; shows *versus* watch shows 150–152

Fénelon, Archbishop 15

Ferrari 25, 170

Ffoulkes, F. 19

firm: analysis, creativity for (*see* creativity for firm analysis); creative value system 136; *versus* creators 115–117, 122–123

Ford, T. 38, 117, 118, 199, 200

Ford Mondeo 92

founders, role of 108–110

Frankfort, L. 90

Fred 220

functionality trap 64–66, 69

Galileo Galilei 65

Gallego, J. 13

game theory 48

Garralda, J. 237

generational change 236–239

Genta, Gérald 29, 117, 222

Index

Gignac, J. 66, 68–69
Gobbetti, M. 171
Godart, F. 106
Google 55, 154, 156
Grant, R. 84, 166
Greenburg, Z. O.: *3 Kings* 187
growth challenge to luxury 39–40, **44**
Gucci 38, 39, 41, 43, 117, 173, 180, 185, 199–201, 210, 238

hard-luxury 168, 173
Harry Winston Timepieces 158
Hayek, N. 188
HBO 156
Henríquez, M. 56–57
Hermès 148, 173, 210, 213–214, 216
Hernandez, M. 200
history of luxury 9–21
HM *see* Horological Machine (HM)
Hont, I. 15, 16
Horological Machine (HM) 126, 158, 159
Hublot 220, 221
Hume, D. 17–18; "Of Luxury" 17; "Of Refinement in the Arts" 17, 18
Hutcheson, F. 15

"iconic" designs, origins of 29
IE Luxury Barometer 228–229, *229*
individual talent 115–117
inequality, luxury as 28
innovation, and creativity 107–108
inspiration 13
Ivy, J. 65

Jacobs, M. 38, 117, 118, 200
Jaeger-LeCoultre 125, 126, 158
Jaguar 92
Joachimsthaler, E. 62
Jobs, S. 65

Kern, G. 199
Krakoff, R. 90

Krug, J. 81, 87, 113, 200
Krug Champagne 56–57, 81, 235; creativity at 113

La Fabrique du Temps 222
leadership: creative, and social change 180–181; and extraordinariness 82
Lee, S. 90, 91
Leonardo Da Vinci 12, 13, 30
Lipovetsky, G. 8, 12; *Le luxe éternel* 9
location 137–139
Loewe 82, 148; annual report on sustainability 237
logos 64
Louis Vuitton 38, 39, 41, 42, 117, 173, 193, 199, 200, 201, 207, 210, 222
Louis XIV 15
luxury: categories, difference across 168–177, *169*; as classic or everlasting 28–29; components of 8–9; as constant change 21–22; as development force before being an industry 26; during Renaissance 12, 18, 26, 104; in early civilizations 9–10; in eighteenth century 14; as enemy of man 10–11; future of 226–240; limits of 88–94; market 19–21, 36–37; in Middle Ages 11–13; in nineteenth century 14; paradigm 48–49, *49*, 65, 67, 93, 105; post-pandemic 229–230; transformations 198–201; turnarounds 198–201; *see also individual entries*
Luxury in the Eighteenth Century (Bergand Eger) 14
luxury managers 21–26, 28, 110–129
luxury rivalry, foundational problems of: poor assessment of threats 186–191; poor strategy formulation 177, 180–184; poor strategy implementation 184–186
luxury strategy: business level of 206–208; components of 200, *200*;

244

Index

corporate level of 206–208; formulation of 166–168, *167*; interpretation of 166–168; need for 55–56; poor formulation of 177, 180–184, *182*; poor implementation of 184–186
Luxus and Kapitalismus (Sombart) 19

Mallevays, P. 220
management: and creativity 117–119; and creator, tension between 38–39
managerial approach to luxury: challenges of 36–43, **44**; change challenge 40–41, **44**; control challenge 42–43, **44**; creativity challenge 38–39, **44**; growth challenge 39–40, **44**; need for 35–58; traditional competitive strategy 50–55; traditional marketing 43–49
Mandeville, B. 17; *Fable of The Bees: or, Private Vices, Publick Benefits, The* 15
Marchionne, S. 170
Marco Polo 139
market: creative 154–155; luxury 7, 16, 17, 19–21, 36, 154, 159, 168, *169*, 170, 181, *182*, 185, 216, 226, 228, 229, 236–240; networked 155–157; traditional 155
mass media 140–141
mass *versus* exclusivity dilemma 40, 92
Matisse 52
MB&F (Maximilian Büsser and Friends) 82, 107, 109, 136, 195, 233; creativity at 124–128, 157–160; modern style 120–122
McDonald's 193
means of luxury 3, 165, 191–198, *194*
mechanical watches *versus* smartwatches 189–191
mechanical watchmaking 79
Melon, J. F.: *Political Essay Upon Commerce, A* 15
Mercedes-Benz 41

Mercedes Benz C-class 92
Michelangelo 12, 13
Michele, A. 180, 199
Microsoft 157
Middle Ages, luxury in 11–13
Moncler Genius approach 122–123, 136
Monet, C. 108
Montblanc 171, 172, 210
Montesquieu 16
Montgomery, C. 208
MontresDior 220
Mugaritz, creativity at 114–115

Nabisco 56
Nagel, C. 213–214
Nakache, O. 53
nature of luxury 3, 167, *167*, 187, 200
Nautilus 117
needs: basic *versus* sophisticated 24; *versus* desires 21, 24
Nenadic, S. 19–20
networked market 155–157
Netflix 156
Netscape 157
New York City (NYC) Garbage 66–69, 122
normal competition 65–73, *69*, 73; characteristics of 69–72, **70**; extraordinariness 82–85, 87

omnicanality 233
operational-driven approach 211–212
opinion leaders 141–145

Pagani (brand) 10, 25, 81
Pagani, H. 65, 81, 87
Parker, G. 156
Parker, R. 134, 141, 144–145
partners 136–137, 214–215
Patek Philippe 55, 117, 148, 190, 193; classic style 120, 121
pathos 64

Index

personal luxury, powerful categories in 171–174
Pertegaz, M. 138–139
PESTLE framework 134
Picasso 52
Platform Markets 55
Plato 10, 11
point-of-sale business model **175**, 176, *178–179*
Porsche 10, 189; Boxster 40, 199, 212; Macan 92–94
Porter, M. 50, 134, 135, 208–210, 212, 218
positioning 50, 51
post-pandemic luxury 229–230
power, and luxury 9, 12
Prada 173
Prestige D'or 222
price premium 52, 53, 72

quality 25
quantity 25

R&C *see* resources and capabilities (R&C)
Raphael 12, 13
RBV *see* resource-based view (RBV)
refinement 17–21, 25–26
relativity, luxury as 9–10, 22, 24
Remo Ruffini 122
Renaissance, luxury during 12, 18, 26, 104
Renova 105
resource-based view (RBV) 51, 55
resources and capabilities (R&C), role in achieving extraordinariness 83–88, **85**
Richmont 207–208, 220
Rimowa 116
Rochet, J.-C. 156
Rolex 174, 193
Romanticism 19–20
Rousseau, J.-J.: *Discourse on the Arts and Sciences* 18
Royal Oak 29, 117

Saint Lauren 116
Salon International de la Haute Horlogerie (SIHH) 160
Salvatore Ferragamo 186
Sennheiser 187
service-based business model 174–175, **175**
SIHH *see* Salon International de la Haute Horlogerie (SIHH)
single investment business model 175–176, **175**
smartphones 75
smartwatches *versus* mechanical watches 189–191
sneakers 23–24, 186, 239
social change 236–239
The Social Network(film) 156
Socrates 10
softluxury 168
de Sole, D. 38, 117, 118, 185
Sombart, W.: *Luxus and Kapitalismus* 19
Standard & Poor, S&P Global Luxury Index 170
Starbucks 55, 155
static *versus* dynamics companies 120–123
status 20
status-driven consumption 63
stereotypes 26–30
Stoicism 11
storytelling, misuse of 183–184
strategy *see* luxury strategy
streetwear 197
superficiality, luxury as 27–28
Swatch Group 88, 193, 220, 221
synergies: corporate strategy diversification 208–216; creating business success from 219; diversified conglomerate, analysis of 216–218; limits of potential 218–219

TAG-Heuer 220
task motivation 104
technology, and creativity 107–108, 124

threat(s): complementary *versus* substitution 186–191, **192**; luxury as 24–25; poor assessment of 185–191; to society, luxury as 11
time dilemma 40–41
Tirole, J. 156
Tisci, R. 171
Toledano, É. 53
traditional competitive strategy: competitive mindset 50–52; economic logic 52–54; external analysis 55; value assessment 53, 54
traditional marketing 43–49, 155; classic paradigm 46–47, *46*; luxury paradigm 48–49, *49*; "value driven by consumers" view, limitations of 47; zero-sum game 47–48
Trapani, F. 221

unfairness, luxury as 28

value assessment 53, 54
value creation process 60–95; benefits, type of 62–64; excess competition 73–78, **74**, *77*; extraordinariness 78–88, *80*, **85**; functionality trap 64–65; normal competition 65–73, *69*, **70**, *73*; *see also* creative value system

value creation synergies: corporate strategy diversification 213–214; diversified conglomerate, analysis of 217
"value driven by consumers" view, limitations of 47
value side synergies: corporate strategy diversification 212–216; diversified conglomerate, analysis of 217
Van Alstyne, M. 156
Vasari, G.: *Lives of the Most Excellent Painters, Sculptors, and Architects, The* 12
Veblen, T. B. 8; *Theory of the Leisure Class, The* 20
Velazquez, D. 108
Voltaire 16, 18
VRIO framework 84, 86, 87

watchmaking, LVMH 220–223
watch shows *versus* fashion shows 150–152
wealth accumulation 20
Wintour, A. 142

Zenith 220
zero-sum game 47–48, 82, 155, 161

Printed in the United States
by Baker & Taylor Publisher Services